GOD'S "HIT[...] [...] [...]T

THE BIOGRA[...] [...] ROLFE BARNARD

ROLFE BARNARD

by
E. A. Johnston

REVIVAL LITERATURE
PO BOX 6068
ASHEVILLE, NC 28816
828-681-0370
WWW.REVIVALLIT.ORG

Published by:
REVIVAL LITERATURE
P. O. Box 6068
Asheville, NC 28816
Web: www.revivallit.org/
Email: revivallit@bellsouth.net

All Scripture has been conformed to the King James Bible.

Formatting by:
THE OLD PATHS PUBLICATIONS, Inc.
142 Gold Flume Way
Cleveland, Georgia, U.S.A. 30528
Web: www.theoldpathspublications.com
Email: TOP@theoldpathspublications.com
Jeremiah 6:16

1.0

Contents

Acknowledgments

I must first acknowledge the King of Glory, my Redeemer Jesus Christ who revealed Himself to me, showed me I was on my way to hell and that I deserved to go there, and who marvelously saved me by His grace and took a lost church member and gave him *life*. I want to thank my precious wife Carla and my dear daughter Carly for their willingness to accept my absence in writing. I warmly thank Dr. John Thornbury for his friendship and research help on his friend, Rolfe Barnard. I am indebted to Wylie Fulton for research material, encouragement and the title for this book! I am grateful to Drew Garner for gifting me books on Baptist history and sovereign grace. I am thankful for Bro. Howell for maintaining the Rolfe Barnard Library on SermonAudio.com. I wish to thank "The Fanal": the Yearbook of Piedmont Bible College and Cathie Chatmon for sending me the cover photo for the book (which is the 1948 faculty photo of Rolfe Barnard when the school was the Piedmont Bible Institute and he was the part-time theology professor and school evangelist). I wish to thank Dr. Paige Patterson and Barbara Walker of Southwestern Baptist Theological Seminary for the faculty photo. I thank E. W. Parks for the Barnard photos! I want to express gratitude for Dr. Bob Doom at Revival Literature for making this publication possible!

A word of encouragement to my preacher brethren. The germination of this project is the result of the following story: While re-reading David Wilkerson's book, *The Cross and the Switchblade,* I was impressed by a facet in Wilkerson's life. Early in his ministry he was a country pastor who spent the hours of midnight to 2am watching television to unwind and relax. One evening God challenged Wilkerson to give that time to Him.

Wilkerson sold his TV and never replaced it. From that point forward he gave God midnight to 2am, and it was during this time that God called Wilkerson to NYC to minister among teen gang members, eventually starting Teen Challenge. I realized that God did not reveal this wider ministry opportunity to Wilkerson until he chose to go deeper with God in a sacrificial daily quiet time. I had maintained a daily, regular quiet time for many years, but lately my time with the Lord was missing something—there was no *sacrifice* attending it. And the God of the Bible delights in sacrifice, for He sacrificed His only begotten Son for sinful man. After reading Wilkerson's story, I made a covenant with God to rise at 4:30am and give God the first hour and a half of each day—walking with Him. It is amazing how God honored that time! During this period I became familiar with a man I had never heard of—Rolfe Barnard. No man told me about Barnard but God did. God called me to write this biography on Barnard and gave me great assistance in performing this almost impossible task. This book would not be in your hands had it not been for a willingness to go deeper with God. Let me ask you a question and please be honest. Does your daily quiet time with God have a sacrificial aroma attending it? Is your sweetheart love for Christ more passionate today than yesterday? His desire is to *spend time with you*. God is looking for a man *to walk with*. Those Enochs will be translated to a deeper walk and wider usefulness to Him for His glory.

Foreword

It is with great joy and God-given enthusiasm that I write this foreword.

I have personally profited from hearing the sermon tapes and CDs of Rolfe Barnard and reading his printed sermons which we've had the privilege to distribute.

The founder of Revival Literature, the late Dr. James A. Stewart, knew and appreciated Brother Barnard when he had the opportunity to preach either in meetings or where Brother Barnard was pastoring. When James Stewart founded Revival Literature part of his vision was to produce biographies of men used in revival, such as Malof, Burns, McCheyne, Spurgeon, and Troup. I know he would be excited to have *God's "Hitchhike" Evangelist* in our series of such biographies.

As source material is scarce, with no journals or personal information from living family members, Dr. Johnston has done a masterful job of telling the life of Rolfe Barnard from his sermons.

I'm praying that this biography will set this generation of preachers afire to preach afresh all the Word of God with both its warnings and wooings. I'm praying the "Lord of the harvest" to raise up in our beloved Republic from coast to coast and border to border a band of fearless, Spirit-filled preachers like Rolfe Barnard.

Barnard, like Richard Baxter of old, would rejoice to have men to "… preach as never sure to preach again and [preach] as a dying man to dying men."

Yours for Revival,
Bob Doom

Introduction

Rolfe Barnard was an evangelist who lived in relative obscurity and died without even a public notice of his death, but of whom it was said that he was the human means of divine mercy to a 100,000 souls, the fruit of an itinerant preaching ministry that lasted over forty years and canvassed much of America.

To say this man Barnard was a controversial figure is an understatement. A Southern Baptist and fundamentalist, Barnard's ministry alienated him within his own denomination and fundamentalist circles. Pulpits were closed to him and peers spoke ill of him. What did he preach which drew such ire from so many? Rolfe Barnard preached the unvarnished doctrines of grace, the gospel of God's glory. He believed in sovereign grace and defended its doctrines to his death. He saw its reality within his own heart and proclaimed the sovereignty of God in the salvation of men—this was the message which upset so many. This was also the message that God seemed pleased to *save many* throughout the ministry of Rolfe Barnard. His primary message was repentance in a day when most preachers no longer believed repentance was necessary to faith and salvation. Even within the sovereign grace movement, which he was primarily instrumental in its formation and served as its figurehead, he came down hard on those who only preached the doctrine of election and did not preach repentance and the need for a changed life. Addressing a group of Reformed pastors during this period he commented, "We must put first things first. The first emphasis is repentance. This generation doesn't need to learn the doctrine of election. This generation needs to be called to repentance. This generation needs to bow to Jesus Christ!" But what alienated him most within his denomination was his prophetic voice which cried out against the spiritual deterioration of Southern

Baptist life, the dilution of the gospel to make it more palatable to the masses, and evangelism which relied more upon man's methodology and emotional appeals more than God's sovereignty and the Holy Spirit's activity in convicting the heart of sin. Rolfe Barnard was not afraid to take aim and shoot down what he saw as the cheapening of grace and the perversion of the gospel, and he simply ruffled some feathers of his peers! Thus he had his enemies. One man was so mad at him that purportedly he came to a meeting with a gun to shoot Barnard! Providentially there was no shooting.

Historian Leon McBeth referred to Rolfe Barnard as "the pioneer of Calvinist resurgence among Baptists in America." It was said of Barnard that he was one of the first proponents of getting Banner of Truth's Puritan books known in the United States before many began to support them. Yet, when I asked my friend Iain Murray what he knew of Rolfe Barnard he replied, "I heard of him but nothing more." I asked another Calvinist friend, Richard Owen Roberts, who has canvassed much of America in his own itinerant ministry, what he knew of Barnard and his reply was, "I have heard the name but know nothing else about him." Why has Barnard suffered from such neglect? To those in the sovereign grace movement of the 1950's Rolfe Barnard was simply a *giant.* He mentored many young preachers and he had a wide radio ministry for years, yet few today know of him. In his own day we have the following story: a local radio personality had heard Barnard as a boy, but over the years—despite much traveling—had never met anyone who had ever heard of this preacher. To the world Rolfe Barnard was a "nobody." He never made a name for himself, he formed no institution bearing his name, and he authored no books. However, he has over 270 sermons on SermonAudio.com and over 180 sermons on SermonIndex.com. These are his main legacy. Some friends published three volumes of his sermons in the 1980's, and these sixty-eight printed sermons are representative of Brother Barnard's ministry. The Rolfe Barnard Library on SermonAudio. com maintains much of the Barnard legacy.

When I began to study the life and ministry of Rolfe Barnard, I was shocked at how *greatly* this man was used of God in the salvation of souls. In many ways he was the Asahel Nettleton of his day. In fact, Barnard and Nettleton shared much in common. Both fought for orthodox religion of their day and faced fierce opposition for their stance; both preached man's duty for immediate repentance; both saw great movements of God's grace (Nettleton witnessed more because he labored during the Second GreatAwakening); and both men were private persons and walked alone. Oddly, although Rolfe Barnard was much loved by the sovereign gracers, some could be at odds with him because he gave a "public invitation" and had a tendency towards too much "preacher and means" when his peers believed all power to regenerate sinners was in the sovereign Spirit of God who operates "as He wills." Some said he was too much like Charles Finney in the methods he at times employed. He was a maverick, a prophet, and a trail blazer.

Listening to a Rolfe Barnard sermon is an *experience* in itself! You will find yourself startled, alarmed, amused, convicted, and occasionally brought to tears. Take time to read his sixty-eight printed sermons, and you will stand amazed at this man's comprehension of human nature and his understanding of the lost sinner and infidel, and admire his great ability as an effective communicator of the great doctrines of the Bible. Barnard knew full well the windings of the sinner's wicked heart, for he was once an infidel himself and knew all the excuses and objections a rebel makes so not to "stack arms" and "throw down his shotgun" at the feet of a Sovereign! Evangelist Barnard possessed a deep desire to see men submit to the claims of Christ in His lordship through repentance and a life of faith. He was a man of prayer who regularly interceded for the lost. But most of all he believed a Christian was someone who had experienced *change* through a new birth from above and had entered into a union with Jesus Christ. He firmly believed that Jesus saves sinners *from* their sins at conversion. He did not hold to the theory that someone could take Jesus as Savior now and at a later time take Him as Lord. It grieved him to see so many church members living in antinomianism. He believed in being a "doer of the Word," often ringing doorbells in the dead of winter to personally invite the lost to a meeting he was holding in their town. He was a man's man but not afraid to weep real tears over the lost church member seated on the front row of the church. Those who were fortunate enough to become converts under his preaching are among his most loyal supporters today.

How can one describe his preaching and still do him justice? I don't know if it can be done but I will try. Rolfe Barnard preached with a Bible in one hand and a stick of dynamite in the other! As the demands of the holy law of God were pressed upon his hearers a combustion began to occur! And as the passion of the preacher rose, sparks would begin to fly as listeners sat spellbound as they drew closer and closer to Sinai "on a smoke" until they could *sense* the terror of the Lord and were confronted with the wickedness of their own heart. At times, this spiritual combustion could be too overwhelming to some of his hearers, and they would have to be removed from a Rolfe Barnard meeting on a stretcher! This occurred on more than one occasion. Do you know anyone whose preaching does that? There were times when some of his hearers were so overcome by the truths they heard they became insensible and landed in mental institutions. In his younger years his preaching could literally shake an entire town! His preaching could be powerful and gripping under the right circumstances, and that was Rolfe Barnard at his best and most effective. He could also be quite ordinary as a preacher, but he kept a lifelong willingness to preach what others would not and face the consequences for his convictions. He was a man jealous for God and His glory! But one thing was certain, if you went to a Rolfe Barnard meeting you did not leave without a strong opinion of the preacher good or bad! His preaching disturbed people. If I could sum up his preaching with one word it would be "disturbing." He was a disturbing preacher. He had a way of getting under your skin like a splinter beneath your finger which gnaws at you and makes you wince. He could get you mad. Get you under conviction. Get you to the foot of Calvary and at the feet of the Savior whose fountain of blood can wash all sins away!

He preached the gospel in its purity and proper order. He believed in total depravity and preached often on the doctrines of ruin, redemption, repentance, and regeneration with the voice of a prophet warning of a judgment to come and a Christ who ruled with all authority from a heavenly throne! His was not a politically correct gospel. His gospel had *power* to save! Little is known of his early childhood. His daughter Joanne recently died before I could contact her for information on her father. What is known about his early life can only be culled from his sermons. He left no autobiography or diary. With the exception of some personal recollections of friends, the information on Rolfe Barnard herein presented is drawn from his sermonic material. Therefore, we will let the man speak for himself throughout this biography. Rolfe will tell us about himself, what he believed, what he preached, and what God accomplished through his itinerant and radio ministry. You will enjoy his Southern colloquialisms and his humble transparency as a poor sinner saved by grace.

Evangelist Barnard had his share of peculiar traits and flaws (like the time he turned his Baptist church in North Carolina into a "experiment," which ended in chaos and disaster and his sudden departure!); he demonstrated on more than one occasion that he had "feet of clay." He was an imperfect man who preached a perfect Christ.

As you read this biography on Rolfe Barnard we hope that the ride will be rewarding, although often bumpy; such was the man known as "The Hitchhike Evangelist."

> E. A. Johnston, Ph.D., D. B. S.
> Evangelist and author
> Memphis, TN

Chapter One

Early Years

O God, thou hast taught me from my youth: and hitherto have I declared thy
wondrous works. — Psalm 71:17

Gunterville, Alabama is a fishing and hunting paradise. Situated near beautiful Lake Gunterville and Gunterville State Park the rural charm of the town that Rolfe Barnard called his boyhood home still abounds in fishing holes and farmland, and it is the heart of rural southern America.

Rolfe Pickens Barnard was born August 4, 1904; he was the third of seven children—three boys and four girls. It was a new century and a time before the sinking of the Titanic, before the First World War, before automobiles and modern technology. It was also a time when life in America, particularly in the South, was still lived at a slow pace where a boy could grow up roaming country lanes and taking time to enjoy God's creation in the outdoors with his hunting dog beside him and the wind at his back. It was also a time in America when there was still a fear of God in the land. It was a time when God still moved in revival—the 1904 Welsh revival brought 100,000 souls to Christ within a year! Rolfe's parents were similar to many other Christian families at the turn of the century who maintained a family altar in the home and raised their children on the Bible.

James and Julia Barnard had a good Christian reputation in Guntersville. James Barnard was the school superintendent and well known in the farming community as a solid Christian man.

When Rolfe became a preacher he often spoke fondly of his father and in a sermon commented, that when his father died and lay in his coffin there was a heavenly glow on his countenance. Later in life Rolfe Barnard passed through the town of Guntersville, but the town had become unrecognizable to him; concrete streets replaced dirt roads and he could not find his way around town. Passing a farm he stopped for directions, parking his car by a fence line while he waited for a farmer to bring his mule team up near where he was parked. As the farmer approached, Rolfe introduced himself. The farmer wiped his brow with a handkerchief and repeated, "Barnard ... Barnard. You wouldn't be related to Jim Barnard, would you?" asked the farmer. "Yes, he was my daddy." The farmer extended his hand, "Well, if you are Jim Barnard's boy you must be *all right*." The Barnard name was still good in that community years later. Little Rolfe grew up in a solid Christian home, and he regularly attended the local Baptist church where his family belonged. One childhood incident clearly stuck out in his mind from this time; he mentions it in his sermon, "How God Saved Me from Infidelity":

> When I was eleven years old, I walked down the aisle of a church one time. A missionary was there and he said, "Are there any here that will make a vow tonight to God?" He quoted that song, "I'll go where You want me to go, I'll be what You want me to be, I'll say what You want me to say." I thought I was saved, but I wasn't. Before I knew it, I was down that aisle and I said, "I will." You may not believe this, but if you give God anything, He never trades back, He keeps it. I had made a vow.

As a boy Rolfe enjoyed reading the stories of Horatio Alger, where a shoe shine boy can grow up and marry the owner's daughter and become president of the company! Little Rolfe fantasized that he too could become a big success, and he expected "big things" for himself in life. Having an academic for a father he excelled in his studies and demonstrated maturity for his age by entering school at age four! The Barnard family relocated to Abilene, Texas when Rolfe was a teenager. Rolfe soon enrolled at Hardin Simmons University to begin his college studies at the tender age of fifteen! Rolfe planned on becoming a successful trial lawyer and he applied himself for a legal career.

Upon graduation, his academic excellence won him a scholarship to law school at Baylor and the offer of a junior partnership in a prestigious Texas law firm! He was on his way to making a name for himself as an attorney and achieving his own version of his boyhood Horatio Alger dreams! But God had other plans for Rolfe Pickens Barnard and being a famous lawyer wasn't one of them.

Unbeknownst to Rolfe his parents had dedicated him, before his birth, to be a *preacher.* When Jim and Julia saw the direction their son was taking by choosing a legal career and not ministry, they grew concerned and shared their prayer with him of dedicating him to the Lord and ministry. This news was not warmly received by Rolfe—he had other plans and being a preacher wasn't one of them! A battle commenced between Rolfe Barnard and his God. Rolfe would fight being a preacher for the next five years, and these five years would be a heartbreak for his parents as they saw their son become a declared atheist and infidel! But Jim and Julia never gave up hope for their rebellious son because they had already given him to God before he was born. No matter how hard Rolfe Barnard would fight against God for the next five years he would eventually realize that one cannot outrun God.

Chapter Two

Infidel

The fool hath said in his heart, There is no God. — Psalm 14:1

Rolfe Barnard commented later in life that Psalm 14:1 was a mistranslation in the King James. The text really read, "The fool hath said in his heart, no God." Barnard commented, "There is no such thing as a true atheist. Everybody deep down believes there is a God; they just don't want any part of Him! I believed in God when I was an infidel but I didn't want Him to run my life!"

Rolfe's college days were crowned with many achievements: an honor roll student, he was tall and handsome and well liked by many. He played lead roles in the school drama productions and he was tough to beat on the debate team which was good preparation for him becoming a trial lawyer. But out of all these achievements he was mostly known around campus for being a proclaimed atheist! What aggravated his college professors most was the fact that he was such a star pupil and campus leader and the school was a Baptist college! But what greatly disturbed the college faculty was that the campus star was leading many astray into atheism. In a later sermon he lamented over this fact that he had "led so many to hell in those days!"

Rolfe was striving against God because he did not want to become a preacher. He did not want to live a life of cornbread and water as a preacher when he had such bright prospects before him at one of the country's most prestigious law firms. He wanted to

GOD'S "HITCHHIKE" EVANGELIST

make a name for himself and grow a big bank account and being a preacher did not fit into his plans so he fought against God. He formed an infidel club and became its president, holding Friday night rallies on campus and swaying many away from Christ. He convinced himself that there was "no God for him" and he fought God tooth and nail for five years! He was gifted as an orator and debater and he could influence many fellow college kids to come over to his side of infidelity. Soon over three hundred students belonged to Rolfe's infidel club! He would stand on a platform and denounce God and dare Him to do anything about it! He spoke about these days later in life in a sermon entitled, "How God Saved Me from Infidelity":

> I knew that being saved for me meant I would have to be a public preacher. And I did two things to try to handle that situation: I became an infidel by day and a prayer by night. By day I got so bitter, I got so miserable that I had to find a refuge, I had to crawl into the dust just to get a little peace. So I found out there wasn't any God, I said. I organized an infidel club in my college; I had three hundred young Baptist college students to join. By night I would pray to God to save me. I was an orator in those days, college debater, college Shakespearean actor. I was a big shot in those days. I was the most prominent man on the campus when I organized my infidel club. I led a lot of people to hell.

One can only imagine the rumors in the Baptist church where Rolfe's parent's were members, that their son was the town atheist! The battle going on inside Rolfe Barnard was a paradox for by day he was an outspoken atheist and the leader of an infidel band; but at night, when alone, he was a penitent sinner on his knees begging God not to destroy him. He would curse God by day and pray to Him by night! A man cannot fight God and win and Rolfe knew this deep down in his heart and he became fearful for his life by blaspheming God during the day. He would pray, "God, if You'll not kill me tonight I'll surrender to You tomorrow," but his promises to God were quickly broken in the morning light. He had simply "dug in his heels" against God's plan for his life. Insights from this rebellious period in his life are seen by his comments

20

from his sermon, "How God Saved Me from Infidelity":

> I have you to understand that I had a scholarship in the best law school in the world. I have you to understand that I had the offer already of a junior partnership in the biggest law firm in Texas when I was out of school. You wouldn't catch me preaching, being a little old hitchhike preacher living on cornbread and water and everybody cursing me and talking about me! Now there was never a day in my life that I didn't want to keep out of hell, but I wasn't going to preach. I was cursing God by day and begging God to save me by night but I ain't going to preach! For five years I tried to get God to save me and every time I said, "I will not preach!" I don't care how little it is, if that is where your rebellion heads up, it must be crushed. If not there is no salvation. I know what it is to pray and cry, seek and everything else. This easy believe stuff to get somebody to cry a little bit and make some kind of profession and call it salvation is deception. You must be willing to *surrender your all* to the Lord Jesus Christ and do His will. Christ must be revealed to you—that is salvation.

When Rolfe Barnard pitted his will against a holy God he hid a secret from his other infidel friends. The smile they saw on his face by day did not reveal the turmoil he was experiencing on the inside. During those college days Rolfe Barnard was the most popular man on campus and he was the most unhappy. He was a man eaten up inside with guilt and frustration. He faced a fork in the road of his life: one way led to success and popularity as top lawyer; the other led to poverty and unpopularity as a preacher. He knew which road God wanted him on but at this time he was unwilling to take it.

Rolfe had a friend on campus who was praying for his salvation. This friend was his English professor. He often referred to this professor later in life as "the one who loved my soul enough to not let me go to hell." We see his remarks from his sermon, "A Burden for Souls":

> I stand here tonight because God set his affections on me and He sent a college professor after me and that college professor wouldn't let me go to hell. He loved me and he wouldn't leave me alone. Somebody wouldn't let me go to hell; that college professor he prayed for me, and wept over me. I don't know why God laid me on that old professor's

heart—I just thank God He did. That professor couldn't save me, but he could weep over me and ask God to save me. He couldn't break me, but he could ask God to break my stubborn will. He would wait for me at night and with tears in his eyes he would say, "Rolfe, I can't let you go to hell."

Chapter Three

God's Bloodhound

For whosoever will save his life shall lose it: and whosoever will lose his life for my sake shall find it. — Matthew 16:25

Many prayers were offered up to God on behalf of Rolfe Barnard during this critical time in his life. The tears that his English professor shed for his soul haunted Rolfe—he just couldn't believe a man would hound him like that! Everywhere he went on campus Rolfe would see the professor's pained face as Rolfe the infidel would deny God. Memories began to haunt him: his parents' dedication of him to the Lord; the time when he was a eleven-year-old boy when he made a public profession in church to follow God.

We see his remarks about these things in "How God Saved Me from Infidelity":

> You may not believe this but if you give God anything, He never trades back, He keeps it. I had made a vow. I didn't know that back of my actions that night, my mother and father never told me (they both are in glory now), but before I was born they gave me to God to be a public preacher. They never did tell me. God knew about it. I'm telling you, if you give one of your children to God, He will take it! Our papas and mommas knew about this in other days. They just said, "Lord, he is Yours." That is serious business. A boy can't win against odds like that; it just can't be done. He has got Mama and Papa and God against him! You had better quit before you start!

Still, oddly, Rolfe Barnard continued to fight against God and refuse to surrender to His claims on his life. He wanted God *on his terms.* He wanted to be saved but he did not want to preach. He wanted to pursue his lifelong dream of becoming a success in life, and he felt the legal profession was the best platform for him to exercise his many talents. He knew there was a surrender involved to come to Christ, and he still refused to "throw down his shotgun" which was pointed at God. This is seen from the same sermon:

> I knew for five long years that salvation for me meant I had to be a public preacher. And I believe it is meant for you to do whatever the will of God is for you. For me it was this: I knew that surrender to King Jesus meant I would have to be a preacher and that was the one thing I was not going to do! So I did what it seems that most professing Christians have been able to do (I couldn't get the job done though!). I tried to get God to save me without throwing down my rebellion, but that just won't work. You just can't do it and call yourself a Christian. If you do, you're certain to go to hell. Until your rebellion is crushed and you surrender to do His will, there is no salvation.

What Rolfe Barnard failed to realize was that he was being chased. The young rebel was being pursued by an agent from the King's army. God's Bloodhound was hot on his trail! And it would not be long until the Holy Spirit got a hold of him and saved him, causing Rolfe Barnard to "throw down his arms" and surrender to the King of Kings who had all claims on his life.

A circumstance occurred in his life at this juncture which was out of pattern from his original plans to go immediately to law school after graduating college. We see a divine delay in his plans. Instead, he took a teaching job in a Panhandle Texas town to pay down his debts before going to law school, and it was there that God's Bloodhound would track the rebel down! It all started when he joined the local Baptist church. We see the somewhat humorous account from an extract from the same sermon:

> I graduated from that school and I went out to the Panhandle of Texas to teach school. I was going to work a year before I went on to law school and pay a few of my debts. I got out there, and of course, I was a good Baptist all that time—I passed for a good church member, so they didn't

turn me out. Anybody that wants to can be a church member now; it is the easiest thing on earth to get in and just about impossible to get out. That's the church now. Well, I was a church member and also president of an infidel club in that school. But I went out to teach school and in those days you had to be a church member if you got a job teaching in the public schools. So the first Sunday, I marched down the aisle and joined the church there by letter. Of course I didn't go back that Sunday night, no use being a fool about this religion business! And I didn't go Wednesday night, when they had a business meeting and elected me to be a teacher of the men's Bible class. That's right! And there I was. I supposed they didn't know anything about me and I could put on a good show you know, and I knew more Bible when I was a kid than those men did, and so we just had a storm! If I didn't go through hell, I'll choose up and take sides. I taught that Bible class and then the preacher resigned and we went two or three Sundays with no preaching. Then one Sunday I went to my boardinghouse from Sunday school and I never did know why but I went to my room and locked it. I could have gotten out, but I didn't want anybody to come in and bother me. I threw my Bible down on the floor and I buried my face in it and said, "Lord, whether You save me or damn me, I will preach from now on!"

The guilt of the vacant pulpit had been too much for him. In his heart of hearts he knew what he had to do and that was to surrender to God and end his rebellion. He was tired of being a "hypocrite and a devil" rolled in one! When he locked himself in his room to have it out with God the battle was fought and God won.

That same afternoon he wanted to share what had happened to him with the superintendent of his church's Sunday school. He walked to the man's home and found him on the front porch asleep in a rocking chair while he awaited dinner. Rolfe walked up to him and awakened him.

"Brother Mills, I've come to tell you the Lord has saved me and I want to preach next Sunday." The superintendent said, "Well, it's about time." I said, "What do you mean?" He said, "Things have been going on." A couple of letters came to Panhandle, Texas post office. One of them was addressed to the Superintendent of the Sunday School of the First Baptist

Church. The other was addressed to the Pastor—didn't know any names. They were identical letters. Some old white-haired woman from Abilene, Texas said, "My boy's coming to your town to teach school. He's called to be a preacher. He's not even saved. He's in an awful mess. Don't let him have a moment's peace." And he said, "Boy, we've been doing it. We knew you weren't saved, but we elected you to teach a men's Bible class. We've been meeting once a week and asking, 'Lord, make the fire a little hotter.' We've been waiting."

God's Bloodhound had finally caught up with Rolfe Barnard. The rebellion was ended. He had "stacked arms" and laid down his shotgun of rebellion and said "yes" to being a preacher! God had crossed him at his point of rebellion and Rolfe submitted and was saved by grace. His days as an infidel were ended.

When word reached his Alma Mater that Rolfe Barnard had finally come to Christ, it sent shock waves throughout the campus! The president of the college quickly telephoned Rolfe to see if what he had heard was true—was Rolfe Barnard the outspoken infidel really saved? When he learned it was indeed true he invited Rolfe to come and preach in their chapel for a week of meetings to tell the entire campus what had transpired in his life. We will let Rolfe Barnard tell the story in his own words from this point (taken from his sermon, "The Character of Hell"):

When I got saved I mailed two letters, one to my mother and one to the head of the English department at my old college who was the human instrument of keeping this infidel out of hell. And the head of the department of English told the president and within an hour the superintendent of the school where I was teaching got a telephone call from the president of the school where I'd been and had been the president of an infidel's club there in that Baptist school. And pretty soon I was called into the office of the superintendent and he said, "The president of your Alma Mater has been on the phone and he's asked that I grant you a week's leave. They'll take care of your expenses and your salary. He wants me to release you to come back to school and speak in chapel every night." And about that time the telephone rang again and it was the president and he asked for me. And after the "hello's" he said, "Rolfe, news has come our way that the Lord has saved you!"

I said, "I believe He has Prixy." We called him Prixy, a term of endearment. He said, "Well, I've asked your superintendent and he said it's all right with him for you to leave and I want your word and I demand that you come next week and speak to us. We'll turn the chapel over to you and we'll meet every night! I want you to come talk to us. I want you to undo much of the hell that you caused here as much as you can!"

That's a pretty hard job to do isn't it? And I went back. They still had an infidel's club. The young man who had been the vice president of it the year before when I started it, he was now the president. He and I were almost blood brothers. He heard me speak in chapel—he had to. He heard me every night. I stood up there in that chapel every night and gave what we call our testimonies, what I believed the Lord had done for me. I didn't know doctrine or nothing but they listened. And I was facing not all of the youngsters who had been in my infidel club, some of them the year before had been seniors and they'd gone on to spread their poison out yonder. But there was still a lot of them and that year the infidel club was bigger than the year I was there! And I stood up there and tried to wash stripes. That's in the Bible, isn't it? And when the last service was over my buddy, now president of the club, asked me, "Rolfe I want the privilege of taking you to the train." And we left early and went down to the train station and got the ticket arranged and sat in his car. And he said, "Rolfe, you've gone off your rocker. You used to be a brain. I hope you'll recover and come back to your senses and get rid of all this stuff!" I pled with him all that week. Monday through Friday I preached to him. I witnessed to him. And I got nowhere. And we shook hands and I got on the train. And five months later a man put five bullets in his chest. And I have terrible reason to believe that five seconds later in hell he lifted up his eyes being in torments. Two young men organized an infidel's club. That was thirty-nine years ago since I shook hands and told that boy "goodbye." I'm here speaking to you, I'm afraid he's been in torments these thirty-nine years. What's the difference? Somewhere in there in the good providence of God I began to spend time in a cold room crying to the Lord for mercy and that boy never did. And he fell and he is still in the same condition he was in when he fell and I believe God changed me.

Rolfe Barnard always maintained a sore spot in his life that haunted him the rest of his days. It bothered him that he had been the means of damning so many young people from his time in the infidel club. He often spoke about this and how he would have to stand at the last judgment and see all those young people that he sent to hell! He was always striving to undo the damage he had done and this haunted him all his life.

After his visit to his Alma Mater he took ordination at the Baptist church in which he was a member. He was preparing himself for the ministry. We have an account of this from his sermon, "The Record of God's Written, Permanent Revelation to Mankind":

I shall never forget when I was ordained. I remember my dear friend who's been in glory now many years preached the ordination sermon. I was just a young fellow and of course knew "everything," therefore knew nothing! I was full of vim, vigor and vitality, and I thought that if they would just turn me loose on this old world about a year, I would have the whole outfit converted. And there I was, I remember that preacher standing up there and among the things he said were, "Son, you don't know what you are getting into. You are yet able to believe, but there will be nights when you walk the floor. Your wife can't comfort you, your loved ones can't comfort you. The heavens will be dark and you will want to die. You will never know what heartaches you are letting yourself in for. You don't realize the opposition of Satan or the absolute depravity of men, even good men. I want to remind you of one thing: Rolfe, always be as narrow as the Bible, don't be any broader than the Bible, and preach the Word!"

Chapter Four

"Booger Town"

Because sentence against an evil work is not executed speedily, therefore the heart of the sons of men is fully set in them to do evil. — Ecclesiastes 8:11

"Booger Town" was the infamous nickname given to Borger, Texas in the 1920's, for it was at that time the world's biggest oil town and the discovery of "black gold" transformed a sleepy ranch into a booming frontier town of 50,000 inhabitants within months. Prospectors and oilmen flooded the area in hopes of quick riches. The new town attracted attention quickly as word got out that money was easy to get and flowing as fast as the oil could come out of the ground! A shrewd businessman by the name of "Ace" Borger bought up most of the 240 acre ranch and created a town site consisting of saloons, grocery stores, brothels, and gaming houses. The town of Borger quickly earned the name "Booger Town" because it attracted the lowest classes of bandits, cardsharks, and prostitutes that could squeeze into the two and a half mile main street which consisted of 264 businesses!

When one studies the history of Borger, Texas it is interesting to learn that in this wild west oil town there was a shooting or knifing every day! The local deputy sheriffs were bought and paid for by "Ace" Borger who had his fingers in every pie in town. Lawlessness was rampant. Death was in the air, literally, as many died from "gas pneumonia" from the drilling fields. But what is most interesting of the secular history of this infamous town is the fact that a prominent citizen is *never mentioned.* In fact, this prominent person was known by everyone in Borger, Texas during 1927-1929. This well known citizen was pals with Frank Hamer, the famous Texas Ranger who shot and killed the outlaws Bonnie and Clyde. Frank Hamer was assigned to be the personal bodyguard to this prominent citizen of Borger who was instrumental in cleaning up the town of its crime! Who is this forgotten hero of this western town? None other than Rolfe Barnard!

Surprised? Rolfe Barnard was sent by the governor of Texas to clean up the town! In 1927 Governor Dan Moody sent a force of Texas Rangers to rein in the town and leading the pack was a twenty-three-year-old Rolfe Barnard! The Red Light district of the town had become so dangerous a killing occurred every day. Rolfe Barnard took signed documents to Governor Moody to bring justice to "Booger Town" and clean it up. Martial law was imposed on the town for a whole month. Two prominent citizens of Borger, the mayor and Rolfe Barnard, led a procession of 1,200 prostitutes out of the city limits! But try as you may you will not find Rolfe Barnard's name in the history of Borger, Texas and this is a shame. For sixteen volatile months he was the pastor of 50,000 people! He started the first church in town. He preached on street corners, in saloons, in houses of ill repute and went to the sinners where they were and preached the gospel to them. While preaching in the town's biggest saloon he stood on a beer keg and his picture was taken and sent to all the newspapers in adjoining states. But no one knows about Rolfe Barnard in Borger, Texas *until now.* Listen to him tell the story from his sermon, "Watching Men Die":

> In 1926, the city of Borger, Texas was at that time the world's largest oil town. An old man by the name of Whitenburg, an old bankrupt rancher, struck oil on his ranch and in one year's time the royalties that he received amounted to 90 million dollars. And somebody came along and bought a town site [Ace Borger] and he made a little town and they named it Borger and in six months time there were 50,000 inhabitants of that fast growing city!
>
> The Baptist Association of that section went out and bought one of the lots in the town for the future erection of a church building. And I'd just been saved, and they asked me

if I would go out and build a church in that wicked oil town. And I did. And I just knew one man in that wicked city and I just had five dollars in my pocket. I resigned my job—I was teaching school—and I went out to build a church. There was a lot that was paid for and I had to raise money to build some sort of building. First thing I did I purchased a dance hall that was vacant and I purchased it on credit, then I hired a man to move it and place it on the lot that had been purchased by the Baptist Association. And then not knowing what else to do, I got a big ten gallon hat and I started begging for money. The main street, the whole town was built on one main street, some businesses had false fronts and the rest of it was wood—they were hastily built and the main street was two and a half miles long. And I went down the street on one side and I knew that God was no respecter of persons so I went into every place of business; places of ill repute, saloons, gambling houses, grocery stores, just name it and I didn't leave anybody out. And I'd tell them I was a Baptist preacher and I was raising money to build a Baptist church and I wanted them to kick in and they did!

Money was loose and free! I needed about a thousand dollars to build that church. By the time I got the length of one side of the street I had thirty thousand dollars in my hat and I was doing good! And I got down on the other side of the street and one little white-haired, pink-cheeked Baptist deacon, I didn't know him but he heard there was a preacher in town and disgracing God! And he finally ran me down and he rebuked me. And I received his rebuke and he said I was doing wrong and I should be ashamed of myself and he'd forgive me because I was so young. He said, "You ought to know that the Lord doesn't want to use the devil's money to prosecute His work!" I said, "He don't?" And he said, "No siree!" And I apologized to the old man and I wouldn't rebuke an elder, except he was wrong. There's a lot of pious pomposity that we don't want any money except the Lord's money; well, I didn't know there was any other kind! The Bible says the cattle on a thousand hills are mine. The Bible says the silver and the gold are mine! The Bible says it's God that gives you power to get wealth! If the devil swipes some of God's money, well, I'll swipe some of it back!

And I remember by the time I came to the middle of the

31

second block where Mr. A. P. Borger for whom the town was named—he bought the town site. He had his finger in every puddle in the city. No prostitute engaged in her traffic without paying him. No saloon sold any whiskey in town without paying him! Nobody had a gaming establishment without paying him. He had a take off of everything; the deputy sheriffs and everybody else was on his pay and he was getting rich. And I wasn't going to *pass him by* and when I got to his place, he had the biggest establishment, and there were 267 of them alike on that main street, and the front of his place was a whiskey place where you could buy whiskey, Texas was dry but they hadn't found that out there, and you could buy whiskey there and the second room was a gaming house and right behind it was a house of ill fame. 267 of such establishments in that city at that time!

And when I got there they were waiting for me! And I went in and there was a big crowd. They had been timing my approach up the street and they were waiting for me. And I told them who I was and why I was there. And they had appointed somebody to tell me that, "We are not going to give you a dime until we get a sample of your preaching!" And that just suited me fine and somebody rolled out a big beer keg and stood me up on top of it and had me hold my Bible kind of pious like, and they had a couple of deputy sheriffs with their ten gallon hats and six shooters and they looked like Hop Along Cassidy, and they took pictures of me and those sheriffs and published them in newspapers all over the west! Showing the preacher with his Bible and the sheriffs with their guns and how they were going to tame that wicked city!

And after they had their fun they said, "Preach to us!" And I preached. And I preached from the text from Ecclesiastes chapter 12 about how, *"Then shall the dust return to the earth as it was: and the spirit shall return unto God who gave it."* And I told them that all of them there would die and they needed to repent of their sins. And I have never seen the Holy Spirit challenged where He didn't come around! He doesn't come around much today but He bothered them *that day* and seven men hit the floor of that saloon and claimed the Lord Jesus Christ. They became charter members of our church that we started! They were our first seven deacons! And from that experience of preaching to those people in that saloon we built a church.

For sixteen months, I was a single man of twenty-three, I was the only preacher in that city. From that experience I learned you can't clean up men or a city from the outside; it just can't be done. Man's got heart disease, he needs a new heart. He needs to hear the doctrine of the new birth! I couldn't clean up that town. We tried three times!

I went to Austin, Texas to meet the Christian governor and I took a suitcase full of affidavits, duly fixed, signed and sealed and before I got back from the governor's office, the Texas Rangers were there. Two Texas Rangers were assigned as my body guards [one was Frank Hamer, author's note]. Wherever I went they went with me or I would have been murdered. And they let me put the first padlock on, and we padlocked 267 of those places! They let me strike a match to 1,200 slot machines and we burned them up! They let me and the mayor lead the procession of over 1,200 public women who were led out of the city limits and we cleaned up that city as clean as a hound's tooth. And it stayed clean two or three days. They kept coming back. New ones would come from everywhere. But I say that city cleaned up three times! And in those sixteen months I preached to everybody in that town. I didn't build a nice little church building hoping they would come. I went down to where sinners were! I preached in every house of ill fame. I preached in the dance hall. I preached on street corners. I preached everywhere, I had a congregation of 50,000 souls! And in that sixteen month period I baptized 2,361 persons.

The intriguing story of the beginnings of Borger, Texas are certainly enlivened by the added first-hand knowledge of Rolfe Barnard. Why has Rolfe Barnard been omitted from the town's early history when he played such an integral role in bringing law and order to this frontier town? One explanation may be that all of the 50,000 residents of Borger at that time only knew him as "the Preacher." There were no other clergymen in this city during this time. Rolfe Barnard was the *man* who did the marrying and the burying. When someone lay dying they sent for "the Preacher"; when somebody lay ill in the hospital they called for "the Preacher"; when somebody needed to be buried or married they called for "the

Preacher." This could explain his anonymity.

The lawlessness in "Booger Town" had risen to such a fever pitch that the District Attorney John A. Holmes was shot and killed on September 18, 1929. When the Texas Rangers came to town to instill martial law it was Rolfe Barnard at the lead with Captain Frank Hamer by his side! For an entire month the Rangers were enlisted to bring order to the town and the main character who was given the high privilege of padlocking all the doors and setting the first match to the slot machines and leading the procession of 1,200 prostitutes out of town was Rolfe Barnard! It was Rolfe Barnard who established the First Baptist Church of Borger, Texas which still stands today. It was he who brought religion to "Booger Town." Hopefully, the history of Borger, Texas can be rewritten to include the name of Rolfe Barnard.

We turn to his comments regarding this sensational time in his ministry with the following from his sermon, "I Remember Dixie":

> In my early ministry, a little over thirty-one years ago, I went to the world's largest oil town that just sprung up in a cow pasture. In a little while there were 50,000 people there crawling over one another's backs to see who could get to hell the quickest. I was the only preacher there for sixteen months and I watched men die. For sixteen months I preached on average three funerals a day. I preached as many as seven funerals in one day! I was just a boy twenty-three years old and I lived with death. I lived in the County Hospital where the old folks would be sent, you know, and there to rot and die and when they were dying they would call for "the Preacher." I lived in the houses of ill fame and the saloons where men would get shot and poor women would get shot or die of disease, and just before they died they would call for "the Preacher" and there they would look in my face and beg me not to let them go to hell. They would want me to pray for them but it would be too late to pray then.

> I remember Dixie. Dixie was the queen of the dance hall girls in my oil field town. When she came to die she was just twenty-three years old. She had already been married seven times, and was now living, of course, in sin with an eighth man. I remember when Dixie sent somebody to me and said she wanted the Preacher to tie the knot, that she was going

to get married again. I sent word back that I would not marry her. She got so mad; she came to see me and said, "It is some note, when a girl wants to be decent and the preacher won't tie the knot!" I said, "Dixie, you can go get somebody else to tie the knot, but I don't want to have anything to do with it." I said, "You can't get married in the sight of God."

I remember when Dixie called for me later. She had been on the dance floor and she was dancing with some man and another fellow came and tried to take her out of the arms of the other man. They got into a scuffle and somebody pulled the trigger, and instead of shooting the man, the bullet went into the vitals of Dixie. They carried her into her bedroom there. There was no use to take her to the hospital. They summoned the doctor and the nurse, and in a little while my phone rang and someone said, "Preacher, Dixie is dying and she is calling for you." I went. When I went, the doctor was gone and the nurse was there. She said, "Preacher, you can come on in; we have done all we can. There is no hope for Dixie."

I went over and sat by the bed. I said, "Dixie, this is the preacher and you sent for me. What do you want, Dixie?" "Oh!" she said, "Preacher, don't let me go to hell!" I said, "Dixie, I wish I could keep you out of hell, but I can't keep you out of hell." She said, "Preacher, won't you pray for me?" I said, "Dixie, I'm afraid it's too late to pray now. God never has saved anybody unless they were brought to repent and to believe in the Lord Jesus Christ."

And so she said, "Well, Preacher, how do you do that?" And the best I could I sat by her bedside in that late midnight hour when I could almost see death in her face. I preached unto her the law and the gospel, and when I finished, Dixie turned (I don't know how she had strength enough to do it) and faced the wall with her back turned toward me. And great racking sobs filled the room, I thought they would tear her body in pieces; great racking sobs came from Dixie's throat. In a little while she turned back and looked into my face, and *I saw hell*. Brother, I saw hell! Oh, I saw hell! And as I demanded that she repent right then and there, Dixie said, "I can't. If I were to be healed I'd go back to my way of life." Then Dixie screamed out of that croaking voice, "Preacher, I can't repent! I can't repent!" And God help me! She died as she said that last, "I can't repent!"

I carry the memory of Dixie's beautiful face around with me, and sometimes, please God, I wake up in the night and I hear that croaking voice, "Preacher, I can't repent; I can't repent!" The last words that girl ever said here on this earth before her body began to rot, and her spirit went back into the hands of God who gave it—the last words she ever said, "I can't repent! I can't repent!"

The impact on the impressionable young, twenty-three-year-old preacher of seeing men and woman die so tragically stayed with him and haunted him for life. The time Rolfe Barnard spent in "Booger Town" was probably the best training he ever received for the preaching ministry. No seminary classroom can train ministers like that!

No seminary classroom can indoctrinate you to death bed scenes and hell holes of infamy where people strive for money and lust and end up dying and going to hell. Oh, Rolfe Barnard would still receive a "formal seminary" education at Southwestern Baptist Seminary in Forth Worth, Texas, but what he had already learned in "Booger Town" put him far above all his classmates. He entered seminary as a *seasoned veteran* preacher who knew what it was like to see hell in the face of a lost sinner who had rebelled too long against a holy God and waited too late to do anything about it. God had set His seal upon Evangelist Barnard's ministry in "Booger Town" for under his preaching there over 2,300 persons had claimed Christ as their Lord and Savior. But this was only the beginning of what God seemed pleased to do in the life and ministry of his servant Rolfe Pickens Barnard.

Chapter Five

The Ten Cent Book

*Thus saith the LORD, Stand ye in the ways, and see, and ask for the old paths,
where is the good way, and walk therein, and ye shall find rest for your souls. —
Jeremiah 6:16*

Rolfe Barnard commented that a ten cent book ruined his
ministry. He could have been a popular preacher had he not read
that book! Once he read that book it changed his "message" from
that point on. He explained this in his sermon entitled, "He Could
Do No Mighty Works Because of Unbelief":

> My ministry was ruined, I suppose, of ever being a popular
> preacher, or making any money and getting anywhere, while
> I was a student in the seminary at Fort Worth. One day I went
> down to a second hand bookstore and browsing around I
> found a book of sermons by Brother B. H. Carroll, one of the
> old giants of the faith, and the founder of the school where I
> was going then. I bought that book for a dime and I still got it.
> I was reading a sermon by that dear man of God and just like
> a key that unlocks a door, *my Lord revealed a truth to me.* I
> was rebelling against what my professors were teaching me.
> My professors believed in the great doctrines of the Word of
> God. What little I have ever learned about them I was taught
> by those men.
>
> I was taught the gospel in Southwestern Theological
> Seminary. I was a student there 1928 to 1930. I haven't
> changed a word of my message since. Those old professors
> taught us boys the gospel of the glory of God. But at the first I

rebelled against them. My professor told me that election was God's purpose in redemption, and he actually taught me that God chose people in Christ, the ones who would be saved. Why everything in me hated that, so I rebelled against it and I argued with them. I had been pastor of a big church and I baptized many, many people; and I was a big shot in those days. To hear such teaching from a Baptist professor and all the attendant things that go along with the foundation of the gospel of Jesus Christ, I couldn't take it. I fought them and I was miserable. I read this one sermon from the pen of our dear Brother Carroll in a sermon he preached. He was preaching on "The Voice of Authority" and he quoted John 5:25: *"Verily, verily, I say unto you, The hour is coming, and now is, when the dead shall hear the voice of the Son of God: and they that hear shall live."* One sentence the dear man said is this: "I well know," said Brother Carroll, "that if my voice is the only one you hear in this gospel service, you will go away from here, nothing bettered, but if in the providence of God, *you hear His voice speak to you, He has authority in His voice, and if you hear Him, you shall live."* That is the heart of the truth of the gospel of our Lord Jesus Christ.

From that juncture on Rolfe Barnard preached the gospel of the glory of God. Much had transpired since "Booger Town"; he had married Hazel Hayes Hilliard at Amarillo, Texas on October 25, 1927, and the following January of 1928 he enrolled in Southwestern Baptist Seminary. The seminary had been founded in 1905 by B. H. Carroll, the man in the ten cent book! These formative seminary days solidified his theological message which he preached from that point forward.

He and Hazel would move around in these early days of their marriage to various pastorates in the Southwest. Rolfe took a pastorate for a while in Portales, New Mexico, then one in Denton, Texas, then two years in the state of Oklahoma in Wetumka. After seminary graduation he and Hazel traveled to New York City to work in the Bowery Mission at the invitation of a fellow seminary graduate. It was in the Bowery that Rolfe saw the results of what sin can do in the life of a man, making his life a hell before he even gets there! He said that in the Bowery Mission every bum wanted to accept Jesus Christ and all would go forward in the public invitation time and then later, that same night go out and get drunk and debased all over again. Rolfe commented that the down and outs were needy for Jesus but their wills were just too far gone. There was no real *change*.

As Rolfe Barnard began his itinerant ministry he realized the *price* that ten cent book had cost him! The message of sovereign grace was unpopular in America and he speaks of the obstacles he faced in preaching a unpopular message. This also, from his sermon "He Could Do No Mighty Works Because of Unbelief":

> The most solemn thing I have faced for thirty years going up and down this country is that life is absolutely in the hands of the Lord Jesus Christ. There isn't any life anywhere else. I have had men cuss me; I've had them to storm up on the pulpit with their Bibles; I've had them to have all night prayer meetings, praying that I would get the light, as I have tried to press upon men and women this truth. The only way on God's earth that this old preacher knows there is any hope of an eternity bound sinner is to recognize and openly confess to this godless world that the Lord Jesus Christ is my Lord, whether I ever get saved or not. God has appointed Him to be my Lord, I know it is so, and I want you to know that I am in His hands. I am subject to Him and He can do with me as He pleases. I am dead and He has got life, and I will never have life unless He gives it to me. Life is in the hands of the Lord Jesus Christ.

> He has got life and bless God, He has ordained that Christ will give life to other people. That is the reason we go up and down this country and wear our bodies out, and fight the preachers and everybody else and tell you that hell is full of people who believed a fact of the death of Christ. But heaven will be full of people who have been joined by faith to the Christ who died and rose again.

One example of how Rolfe's "message" kept him from ever having a big popular ministry occurred at a conference when he preached plainly on the doctrine of election and some "big names" in fundamental circles disowned him and spoke against him. He was unfairly labeled as a "Hyper-Calvinist" who preached error! From that point on (1949) the large conference platforms were closed to Barnard and he became known as a *controversial figure*. The "ten cent book" indeed had a big price attached to it but it was this message of God's sovereign grace which launched him into a deep and penetrating ministry of being used of God to awaken men to their lost condition and to face eternity.

One of Brother Barnard's delights was ministry to ministers. He taught many young preachers the doctrines of grace and the following sermon extract is an example of his preaching at this time, taken from his sermon, "Awakening and Exhorting":

> I once knew someone who was greatly disturbed that I preached election and the responsibility of man. I want to sound a word of caution that Baptists are likely to fall into the same pit as the Jewish elect nation did and brag on ourselves and crucify Christ at the same time. It is a Bible fact that a perverted conception of the doctrine of election led to the crucifixion of the Son of God. God help you get it right. And keep your mouth shut unless it grows extremely missionary, evangelistic, intercessory churches.

> As long as Mr. Wet Eyes and Mr. Amen are absent from our congregations we're still going to be dead. That person who believes that in the province of God that he has forever been the object of God's affection is under a tremendous debt. That if God should show mercy to you, He wouldn't have much trouble saving anybody else. And you are a disgrace to the name of Jesus Christ and any of the precious doctrines that buttress His ministry, if that doctrine doesn't lead you to long that every other human being shall drink at the same fountain where your thirst for God was quenched, and I wish we could come back to that.

> So many young preachers go off half-cocked and take a doctrine and beat hell out of everybody with it but the doctrine's no good except as a foundation for Christ. And I long for us not to have to say but the heart of missions and evangelism is the movement that we sometimes call Calvinism. I never admit to that term now because the average Calvinist believes in the grace of God as an excuse to live like hell. And I don't like that. We're filling hell with the carnal doctrine of security of a believer which is not what the Scriptures teach. And we need to be humble. God help us to measure up to the fact that

if you have any life from God you can't brag about it; it was given to you. And I wish we'd be merciful to others who have not yet come to the light we may think we have and know that it is our job to adorn the doctrine of Jesus Christ. There are just two weapons, my friends, that the church of the Lord Jesus has wherewith to prosecute the task that the Lord gave us. They are preaching and prayer. Strangely enough we've been getting along without both for nearly sixty years. Our preaching has been mostly a religious whine and an attack on somebody who ain't present. And we've majored on minors. And we are out at the fringes and we are isolating ourselves to the mainstream Word of God and we have got so separated that sinners start running every time they see us coming. We are so little like Him who was a friend of sinners.

It is obvious that Rolfe Barnard lived out what he believed to be a vital life change that transpired at salvation. He preached with authority because he knew it was Christ preaching *through* him and that in order to be an ambassador for Christ that before one entered the pulpit he had to first spend time on his knees and weep over the lost before preaching to them. Rolfe knew full well that mere doctrine alone could not save anybody. Merely believing the doctrine of election never saved a soul. One had to have Christ *revealed* to them through the preaching of those great doctrines in order for the lost sinner to hear *His voice* through the human instrument standing in the pulpit.

This understanding placed Rolfe Barnard in direct succession to other Calvinist preachers such as Whitefield, Spurgeon, Edwards. These men had a lively faith and preached a vital gospel of God's sovereign grace. Barnard knew the doctrine of election alone preached to the head was deadening to the soul. He comments on this from his sermon, "Awakening and Exhorting":

The truth in itself is the coldest deadest thing this side of hell! And there is nothing on God's earth that does as much harm as a professing Christian expounding truth without a sob in his voice—that's the God's truth! Give me a "deep creek" Arminian every time to a "dry eyed" Calvinist. Truth not saturated in intercessory prayer burns everything it touches! And we desperately need to get on the mourner's bench there. Our churches have turned into societies where we congratulate ourselves instead of bleeding hearts stretching out to reach a world of sinners.

Rolfe Barnard's theology was not contained to ivory towers but lived itself out practically and passionately for the perishing souls in his generation. The "ten cent book" was a way of life. And there was another Book that Rolfe centered himself in and saturated himself with—he was a man of one Book. He knew his Bible. He believed in its great miracles, its great truths were a balm to his heart, and the Word of God was the foundation for his entire ministry. To get a sense of this look at his comments from his sermon, "The Record of God's Revelation to Sinful Men":

> I remember many years ago I was a student in the seminary at Fort Worth, Texas, and I had what they called a student pastorate. I lived in Fort Worth and went out on the weekends and preached to the people. One day I got a telephone call and they said, "Mr. So-and-So is dead and we want you to come and preach his funeral." I left my classes and got on a bus and went out to my little church about sixty miles from Fort Worth, and I went into the home. There was that dear widow with a lot of dear children, and there in the casket, already laid out, was the still body of her husband. I was a very young preacher. And I remember that pretty soon after I got there, this dear woman brought me the Book and just handed it to me and said, "Pastor, read out of the Book. Read out of the Book." Why sure! Read out of the Book. It is God's record. Don't let anybody rob you of that. When death comes, read out of the Book. It is God's Book. If you need a Savior, read about One in the Book. It is God's Book. If you wonder about the future, bless God, read out of the Book. It is in God's hands. I still believe in the good old Book.

The advice that, "when death comes, read out of the Book" would prove a reality in the life of Rolfe and his young bride Hazel. They would experience the tragedy of the death of their first child. Their precious, darling daughter, Patty Sue would die at the tender age of three and a half years. Rolfe would occasionally mention this solemn time of personal loss to them. He was at a preaching engagement and he received a phone call that if he wanted to see his daughter alive he must come at once. He borrowed a car and drove all night and finally got home in time to see his weary wife sitting by the bedside of their dying daughter. Rolfe held little Patty Sue's cold hand and as he looked into her pain-filled eyes he felt helpless to relieve her suffering. She could not speak but her eyes were speaking to her daddy to help her! But he could give no help other than sit there holding her hand and witnessing her death. God would be pleased to bless Rolfe and Hazel years later with another daughter, Jo Ann. But the death of Patty Sue brought the stark reality home that when death comes it is time to turn to the Book! There is solace in the Word of God. We have his account of this trial from his sermon, "Death":

In our young life, Mrs. Barnard and I sat where you're sitting, as they brought the casket with the body of our first born into the little tabernacle style church house where I ministered. Another minister stood up and preached what they call a "funeral sermon."

We were young, we'd had our youngster three and a half years, and now, we didn't have her. They wheeled the casket out and put it in a hearse and we followed it to a cemetery and they lowered the casket with flowers on it and sent us home. They didn't want us to see, didn't want us to hear the clods of dirt falling on the casket of the body of our baby.

We had the funeral in the morning and my wife and I slipped away later and went out to the cemetery. Already flowers were beginning to wilt under the sun. At that little mound covered with flowers we knelt on either side, and through our tears, the woman—there is something about the feminine sex, apprehends truth like this that we men don't know about—my girl bride, bereft mother, said, "It's all right, Rolfe. Patty Sue isn't here. She's with the Lord. She's with the Lord." And that's so, dear ones, that's so. She is asleep waiting for the time when the One who said, "Our friend Lazarus sleepeth, I go to awake him." He shall speak and she will awake! She'll awake.

God used this awful trial to make His servant more like Him. God brought comfort to the grieving parents that were soon to be separated for a season—because of World War Two. Rolfe would join the Army as a chaplain and he would reach thousands of G. I.'s with the gospel of God's glory.

Chapter Six

Army Chaplain

And as it is appointed unto men once to die, but after this the judgment.
—Hebrews 9:27

With the outset of World War Two and as America sacrificed her young men to the war effort, Rolfe Barnard saw a great need emerge. He saw that thousands of enlisted men were going out to fight on foreign soil to defend their country and many would never return alive. Rolfe wanted to get to as many as he could before death confronted them. Some of the greatest lessons he learned emerged from his experience as an Army chaplain.

Before he enlisted in the Army he set up a tent near the perimeter of a Air Force training camp in Montgomery, Alabama. The camp of thirty thousand men gave Rolfe plenty of opportunities to preach and witness to the young soldiers as they entered and left the camp. But after a while this ministry door became closed. At first he moved his ministry around to train stations where he could reach the young enlisted men. He had a makeshift platform with loud speakers and he would preach. But soon this too was no longer effective. He realized he had no other choice but to "join up" if he was to reach these men before they died on the battlefield and entered eternity. Rolfe Barnard enlisted in the Army as a chaplain. He speaks of this experience from his sermon, "I Was an Army Chaplain":

> I entered the chaplaincy to preach to men who were going to shed their blood for their country. First I got some big

tents and went to places adjacent to military training camps. I saw that if you could confront young men who were on their way to kill or be killed with Christ and the Christ of the Bible, some of them would listen to you. Finally the Army shut this opportunity down so I had to get "inside" and I'll hold my nose, and I'm going to try to preach to these boys.

So I got in the Army. I found out the desperate moral religious condition America was in. I lived in the atmosphere of training boys to kill. And I learned there that holiness is sneered at and righteousness is an unknown word and this generation is going to hell with a little religious profession while we rot in moral corruption. I saw in the Army the product of Sunday morning easy believism without transformation of character and calling it salvation. I saw the promotion of fornication and adultery in the Army. I was stationed in Montgomery, Alabama with thirty thousand soldiers. My Catholic chaplain supervisor said, "Brother Barnard you work harder than any of the chaplains I've got, reach more men and raise more hell than all my two hundred chaplains put together." He said, "I don't understand a fellow like you. Are all Baptists like you?" I said, "Oh, no, I don't guess the world could stand anybody else like me." He said, "I don't understand your philosophy. Unless a soldier can go to town on Saturday night and get him a quart of whiskey and a blonde woman life ain't worth living." He was the supervisory chaplain!

I won many Catholic boys to the Lord but I made them promise not to tell because they would have been court marshaled and so would I. They would have court marshaled me for talking to a Catholic boy about his soul.

I went to Harvard University to learn how to be a chaplain. They had chapel every week: Jew, Catholic, and Protestant all in the same service. The chaplains were instructed not to be seen drunk in public; if you had to get drunk do it in your room! Now the boys that were real Christians were a minority and they were made fun of—they were called "Holy Joe's."

Back at training camp I had a unique experience. For nine months I preached to these boys knowing I would never preach to them again. For nine months every Sunday I preached to a different group of soldiers, sixteen hundred at a time in chapel, they would march them into the theater and I would preach to a different group each Sunday knowing I would never see them again. We had a thirty minute service and I broke all the rules! I refused to lead in the "Lord's Prayer" because I'm not going to allow an unsaved man to say "Our Father," because God isn't his father. I'd buck 'em! They wouldn't let me give an invitation but they couldn't keep me from doing this—I would say, "Now if any of you boys are interested in faith or the lack of it in the Lord Jesus you write your name and squadron number down on that card and after the service pass it to the ushers and they will take it up at the close of the service. And I'd get hundreds of these names everyday! What I did as chaplain, instead of handing out drinks and cigarettes and sponsoring dances and all that junk I just had a prayer meeting going on all the time! I'd have a prayer meeting there in my study. I'd get on the phone to a squadron commander and read a boy's name off one of those cards and say, "This is Chaplain Barnard. I want you to send so and so over to see me" and they would have to do it! And there comes this boy and we'd lock the door and he wanted to know the Lord and I tried to show him.

During the war I heard of a terrible casualty of eight of our bombers that were shot down over Germany and we lost five hundred boys. And I thought about how many of those boys when I get to the judgment and they find out I had one chance to preach to them and they think I'm an old sourpuss but they didn't have many opportunities to hear a chaplain preach on Christ and hell! When I get to the judgment I'm going to be looking for the thousands, looking how many of these precious boys I'll have to see sent to hell! Be a witness against them! I didn't talk to them to tell them how to be good—I just had a simple message—there's just one remedy for deep, dark-dyed sin and that's to have the merits of the Lord's life laid down, applied to you so that when a thrice holy God looks on poor old Rolfe Barnard He'll say, "When I see the blood" that is my only hope! And it's yours! That is the only way God can avoid sending you to hell; that is to have His Son upon a cross and have you be a partaker of that cross—Blood, Blood, Blood!

One day Rolfe's commanding officer sent him on a secret mission to a training camp where five hundred soldiers were waiting to be shipped out. Chaplain Barnard was to deliver the letter giving them their shipping orders! He also was allowed to preach to those boys before they shipped out the next day. They all sat in a grove and Chaplain Barnard got up on a little platform and a soldier played a pump organ while another soldier sang, "There Is Power in the Blood." Then Rolfe preached the gospel to those soldiers. The boys knew the danger that awaited them and there was a certain solemnity in the air that afternoon as the Christ of the cross was proclaimed with all authority by the faithful servant of God in an Army uniform. As the soldier boys sat on the grass Rolfe Barnard called out to them in a final plea, "It's Christ or hell!" And then they parted company never to meet again.

Rolfe's experience as an Army chaplain gave him the largest preaching platform of his life. For over a nine month period he had the awesome privilege to preach to 58,000 men! He took his work seriously. He had joined the service just to reach those men! He pleaded with them as a dying man to dying men and presented Christ of the cross risen in all His authority! The eternal impact of this time of ministry will be revealed at That Day. But for Rolfe Barnard he would carry those special memories with him for the rest of his life when he wore an army uniform and preached to young soldier boys the risen Christ.

Chapter Seven

Piedmont Bible Institute

And the things that thou hast heard of me among many witnesses, the same commit thou to faithful men, who shall be able to teach others also. — *2 Timothy 2:2*

Soon after the War, Rolfe and Hazel settled in the state of Oklahoma where he was the pastor of a Baptist church there. But late in 1946, Brother Barnard received an invitation from Piedmont Bible Institute in Winston-Salem, North Carolina to come and be their school evangelist and a part time theology professor. They prayed about it and felt God's call to pack up their belongings and make the move to Winston-Salem which would be the Barnard's home for the rest of their lives. This move would broaden his ministry and introduce him to wider circles within the fundamentalist camp. Barnard would be on faculty there from 1946 to 1949 and it would be a good move for both of them. His connection to Piedmont Bible Institute gave him instant prominence within the community and Hazel made friends with the wives of the faculty members.

Rolfe soon found he was in demand as a preacher in the Winston-Salem area. He would teach school by day and preach in area churches in the evenings. It was during his time at the Bible school that he began a local radio ministry which in itself broadened his ministry platform in North Carolina. Rolfe's radio ministry was controversial. He preached on repentance and election and sin and hell! Many tuned in to hear this Southern preacher sound forth over the radio each day! And many came to know the Lord during his useful time in the Piedmont area. Many church members were saved under his awakening preaching. We get a glimpse of this from his sermon, "Who Is Going to Heaven?":

Some years ago I was the school evangelist and part-time teacher in North Carolina. I would drive at night to hold meetings so they arranged for some of the students to drive for me to help save my strength. One night a boy by the name of Roger Merritt drove for me to the preaching service. And when we got back from the service as he got out of the car he slipped me a little bill of money. He said, "Brother Barnard, my wife and I have been saving for some time; we want to give you a gift." I thanked him and put it in my pocket. He was going to school on the G. I. Bill, and he had a wife and four children. He was selling shoes in his spare time and living on his G. I. Bill and going to school to be a preacher. And he didn't have much money, so I thought he might have given me five dollars.

I went home and I was dressing for the night and I put my hand in my pocket and there was that bill. I took it out and looked at it and it was a one hundred dollar bill! It scared me; I thought he made a mistake so I called him. I said, "Roger, do you know what you did?" He said, "What was it?" "Did you know you gave me a hundred dollar bill?" He said, "Sure. We have been saving for months." I said, "I just know you made a mistake. You haven't got that kind of money, I am going to bring it back to you." He said, "You wouldn't insult us, would you? We have got so much joy out of saving it; we wanted you to have it. We love you."

Have you ever had a little part in bringing somebody to Christ? If you have, they love you. That is wonderful. When he decided to be a preacher his wife rebelled. She said, "I didn't marry a preacher. I am not going to take it and I am not going through all this going-to-school business." She wouldn't let him have a family altar. It was pretty bad in the home. I went to his community and held a meeting; she came to hear me one night, and she got mad at me. She said, "I wouldn't go back to hear that fool anymore." But she did and God saved her. He said, "We have a family altar now. We read the Bible and pray together. We got a little heaven in our home and we love you." He said, "You know my mother and you know what happened to her. You keep that hundred dollars because we love you."

His mother was in her seventies; she had been a charter member for over forty years of the church where I was preaching. And one night I preached and I said, "If there is somebody here troubled and you need help and you want prayer, raise your hand," and old Mother Merritt lifted her hand. We sang an invitation song and Mother Merritt walked down to the front and knelt at the pew. After the service was over somebody walked up to her to help, but she said, "No. Nobody can help me."

The second night she did the same thing. I have you to understand she was "the Christian" of that congregation and everybody looked up to her. A blessed woman. The third night, my soul, there was no small controversy everywhere. They were saying, "That fool preacher has got Mother Merritt confused. If there is a Christian around here, she is one. He can't be preaching the truth or she wouldn't be disturbed." She just kept coming night after night, she would lift her hand, and in her trouble she would get down there and pray. You are not saved by praying, but you are not saved apart from praying. It is the heart's cry of the sinner to the Lord.

My, she got me a crowd! They were coming to hear that fool preacher that had got Mother Merritt disturbed. I couldn't disturb anybody but God can. One night I thought maybe I could help, so I knelt down by her and said, "Mother Merritt, can any of us be of any help to you?" She said, "No, preacher, this is something I got to wrestle through. I have been trying to serve the Lord for over fifty years and I have never had a minute of the peace of God. Just leave me alone." She pointed above and said, "Only He can help me. You preach that He speaks peace and He has never spoken peace to me, and you preach that there is peace. God says, 'My peace I give unto you.' I am going to get in touch with Him. If He is the One who speaks peace, I am going to seek Him until He speaks peace to me."

The meeting went on and Sunday morning they asked me

to speak in Sunday school, so I came a little early. I got out of my car when down the steps of the church came Mother Merritt. She was German, had silver white hair, and beautiful pink cheeks. She came walking to me like a sixteen-year-old in her seventy-year-old body. She came up to me and said, "Brother B'nard, this morning at eight o'clock whilst I was washing the breakfast dishes, the living Lord did speak peace to my soul."

And He is still in that business! Bless God, He is alive and He is the God of all peace!

Soon the name of Rolfe Barnard was well known within the surrounding community and the Barnard family were happy to call Winston-Salem home. Although he would spend the remainder of his life as a "hitchhike evangelist" living out of strangers' homes and hotel rooms, he always looked forward to returning to his home base in North Carolina. Hazel would at times accompany him on his itinerant ministry, for she was a gifted pianist and she would play the piano and Rolfe would sing solos at the meetings! Rolfe had a pleasant singing voice and he enjoyed singing to his Lord. Soon there would be "another sound" attending Rolfe Barnard's meetings—the sound of rustling in the tops of the mulberry trees.

Chapter Eight

An Awakening Ministry

And he came thither unto a cave, and lodged there; and, behold, the word of the LORD came to him, and he said unto him, What doest thou here, Elijah? And he said, I have been very jealous for the LORD God of hosts. — *1 Kings 19:9-10*

For the forty year period from 1929 to 1969 Rolfe Pickens Barnard was the *only* itinerant sovereign grace evangelist in America. He had a prophetic ministry which God used to awaken lost church members and bring them to Christ. The post war years of 1947 to the mid 1950's was the most profound of his preaching ministry; revival blessings attended much of his preaching during this time.

Rolfe had a series of radio messages entitled, "John the Baptist Comes to Town" and one could compare Barnard to the prophet because when evangelist Barnard came to town there was a shaking from on high! This happened on more than one occasion and it was not limited to a particular geographical area. God seemed pleased to send revival to various congregations and towns and He used Rolfe as the human instrument. There were "stirrings" from Boston, to the Midwest, and down to the South. There are many accounts of what God did when Rolfe Barnard came to town; we will share one such account from a man converted under Barnard's gripping ministry. The following was written by Dr. John Thornbury, author and pastor, and it is taken from Volume One of the *Sermons of Rolfe Barnard.* It describes in part the revival which occurred during a tent meeting. Men were gripped with the conviction of sin and unable to sleep at night. There was an awful sense of God as lost church members realized their dreadful state and were faced with the issues of eternity. Here now is Dr. Thornbury's compelling story:

I well recall when Rolfe Barnard first came to my hometown, Ashland, Kentucky. It was the spring of 1950. I was a teenage boy and attended, along with my mother, younger sister and brother, a large Baptist church. It was one of the most influential churches in eastern Kentucky with a membership of about 1,000. Some way, I do not recall how, they scheduled Rolfe Barnard to come and speak.

In those days evangelistic services were conducted annually, sometimes more often. They were known as "revival meetings." Some of the most prominent evangelists in America came to our church. Evangelistic services were extravaganzas; there was almost a "show biz" atmosphere. They featured fancy musicians, former boxers, convicts and entertainers as speakers, and all kinds of gimmicks and goodies for the youth. Aeroplane rides were offered for those who brought enough people to church and there were rewards for those who induced others to walk down the church aisles after the sermons. It was the big boom and everyone seemed to enjoy it. I do not recall there being much permanent good effect of these "revivals." After all the excitement died down, people usually went about their sinful ways of living as before.

Like all the guest-evangelists who came, the picture of Barnard was placed on posters and nailed all over town. Beneath his picture was an interesting slogan. It said, "The evangelist who is different." Exactly what was different about him the posters did not say. The man looked to be in his late forties. The only thing noticeably different about his appearance was that he came across as somewhat somber— there was a slightly menacing look on his face. Normally, evangelists had broad smiles and shining faces advertising the jolly good fellows they were.

After a few sermons in the church, folk knew just how different Rolfe Barnard was from the evangelists who had visited the church before. There was none of the flashy demeanor, but a grave and dignified bearing like one who had been sent on a mission. One soon got the impression that he was not there to whip up religious excitement but to deliver a message from God.

The message was as startling as it was different. It centered around the character of God, a God about whom most had never heard before. The deity most were acquainted with was a nice sort of fellow who did his best to save people, but was often frustrated in the attempt. Many times I have heard preachers say, "God has done all He can for you, now it is up to you." I used to listen with astonishment to this statement, for I wondered why I should seek help from a being who could not help me. Barnard, on the other hand, preached a God who was sovereign and omnipotent, One who dispensed His mercy according to His own discretion. He preached that sinners were not to come to God with the idea of helping him out of his dilemma, but they were to come as guilty sinners, suing for mercy. He exalted the holiness of God and the strictness of His law. This, you can be sure, was different.

Rumors began to spread all over town that a Calvinist had come to Ashland. Some reacted with amazement, some with confusion, others with down-right anger. But a small group rejoiced and said, "We have been waiting to hear this for years." My father, who believed in the doctrines of grace, started attending the services and announced to all of us that there was one at the church preaching the theology in which he believed.

The pastor, after much heart-searching and Bible study, came to believe in the doctrines of grace as a result of this meeting and invited Barnard back in the summer of 1951 to hold a tent meeting in a large park down-town. In the intervening months a division developed over the so-called "five points" of Calvinism with the majority becoming more hostile. The pastor was a very talented and gracious man with a winsome personality, and he tried to woo as many as possible to the "new" view, but most stiffened and gave him trouble.

The church had a very active youth group, including a choir. I was a member of this choir and also sang in a quartet with others about my age. I had been baptized at the age of twelve but was utterly without any vital relationship to God in my life. There was in fact a terrible, aching void in my heart which I could not understand. Still, I did not even want to consider that I was not a Christian.

The two-week meeting in the park was a memorable event. The crowds were fairly large, considering the type of preaching which was sounding out. Barnard boldly preached the gospel as he understood it, often denouncing the superficiality of modern religion. We were all fascinated with his style, though he seemed awfully stern and rough. Plain truths of the Word of God were set forth, even the harshest, in their naked reality. One of his favorite texts was "God will have mercy upon whom He will have mercy."

Shortly after the meetings started, there began a breaking up. Many, mostly adults, began to go forward after the messages and state publicly that they were lost and wanted prayer. These, and others who sat trembling in the audience, were under "conviction of sin." The amazing thing is that most of them were church members. I remember one night the piano stopped playing during the invitation and the pianist went to the front seat and sat down sobbing. We all knew she meant that she wanted to be saved. Prominent church leaders such as deacons, Sunday school teachers, and youth workers began to acknowledge that they had been false professors or deceived about their state before God. Our male quartet was singing each night under the big tent, and as it turned out later not one of us was converted at this time. One night Don, one of the members of the quartet, went to the front where the pastor and evangelist were standing and asked for prayer. It was announced that he was lost and needed Christ. It was at this point that I became involved in the picture. God was about to set me straight.

At that time I had the notion that anyone who had any religious feelings such as "seeking after God" was a true Christian. I misunderstood the text in Romans which says that there is none that seeketh after God. At any rate, it rankled me somewhat that my friend had been disturbed by the evangelist. At this very time my own soul was torn asunder because I had no real assurance of salvation, but I had a reputation of being a young theologian who believed in Calvinistic doctrine. I thought this would be a good time for me to show my skill in counseling and to help my friend who was in trouble.

I went to the front of the tent where Barnard and the pastor were talking to Don. Butting in like the immature, upstart youth I was, I said to him, "Don, you do not need to worry. You are seeking God. The lost man does not seek God. Therefore you have the life of God in you, and you are saved," or words to that effect. Never, till the day I die, will I forget what Rolfe Barnard said to me. Looking straight at me with his piercing eyes, he said, "Young man, a believer is not seeking Christ, he has found Christ."

Ten pointed arrows piercing my body, or a jolt of electricity would not have shaken me more than those words. Barnard had not only corrected a false notion which would have led Don astray but also he put his finger on a raw nerve in my own life. With this statement, through the work of the Holy Spirit in my heart, he stripped aside the shroud of pseudo-religion in which I had been hiding and left me standing exposed to my true condition. I did not know Christ.

I was angry. As my parents drove home, I said little, but within I was seething as I resisted the pricklings of the Holy Spirit on my conscience. Was this abrasive preacher right? Was it true that seeking is not enough, one must actually find Christ? If so, I knew I was lost, a fact I did not want to face. That night I told my mother that I wanted her to pray for me, because I thought I might not be saved. I expected her to have some words of comfort, for after all I was a good boy, supposedly, one of the model young men in the church. She had no soothing balm for me, but only said, "Son, I'll pray for you."

What went on in the twenty-four hours would take many pages to tell, but briefly I will say that I spent the most miserable night of my life that night wrestling with the condition of my soul. The next morning somewhat humbled, I told the pastor and the evangelist (there were morning services) that I was lost. I recall well the pastor's words. He said, "John, this is not surprising, since most of our best young people are coming to realize that they have never had a real experience of grace."

There were no words of counsel given me except these, "God saves sinners." This is all that was said to me about how to get relief. This seemed like a brush-off, but I went away. Before the day was over God used the words of the song, "Jesus Paid It All," to bring peace to my heart. Through this song, Christ and His substitutionary work came before my mind. The Holy Spirit seemed to be telling me that it was for me that Jesus had died, and that all my sins were put away forever. That night I joyfully confessed Christ to the crowd and later was baptized, along with twenty or so others who were converted in the tent meeting.

I have given this firsthand account of Barnard's ministry in one city because it illustrates in a capsule way the leading elements of his evangelistic preaching. What happened in the church in Ashland is a sample of what occurred in dozens of places throughout America and parts of Canada. While different churches and communities responded differently to Barnard's preaching, there were many instances in the 1950's and 1960's especially where churches were claimed for truth and many sinners were converted. According to an article written by R. T. Kendall in 1969, shortly after Barnard's death, Barnard estimated that about 100,000 people professed faith in Christ during his forty years of preaching.

The impact of Rolfe Barnard's ministry, as told by Dr. John Thornbury, typifies all the elements involved in a "Barnard Meeting." As Rolfe preached the great doctrines of the Bible and proclaimed the absolute sovereign character and attributes of a holy God, there was quite a stir in the church! First, some unconverted church members would grow angry at both the preacher and God. They had never heard such biblical truths before! Then there was a wrestling within the sinner for their hearts would accept the truths but their minds would argue that "their God" would never act that way! And it was usually true; *their god* would not but the God of the Bible would! Unconverted church members would be shaken to their core over the realization that the foundation they were resting upon was that of sand. They then would be confronted through Barnard's preaching of a living Lord who reigns in glory and who has all authority in His hands to give life or withhold life to whom He pleases—there was nothing in man to merit His grace and mercy. This would shut sinners up to God and cause them to stand guilty against the utter severity of the law of God and the claims of Christ in all lordship!

The following amusing account is reminiscent of a Charles Finney meeting where all hell breaks loose in the meeting! What is startling about the following story is how Rolfe Barnard preached while sick with the flu and God used the flu bug to protect Barnard from the growing animosity of the deacons in this particular church! This account of another move of God among His people is taken from his sermon, "The Father's Answer to the Claims of the Sovereign Redeemer":

That is the cry of our hearts as we go up and down the land. I am trying to preach for the Lord as He would want me to do. Now I am trying to say to you that you are going to go to hell as sure as I am preaching to you unless it becomes a personal reality with you that Christ died for you; that He was raised for you; that He intercedes for you; that He is coming for you; that you are His and He is yours. I pray that the Spirit of God might make that real to somebody as this message goes out. Oh, my soul, the reality that is in Christ Jesus! Do not be satisfied with anything else!

I had the flu years ago, and I closed a meeting with the flu racking my body on a Sunday night. I rested a little while Monday morning. But at eleven o'clock Monday morning I got on a train at Winston-Salem and journeyed to Illinois in my flu-weakened condition. I got there about noon on Tuesday and the pastor met me and took me to a room and called a doctor. The pastor told me there wouldn't be many people to hear me preach that night because they were having some sort of an entertainment at the school. While he apologized, the doctor treated me. I went over that night and preached. I must have preached a powerful sermon because all hell broke loose! The chairman of the board of deacons stood out on the steps after the service and raved and raved, and said, "That man is a false prophet and he is going to tear our church up." I didn't know all about this. I had gone back to the room to my sick bed. This deacon said to the pastor, "Here is a check for $400. I will give it to you if you will pay that preacher off and don't let him preach any more." You know I must have preached a powerful sermon—just one little sermon!

They didn't tell me anything about that and the next night I went over and preached. And it must have been powerful too. I did not understand it, but as soon as I was ready to pronounce the benediction, the pastor said, "I want to meet all the deacons down in the basement." I didn't know what was going on. I slipped out the back door and went back to bed. I was pretty sick. They told me later about how the pastor walked the floor and said, "That preacher is going to ruin us and he is going to tear our church all to pieces," and everybody agreed with him except an old silver-haired deacon. When they got around to him, he said, "Boys, you fellows had better let that preacher alone. *He is preaching the gospel.* You folks have never heard it, and you had better not put your hands on him." I didn't know about all of these things. Thursday night came and the house was just packed and jammed. I wondered what was going on. But unbeknownst to me all of this was going all over the city and here they were coming. Friday night came and the house was packed and jammed. I still didn't know what was going on. Saturday night came, and, lo and behold, the house was crowded and a fellow got up to sing a solo. He didn't mean to do it, but he sang in the power of the Spirit. I saw God take a song, sung in the Spirit, and apply what I had been preaching and pierce hearts with the truth of the gospel. As he stood up there and began to sing, the Holy Ghost took charge of him. He began to sing:

Love sent my Savior to die in my stead,
Why should He love me so?
Meekly to Calvary's cross He was led;
Why should He love me so?
Nails pierced His hands and His feet for my sin.
(Not for somebody else's).
Why should He love me so?
He suffered sore my salvation to win,
(Not somebody else's!)
Why should He love me so?

While he was singing all hell began to pop! The organist quit playing and screamed out, "I am lost! I am lost!" That is the sweetest cry that I ever heard this side of eternity. That is the prelude to the cry, "I am saved." She began running to the prayer room. It was the pastor's wife. Then I heard somebody else sobbing, and that poor pastor said, "Oh, my God, I am lost! I'm lost! I'm lost! I'm lost!" And here he ran. Then I saw 14 Roman Catholics; I saw the Sunday school superintendent; I saw seven deacons; I saw (I don't know just so many) as they screamed out before that man could finish his song. They were in the prayer room on their bones sobbing out their souls to God. Because of my preaching? No. Because the Holy Spirit took a song, the truth of it, and made this thing personal and brought the truth of the gospel and pierced the hearts of those people. Some people there saw for the first time in their lives that Christ died for them; that He agonized for them; that the nails were put in His hands for them; that He was raised for them.

One can see from this remarkable account one of the reasons why God seemed pleased to smile upon the ministry of His servant, Rolfe Barnard; he took no credit for what took place. He knew that what transpired in the lives of those awakened-sinner church members was all of God! Rolfe Barnard knew full well that God will not share His glory with another! Many evangelists see little fruit from their preaching because they are too quick to boast how many they won to the Lord last meeting. Rolfe knew better.

Strange incidents would occur in a Barnard meeting! At times, stretchers would have to be brought in to carry out slain sinners. Other times, demon possessed individuals would cry out and attempt to attack Rolfe Barnard! But one of the eeriest of all is the startling account of how God struck down and removed some church members who were opposing a Rolfe Barnard meeting! There are accounts that when the fiery evangelist Sam Jones held crusades, if there arose opposition from individuals—God removed them! Barnard had much in common with Sam Jones, besides their legal backgrounds.

The following story is taken from his sermon, "Sudden Death":

> The pastor of a church in a certain place asked me to come and hold meetings. Before I got there, seven deacons of that church had come to the pastor and said, "Now Brother Pastor, we are not going to oppose anything, but we don't

believe in what you call evangelistic campaigns. So we will not be back until this preacher is gone and the meetings are over." The pastor said, "Well, I hate to see you take that attitude, but if that is what you want to do, I appreciate you coming and telling me."

Well, if they had done what they said, it would have been all right. But we couldn't get a crowd for a few nights and we were hitting it pretty hard. So those fellows were glad and got to bragging about how we weren't getting anywhere in the meetings. They violated their word that they wouldn't oppose us.

The pastor came to me and he was brokenhearted and he said, "Brother Barnard, this is killing me, what can we do?" I said, "I don't know. Are you game for us to get down on our knees and ask God to save them or kill them?" He agreed, and we got down on our knees and said, "Lord, You know what these fellows are doing. They are ruining the meeting, they are making fun of the gospel, the church, and the Lord Jesus Christ and God's preachers." They were just filling the whole town with this, and everybody was talking about how the meeting was no good, and those seven deacons making fun of it. And so we said, "Lord, save them or kill them!"

Neither one of us was supposed to tell about that prayer, and I don't think I did, but somebody did, and those deacons heard about it. They just heard half of it, though, and so they just had a big time. They said, "The preachers up there are praying for God to kill us!" But we were praying for God to *save them* or kill them, to get them out of the way. They were bucking God, they were hardening themselves against God. I think that is dangerous. They just laughed and had a big time about it. But in four days time, the pastor had *seven different funerals*, and they were the funerals of those seven Baptist deacons. Every one of them died a horrible sudden death! God kills people that harden themselves against His claims for Jesus Christ!

As dramatic as that story is, one can just imagine the effect that those deaths had on that community as people realized the solemnity of making fun of the things of God. The sudden death of the seven obstinate deacons is startling for it brought a whole town to face the God of the Bible!

The next account is how God *saved some men* before they tragically died. Rolfe Barnard saw God move in a saving way early in his ministry while he was still a seminarian. This remarkable story is taken from Rolfe's sermon entitled, "God's Call":

In Texas many years ago while I was a student in Southwestern Seminary there was a little mining town nearby. And I went one summer while I was in school and held what is called revival services. I began the meeting there on Sunday night. I got up that night and I preached; I remember I preached on hell that night and dismissed the congregation, praying that the Holy Spirit would speak to hearts and disturb people.

As we stood there something touched my shoulder. I looked around and the old white-haired pastor stood there, his face drenched in tears. He said, "Brother Preacher, might I say a few words?" Of course, he might, and he said, "Folks, let's don't go home for a few minutes. I just can't let you go right now." Somebody happened to look at his watch and exactly thirty-three minutes later *a lot had happened.* That pastor stood there with his face in tears, and he pointed men out and called them by their given name. I had never seen anything like it! He had been pastor there over thirty years. He knew them by their given name. He said, "Bill, I just can't let you go tonight," and he preached to Bill, and here came Bill. "Jim," and he did that to *thirty-three men,* one by one. Nobody left. He just called those men by name and talked to them, and here they came.

Thirty-three minutes later thirty-three men were lined up! I don't know whether they got saved or not—I'll find out at the judgment. I simply know this—they claimed to. There was power there that night. There was *Somebody there* beside us. God used that preacher to talk to those men through him. He couldn't use me, but He used him. We had an old fashioned hand shaking! We had thirty-three men professing their faith in Christ!

Everybody made their living in the coal mine. But Monday night I didn't preach. I was going to preach, but they didn't have service Monday night. At 4:26 p.m., Monday, one of the mines had an explosion and caved in, and some men were buried in that mine. And the whistle blew and sirens and alarms went off in that little mining town; and all they did was to gather at that mine with all their equipment. And while they worked feverishly, some prayed, some cried, and some cursed!

But they worked to get down to where those men were trapped. The time keeper or whoever is in charge of time consulted his books and knew there were thirty-three men trapped down in that mine. They worked feverishly and finally they got to them, and one by one, they hauled up the bodies of *those thirty-three men* who were crushed in that mine. Every one of them were dead, and they were the thirty-three men that lined up there and said they had received Christ!

What set Rolfe Barnard's ministry apart from his peers was that God chose to honor his preaching with supernatural events! Rolfe preached what others would not preach and God honored that. He never diluted the gospel to make it more palatable to his hearers. He preached a scandalous cross with a bloody Jesus! He preached a risen Lord who reigns in glory! He called sin black and hell hot! He pulled no punches for man's sake.

The next story tells how God awakened the worst sinner in town where Rolfe was holding some meetings up in Canada. It is found in his sermon, "Sovereign Mercy":

I'll never forget a poor fallen woman in Canada. I was up there preaching in a church where no one had been converted in nine years. They were mighty orthodox, mighty separated, and mighty dead. I said to them, "You ought to get acquainted with folks," and they took me seriously. So we went out ringing doorbells up there and inviting people to come hear me preach. It was twenty below zero and I was going around with a deacon from house to house and we came to a wicket gate. I unlatched the gate going up to the house and started to go in. The deacon said, "Brother Barnard, don't go in there." I said, "Why not?" The deacon said, "I don't want to say, but don't go in there." I said, "Why not?" "Oh! I couldn't tell you, but please don't go in there." I said, "I'm going." He said, "It will ruin the meeting." I said, "Why?" "Well, preacher, that is the most notorious woman in this section of Canada. Oh! If you went in there, it would be terrible."

I said, "I'm going." And I went and knocked on the door and a nice looking woman, not yet betrayed by her sinful life, came to the door and said, "Hello, big boy." I said, "Howdy. I am a preacher and am holding meetings down here at the church. I have come to invite you to come and hear me preach tonight." She began to laugh and I said, "It's no joke." She said, "Are you really a preacher?" I said, "Yes." She said, "I believe you are." I said, "Yes, I'm from the South, and I'm preaching here." "Oh!" she said, "I heard about that fellow from the South, and you're him?" "Oh, yes." She said, "Do you know who I am?" I said, "Yes. I've been told that you're the most notorious woman in this section of Canada." She said, "I guess that's right. Do you mean you want me to come up to that church building tonight?" "Yes, I want you to come because I want to preach to you." She said, "Why, if I come up there, it would shock them to death." "Well, they need a good shock and I want you to promise me that you will come and I double-dog dare you to come! Promise me you will."

And bless God, she did. I've never seen the Holy Spirit challenged when He didn't work. I preached that night and before we could get started singing, *here she came.* Just running down to the front and fell down there and sobbed and sobbed and sobbed, and after a while she stood up, tears running down her cheeks, the glory of God on her countenance and she witnessed a mighty good confession.

The congregation was singing people, so they began to quietly sing "Amazing Grace, how sweet the sound, that saved a wretch like me. I once was lost, but now I'm found; was blind, but now I see." They had an old eighty-year-old woman there and she was the mother of Israel of all that section. A fine woman. I wondered what that nice gang of church members were going to do. There was that ex-prostitute standing there claiming the grace of God had done its work of Christ in her life. Tears running down her cheeks, she just stood there while they were singing. Nobody moved. I looked back and saw that mother of Israel pull her glasses up and wipe her eyes. Then pretty soon she pulled them off and took her handkerchief and wiped her eyes. Pretty soon, here she came down to the front, put her arms around that ex-Magdalenia, kissed her on both cheeks and loudly enough so the congregation could hear her, she said, "Welcome, Sister; welcome, Sister." Praise God! At the foot of the cross, objects of the mercy of God; the best and the worst woman in town in the same crowd.

The difference, "the mercy of God," which because His blessed Son hung on a cross, He's able and willing to show mercy, God's sovereign mercy, to the worst sinner that ever stayed out of hell a little while. And when that woman did that, the people's hearts were broken and sinners all over the congregation began to cry out and once again we saw the glory and the wonder of that simple Scripture, *"Whosoever shall call upon the name of the Lord shall be saved."*

Rolfe Barnard was willing to *go after lost sinners and bring them in.* He put shoe leather to his beliefs, practicing what he preached. Through Barnard's preaching God would often bend an entire church and transform it from dead formality to vital, spiritual life. Evangelist Barnard cried out against church members who neglected to make the Great Commission a reality in their lives. He often said that if a church could not wet the sanctuary's carpet with their tears over the lost and go out and reach them then they had no business calling themselves a church!

The next story illustrates how the entire *life* of a church was radically impacted under his preaching. He was up in Boston, Massachusetts, preaching in a place he had never been before. He was from the South and the "Yankees" in that congregation were nice people but they were not obeying what he had been preaching and he wanted to call off the meeting and go home! What occurs is extraordinary as the "Hitchhike Evangelist" once again gets to witness God move in revival in the life of a church! This story is "classic Barnard" and typifies his ministry at its most powerful and penetrating heights. The following sensational account is taken from his sermon, "A Burden for Souls":

God is not going to put up with this stuff we've been calling Christianity forever. We are headed for judgment like we have never dreamed of. And our only way of escape is for Christians to start acting like Christ. Jesus came down here because God so loved the world; He didn't come down here to condemn the world but He came down here that the world through Him might be saved. God help us to be a little like the Lord!

I was up in Massachusetts, the first time I held a meeting in New England. Being from the South they found it a little difficult to understand me; I found it very difficult to understand them. They were very nice people and very cultured, very dignified, very quiet and reserved. As I remember I started the meeting on Sunday morning, my wife was with me. I preached Sunday morning and Sunday night, Monday night, Tuesday night, and Wednesday night. And after the service Wednesday night I said to the dear pastor, "Brother Pastor, I believe we ought to close the meeting tomorrow night." He said, "Oh no! No, we couldn't do that." I said, "I was just making a suggestion. My judgment is that we ought to just close out, and I will go back home."

"Well," he said, "What on earth is the matter, Brother Barnard?" I said, "Well, we are not getting anywhere; I don't seem to be able to get over to you and the people, and so far you have not done one thing that I have asked you to do." He said, "Well, Brother Barnard, you are a little strange to us." I said, "Well, I am going this way and you folks are going that way. We sure won't have the blessings of God that way. Somebody is wrong around here and I am a visitor at your invitation, and my messages and what I ask you to do, you don't do a thing about. I think I ought to just close my part of the meeting and if you folks want to go on with it, you can." And he was greatly disturbed. "Oh," he said, "it would just ruin everything if you did it. What on earth is the matter with you, Brother Barnard?" "Well, you just won't do a thing I ask. And I either ought not to ask you some things or I ought and if I ought to ask you to do some things and if it is right that I do, then you ought to do it; and if I am asking you to do things against the Scriptures you ought to run me off."

He said, "Well, what are you talking about?" I said, "You won't meet to pray. I haven't seen your church on its face, weeping its heart to God. I have been asking you to do it and God is not going to bless people if they are not that kind of people. You might have some more people to join the church, but God is not going to save people in an atmosphere of dry eyes and prayerlessness. I've been asking you to go out here and talk to people and witness to them and bring them in your cars and invite them to the services." He said, "Brother Barnard, we've never done anything like that in our lives." I said, "I am beginning to believe it. Well, my wife and I are going on to our room and if it is all right I will preach tomorrow night, then we will close the meeting."

We went on to the little apartment they had for us and after a while somebody knocked on the door and the pastor and deacons came in. They were greatly disturbed. They said, "Brother Barnard, we just can't afford to close the meeting; it would just hurt everything. People would wonder why." I said, "Well, I don't know what to do." And they said, "Brother Barnard, if you will stay (they weren't thinking about me; it was the reputation of their church), if you will not close the meeting we will do anything you ask us to do." "I don't want you to do anything just because I ask you. I wanted you to do it because it is in the Bible and God wants it!" "Tell us one more time what it is." "I don't want you to do it just to save the reputation of the church, but if it is so, if I have asked you to do what God's people ought to do and you don't you insult God by not doing what you said you would do in a revival effort. It is a shame and disgrace to say we are going to try to have a revival and not have it, because that is a slam on God. He is supposed to be a God that hears prayer and a God who works miracles, isn't He?"

He used to. A church is under obligation to get its prayers answered. So we turned to Acts 5:42 and read, *"And daily in the temple, and in every house, they ceased not to teach and preach Jesus Christ."* They said, "We never have done anything like this, but it's in there, isn't it?" I said, "Yes." And they went out and Thursday night the church was full because they had went out and invited them to come, and they began to do what the Bible says.

And I preached that night and before I got through preaching a little girl began to sob and when we stood up to sing she came running down to the front and just fell down on her all fours there. And after a while I went down and talked to her and after a while she stood up and said, "Jesus is here!" We found out that she was a little sixteen-year-old Italian girl and that was the first gospel sermon she had ever heard. Some of the girls went and brought her. She didn't know "A" from "zero" but you see a sovereign God, He can do things as He pleases! Sometimes it takes Him forty years to save a man and sometimes He saves him the first time he hears the gospel. I think the little girl got saved, of course, I won't know until I get to the judgment, none of us will. But it *scared them*. They had never seen anything like that, so I had them to do like they do down South, I had them to come around and shake hands with her.

Friday night the little girl wasn't at the service and Saturday night she wasn't at the service so I got a little worried and I went to the pastor and said, "I am troubled about that little girl. Do you know where she lives?" He said, "No, preacher. I'm sorry, we got so excited about what happened. We never saw anything like that and nobody asked her where she lived. We don't even know her name. I feel awful bad about it. I'll tell you right now, if she is not here in the morning we are going to organize and we are going to search this city and find that little girl. I am troubled about her."

Sunday morning came and she was sitting in the congregation and it so happened my wife was sitting close to her. And that morning I preached on "Hell, the Sinner's Long Home." And after I had been preaching about twenty-five minutes, they said that little Roman Catholic Italian girl which Thursday night had stood and said, "Jesus is in here"; she began to cry, then she began to sob and pretty soon her body was just rocking with sobs. And my wife put her arm on her shoulder and pretty soon my wife rose and the little girl and they broke up my sermon as they came down that church aisle! My wife brought her upon the platform with me, rolled up her sleeves, had her turn around and rolled her dress down as far as modesty allowed, and let me look at her face. Her back was just terrible whelps and they were festered and fevered, her arms were cut, and her face was cut. And she stood up after a while and *I saw a church born*. She told what had happened to her—to that nice Sunday morning crowd of Baptists.

She said, "Thursday night I ran home, I was so happy! Mama and Daddy, my brother and my two sisters were in the front room. I went in and told them that Jesus Christ *had come in here*, and He is mine and I am His." She told them what had happened and the daddy asked, "Where have you been?" She said, "I went down to the Baptist church. They are having meetings down there. I never was in anything like it, Daddy! All I know is that Jesus is in here!"

And her daddy got up and went and got an old black snake whip. He commanded his girl to stand and she did and he whipped her with that black snake whip until she lost consciousness. She said, "I don't know how long I lay there but I was awakened by pain and I opened my eyes just in time for my two sisters, standing on either side of me, kicking me in the ribs. Then my brother came and spat in my face. My mother came and cursed me. And my daddy told me to get up. I don't know how I did, but I did. He looked me in the face and said, "If I ever hear you talk like that again, I'll kill you! Go to your room!" She said, "I went to my room and he turned the key in the door. I didn't have any medical attention Thursday night. Friday morning my daddy came, unlocked the door and handed me a piece of bread and a glass of water. I stayed in the room all day Friday and Friday night. During that time those whelps were feverish and festered and I was in mortal agony."

She continued, "Saturday morning he came and I was waiting for him. I was desperate. As he turned the key in the lock and as he put his hand on the door he turned it, I let him turn it just enough, I knew it was open, then I jerked it right quickly and he fell in the room. I darted out, I had so much fever I guess I had super human strength. I ran out of the house. I wandered around in the city and found an old empty freight car and I stayed in it all day. When the sun went down I went to a pharmacy, the pharmacist knew me and he treated my wounds some, and I slept that night in the empty freight car.

Sunday morning I was hungry, I was sick, and I was hurting and I said, 'What shall I do?'" And then she said, "I remembered the Jesus people. And I said I will go up where the 'Jesus people' are. They will help me." Then she came to church and took her seat. She was in pain and feeling sorry for herself and afraid to go back home. She said, "I felt so sorry for myself, then I began to listen to the preacher and he talked about hell— that awful place." After a while she said, "I wish what would happen to me and to you, I forgot myself and all I could think of *was the daddy that whipped me, the mother that cursed me, the sisters that kicked me, and the brother that spat in my face and I thought they are going to that awful place the preacher is talking about!"*

And then so help me, that little Italian girl lifted up her hands and began to weep and she broke the heart of that crowd! I saw them fall on their knees, *and I was in a prayer meeting.*

She said, "Oh, Jesus people, won't you help me keep my people from being sent to hell!" That little Italian girl didn't know much, but she knew Jesus *was in here* and her loved ones were going to be sent to hell, and she didn't want them to go. She thought she could say, "Oh, Jesus people, you will help me, won't you?"

We closed the meeting on Sunday night and I was to get in New York on Monday. The pastor said, "Let me get on the telephone and call them and say you won't be there until Tuesday. You just have to stay over Monday night; we are going to have baptizing and I want you to have the great pleasure." I said, "All right, I will." We made the arrangements and they took a vote that everybody come Monday night that was going to be baptized. The deacon got up and made a motion to authorize the evangelist to bury in baptism.

Monday night came and I went down into that pool and five people came there and I got them all down in the pool together. I baptized them. *I baptized that little sixteen-year-old girl, then I baptized her mama, I baptized her daddy, I baptized her two sisters, and then I baptized her brother.*

When Jesus, in His earthly ministry, entered a village those that *encountered* Him were *changed.* Jesus transforms the lives of those He touches. This story of the little Italian girl and her family is not only gripping but it demonstrates the power of the gospel and the power of prayer. It also demonstrates what God was pleased to perform through an evangelist who truly *believed* God was a God of miracles. Barnard possessed the faith necessary to *see God move.* This is what separated him from many of his peers—he really lived in the supernatural to such a degree he expected God to act like God!

When Rolfe Barnard said his "goodbyes" to this Boston congregation they were not the same people as when he first encountered them. That Baptist church in Boston no longer had a dry carpet in their sanctuary; they had learned how to weep over the lost by witnessing a holy God move in their midst to the salvation of souls. They were always thankful to the strange evangelist from the South called Rolfe Barnard.

There were times in Rolfe Barnard's ministry when not only a church would be stirred by God but an entire town! We have not over-mentioned the term "revival" because it is so little understood today to mean nothing more than a series of protracted evangelistic services of high emotions. Historically, a genuine revival of religion is when God visits a community and there is a real sense of the awful presence of God. There is a solemnity and a God-consciousness which pervades that community. This seems to be the case in the following story of when God visited a community where Rolfe Barnard was preaching. The account of this move of grace is taken from his own accounts from his two sermons, "Do You Know God? and "Should God Punish Sin?." What makes this narrative so startling is the fact that the story begins with the people of the town signing a petition to run Rolfe Barnard out of town! Over three hundred people signed it. God brought such conviction of sin to that little town that people could not go to their workplaces because they were so greatly disturbed over sin. Here now is the narrative of a touch of revival during a Rolfe Barnard meeting:

I've never seen much of the breath of revival. Once in a while God has been good and it seemed that He opened the windows of heaven and brought a spirit of prayer and confession, making things right on the part of His people. The Spirit of God was out-poured and then it is wonderful to be around; it makes you hungry to see a revival.

I went some years ago to hold a meeting under these circumstances. I had been in the town in a church meeting and God was pleased to bless and there was no small stir in the city. On Tuesday night of the first week they started a petition down at the big mill where everybody worked. And they had several hundred people sign it by Wednesday, and the petition was to *run me out of town!* Wednesday night they said I was radical and a fellow that believed in holy living, and that unless you are crying for perfection you are not saved.

They said, "That fellow preaches that you can't have any sin. That if you can be content to indulge in any sin, you are lost. If any sin comes to your knowledge and it doesn't break your heart, so you can turn and forsake it, you're lost. You do not know God." They said of me, "That fellow is a holy roller." Isn't it awful that Baptists, who in all their creeds say they believe in Bible salvation—yet they are making fun of Bible holiness! Hebrews tells us, *"Follow peace with all men, and holiness, without which no man shall see the Lord."*

And so they were going to run me out of town but God came to my rescue! My soul, He turned defeat into victory! I've never seen anything that tasted like revival until God's people got out on a limb where they would be disgraced or God must come to the rescue. So God's people were asking God for something definite and *the whole city was disturbed.*

When the scheduled meetings were over, the pastors of that town asked me to meet with them. They said, "We would like to talk to you about coming back for a citywide meeting." I know most citywide campaigns are a joke. But they said, "We would rent the city auditorium, and we would buy you an hour's time on the radio and we promise to pack the place out. And we will get our people behind it and be on our faces before God, if you would come for a month." But they said, "Now we want to make two requests of you before we agree on this meeting." They said, "We are not trying to tell you how to run your business but this is our deep conviction. Would you come to our city and agree before you get here that you would preach three weeks on one subject and not give any kind of invitation? Would you come over the radio every day and every night in the auditorium and preach on one subject: Will the God of the Bible punish sin?"

We've whittled us out a little god that won't punish sin. Nobody is screaming for mercy now, because they don't believe God will punish sin. Nobody is screaming for mercy now because they don't believe God hates sin. They said there was no use trying to get men saved, for they have nothing to be saved from! For if God won't punish sin, there is no need for a Savior. Those preachers said, "We are preaching our hearts out here and people don't want to be saved. Nobody wants to be done with sin; nobody desires to be turned to righteousness. And the reason for it is: nobody believes that God will punish sin."

And so they explained, "Instead of trying to get people to accept Jesus as Savior when they feel no need of Him, come and preach three weeks on the radio and in the auditorium on the subject: Will God punish sin? We would pray for you and stay on our faces praying that God Almighty would take the truth over the radio and in the auditorium and men and women would go to their place of business and back to their homes and get to the place where they couldn't sleep, facing the awful fact that the God who revealed Himself in the pages of this Book that our mothers stained with tears, and our forefathers gave their life's blood to defend—That God Will Punish Sin!"

Those preachers said they believed somebody might feel the need of being saved. And I went the next year and did as they planned and one time in my life *I saw Holy Ghost conviction!* I saw men so disturbed that they could not go to their place of business. I saw people going in the hospital stricken with the fear of God. They said some people went crazy—one woman was sent to the asylum and hasn't got through cursing me yet! But *conviction seized that town.* Businessmen were saved. Church members were saved. Young people were saved. People everywhere were saved! We never did give any kind of public invitation in that revival. As long as you have to invite people to come to Jesus, you are not seeing true Holy Ghost conviction and real revival!

Everyday for an hour on the radio and at night under the tent I became an authority on what the Bible says about "God Will Punish Sin." I preached everything I could find in the Bible on this subject and there is plenty of it. And after I would get through preaching every night, I would say, "Good night. Go on to hell! That's were you seem to want to go." That was my benediction. That's pretty rough, isn't it? Well, that is a little different than saying, "Oh, won't you take Jesus?" They don't want Him, and Jesus isn't found that way.

But the Holy Spirit didn't let me preach for the entire month. On Tuesday night of the fourth week, I was just preaching up a way, and a man way back there got up and came running down the sawdust trail and came up on the platform. He pushed me aside and said, "For God's sake, preacher, I got to say something!" He was the president of the biggest bank in that city. He was a teacher in the Sunday school and deacon of a church. And he had stolen $250,000 from that bank and nobody knew it.

He got to listening to me on the radio and got to worrying about that. Then he got to coming to hear me preach under the tent. All I would say, "God is going to punish sin. I can prove it. He always has. He is doing it now. And He is going to do it." I quoted 1 Timothy 5:24: *"Some men's sins are open beforehand, going before to judgment; and some men they follow after."* And he got in a terrible shape. His little Sunday school teaching wouldn't help him; you know that won't save a man. The fact that he was a deacon, that wouldn't save him. The fact that he was president of the bank, that wouldn't take care of it. And he got to where he would come hear me preach and he would go home at night and lock his door, get his Bible and get down on his knees, and he would just beg God to have mercy on him and save him. There is no way on earth you can do business with God without coming clean with Him; the whole outfit has got to come out! Yes sir! He just couldn't get God to trade with him at all. And he got so miserable that the day before he came and interrupted my sermon, he wrote a letter and put it in the mail and admitted that he had stolen $250,000 from the bank, and got in touch with the Chief of Police and the powers that ran the bank. There were some policemen there in the congregation waiting to arrest him that night and he knew it.

He came up on the platform and confessed his awful sin, then he just fell down like a sack of sugar and sobbed like his heart would break. He looked up through his tears after a while and said, "Is there anybody that can pray for an old sinner like me?" I saw several thousand people under that big tent— saints and lost people, hell rousers and everybody else—they just fell on their knees on that sawdust and begged God to have mercy on that old sinner who brought his sin out in the open and came clean before God. And God was

GOD'S "HITCHHIKE" EVANGELIST

pleased to have mercy on him and *saved him.*

They arrested him and tried him and sent him to the penitentiary. That was in 1951 and he has been in the penitentiary ever since. Next year he is going to get out. I get a letter once a month from him. I have for all those years. He is the happiest prison inmate you ever saw! He's been in prison all these years, but bless God there ain't no prison like sin that binds us! It is a lot better to spend the rest of his life in prison than spend eternity in hell.

We had to go on three more weeks. People would go to work and go to the foreman and say, "I can't work," and they would come to the tent. For three weeks all we did was pray with and counsel men and women coming and saying, *"Could it be that He would have mercy on me?"*

Yes, God shook that town and saved the biggest crook in town. He saved a lot of little crooks too! All sin is crooked. The shortest definition of sin is found in the book of Isaiah in verse 53:6: *"All we like sheep have gone astray; we have turned every one to his own way."* Sin is going our way when we know it isn't God's way. Rolfe Barnard knew full well that God must punish sin. He had witnessed God free men from sin through a saving knowledge of Him. He also knew that a gospel that did not proclaim that God will punish sin is not a true gospel but false and one that will make false converts who claim they know Christ but continue in sin. Rolfe Barnard preached the Jesus who *"saves his people from their sins."*

God not only saved people in a Barnard meeting, He *removed them by death.* Time and time again we listen to Brother Barnard tell of individuals who refused to submit to the claims of Christ in their life and met with a fatal accident. This occurred on several occasions. He would often quote from the book of Proverbs: *"He, that being often reproved hardeneth his neck, shall suddenly be destroyed, and that without remedy"* (Proverbs 29:1). He would place emphasis on the word "suddenly" be destroyed. He had seen it occur so frequently in his ministry that he trembled when he saw someone defiantly fighting God's claims on them.

This last story is a vivid example of how dangerous it is to run away from God. It is the tragic story of a father who would not heed his family's pleas to turn to Christ. It is taken from the sermon entitled, "Sudden Death":

God does reprove sinners, but you know how people in our day meet God's reproof? They harden themselves. *"He, that being often reproved hardeneth his neck"*—God does the reproving and man does the hardening. He says, "God is not going to move me. I wouldn't mind being a church member and I don't mind what they call being saved now, but God is not going to change me! God is not going to give me a heart of flesh; God is not going to plant a holy disposition in me. God is not going to start the work of making me like His Son. No, I will not be changed, so I will fight this business. If God thinks He is going to run my life, He has got another thing coming!" That is how men talk today.

Men harden themselves—they can't be neutral, so they harden themselves. They can't get rid of God, so they harden themselves against the reproof of God. They say, "I don't believe in God," but they go to bed at night and wake up scared. Then they will pray to that God to keep them out of hell (like I used to) before morning! Men harden themselves. Am I talking to you? Every time God warns you, do you grit your teeth and spit in His face and go down the road that leads to hell? You know, you have to harden yourself to do that!

I remember in a certain city after I had brought a message one morning in an evangelistic campaign, I was shaking hands with some people and I felt something pulling on my coat. So I looked down and there was a little three-and-a-half-year-old girl, curly haired and beautiful, a little gift from heaven. And I picked her up in my arms and she put her little arms around my neck and began to cry,"Oh, Brother Barnard, I want my daddy to get saved. Oh, Brother Barnard, I want my daddy to get saved!" Now the little girl didn't know exactly what it meant to be saved, but she knew that life in her home was hell, and she knew something needed to happen to her daddy. She was pitiful and she just broke my heart. Her mother soon came and she began to sob, and she took the little girl out of my arms.

Then I said to this wife and mother, "I will be on the radio this afternoon at three o'clock." I said, "Your husband curses preachers, he curses God, and he has ordered me and your pastor out of his home. He never goes to any assembly of God anywhere, and he brags about how tough he is; but sometimes he will listen to the radio. You make it convenient and maybe he will listen to me this afternoon and I am going to preach to him."

Well, that afternoon over that radio I stopped about the middle of my sermon and asked the audience to pardon me. I said, "I believe there is a man listening to the sound of my voice now, and I believe God sent him the last call this morning." Then I told over the radio how that little three-and-a-half-year-old girl had come and climbed up in my arms and put her arms around my neck and cried, "Oh, Brother Barnard, I want my daddy to get saved, I want my daddy to get saved." I said, "I believe that daddy of the little girl is listening to me now." I said, "You wouldn't listen to God. You haven't listened to the pleas of your wife and little child. You haven't listened to anybody, but now here is God talking to you through the tears and heartbreak of your little three-and-a-half-year-old girl. If there is a spark of manhood in you, get down on your knees and begin to repent of your sins and cry to God for mercy!"

You know what he did? He got up and turned that radio off, slammed his hat on his head, opened the door and cursed me, cursed the radio, cursed God, and cursed his wife. And slammed out of there and went to the nearest honky-tonk and within twenty minutes after he got out of the house, a man *pumped five bullets in his body*. You say, "That was accidental." No sir! Bless the Lord, *"He, that being often reproved hardeneth his neck,"* what is going to happen to him? Judgment is coming! God is going to get a hold of him as He did that man. God *kills people* who harden themselves against Him.

The result of hardening yourself under the reproving, convicting, pleading, persuading power, and the person and presence of God in the Holy Ghost, is *sudden death*. God warns. He said, *"I kill, and I make alive."*

Rolfe Barnard took the injunction seriously of the apostle Paul, *"Knowing therefore the terror of the Lord, we persuade men;"*

(2 Corinthians 5:11). Rolfe had seen his share of the modern day Ananias and Sapphira (Acts chapter 5). He had seen God gloriously save men and he had seen God justly destroy them! And he knew that the God of the Bible kills people!

Chapter Nine

Sovereign Grace Movement

No man can come to me, except the Father which hath sent me draw him: and I will raise him up at the last day. — John 6:44

Rolfe Barnard was a pioneer of Reformed theology in Southern Baptist life in the 1950's. He saw a deterioration of preaching the "old truths" of the gospel of God's grace and it concerned him greatly. He saw what he considered to be a "perverted gospel" emerge that placed man at the center and removed the necessity for repentance. In this "newer" gospel, God was no longer the center and His glory no longer sought in the proclamation of it. He felt evangelism of his day produced more false converts than sincere converts. But what alarmed him most of all was the number of young preachers entering the ministry proclaiming this "newer gospel." Barnard knew that God had in former times blessed America with spiritual awakenings under the preaching of these "old truths" by men like Jonathan Edwards and George Whitefield. Barnard often talked about the gospel of David Brainerd. It troubled him that so few preachers believed what the Bible had to say about salvation.

Rolfe Barnard was a Southern Baptist. The Southern Baptist Convention was founded in 1845 in Augusta, Georgia, and during its first two generations its founders believed and taught a Calvinistic theology of God's sovereignty in the salvation of men.

The doctrines of grace were commonly found in their confessions and associations, in their seminaries and in their preachers. A shift in theology from its Calvinistic moorings occurred in the middle half of the nineteenth century, beginning in seminary life, with some "modifications" of Calvinistic theology. The drift away from Calvinism has continued from that point.

In the days of Rolfe Barnard, to claim you were a Southern Baptist *and a Calvinist* was practically heresy! Evangelist Barnard spent his entire ministry laboring in hostile territory to the message he preached. He faced tremendous opposition from colleagues who shut him out of their conferences and pulpits because of the truths he proclaimed. Some Baptist leaders were so afraid of Barnard they sent out letters warning churches not to host Barnard or have him in their pulpits! He was labeled a "Hyper-Calvinist" who preached error and to avoid him at all costs! He became known within Southern Baptist life as *an enemy to evangelism.* And, of course, he was an enemy to the modern kind of evangelism—if it were up to him he would have stamped it all out!

In the 1950's he began a movement which grew in size and influence. He began to organize "Sovereign Grace Conferences" as annual events, bringing like-minded pastors and evangelists together for fellowship and learning. The first conference was held in Ashland, Kentucky. Then one was held in Birmingham, Alabama and the next year in Pine Bluff, Arkansas. Soon there were "Sovereign Grace Conferences" in the Rocky Mountains, North Carolina, Ohio, and other parts of the country. The emergence of a return to Calvinistic thought within Southern Baptist life was pioneered by Rolfe Barnard although few acknowledge him today. The conferences began to wane in size by the mid-seventies as the pastors who sponsored them retired or died. E. W. Johnson's conference in Pine Bluff, Arkansas continued up to his death in 2001.

Although Barnard was the founder of the sovereign grace movement, he preferred to leave that mantle in the care of others while he went up and down the country preaching the doctrines which he believed. It is fitting at this time to include an article written by Rolfe Barnard which conveys his thoughts on sovereign grace, the subject which lay at the heart of the gospel of God's glory and was so dear to his own heart. The article was provided by the Rolfe Barnard Library.

Some Implications of Sovereign Grace
by Rolfe Barnard

Why do we use the double term **sovereign grace**? What does it mean and what is implied by the epithet "sovereign" as attached to the term grace?

The answer is immediately at hand. The whole so-called Christian world professes to believe in *salvation by grace*. Only a remnant within the whole believes in *sovereign grace*. I am happy to be found among the latter group. The popular conception of salvation by grace is that God used to be holy, but now He has found a way to let men off easier. Nearly all of the major groups talk of salvation by grace and it means, usually, whatever the holder of the view thinks it means. I am trying simply to say this: there seems to be no division among professing Christians as to salvation by grace, as the term is used, but there is great difference as to "sovereign grace"! Because I believe there is no grace but sovereign grace, I used the term and dedicated my own ministry, unprofitable as it is, to the expounding of **sovereign grace** and to the calling of the ministry back to similar action.

(1) What do the terms "grace" and "sovereign" mean? One of the attributes of God is goodness. The goodness of God is the divine essence seen as energized benevolently and kindly toward the creature. "I will be gracious—I will be merciful," saith the Lord. The Lord is plenteous in mercy— The Lord delighteth in mercy. Mercy and grace are varieties of God's goodness. Grace has reference to sinful man as guilty, while mercy has respect to sinful man as miserable.

(2) This attribute (goodness) expressed in grace and mercy is free and sovereign in its exercise. *"I ... will be gracious to whom I will be gracious, and will shew mercy on whom I will shew mercy"* (Exodus 33:19). The goodness of God is infinite and circumscribed by no limits, but the exercise

of His goodness may be limited by Himself. God is necessarily good in His nature, but free in His communication of it. If the Bible is plain about anything it is plain about the fact that God must be just toward all men; He may be merciful to some. God owes all men justice; He owes no man mercy or grace! A sovereign God exercises mercy and grace as it seems good to Him. *"At that time Jesus answered and said, I thank thee, O Father, Lord of heaven and earth, because thou hast hid these things from the wise and prudent, and hast revealed them unto babes. Even so, Father: for so it seemed good in thy sight"* (Matthew 11:25-26).

(3) Actually God exercises mercy in a general manner toward all men. Anything this side of hell is mercy! Mercy is found in and by the works of creation and providence and the delay of punishment, but saving grace and mercy in Christ are only exercised in redemption and regeneration toward those whom a sovereign God is pleased to save. Ephesians 1:3-6; Romans 9:11-16. This is our battle cry! How seldom it is heard, yet it is the very truth of truths.

If you will consider the history of the preaching of sovereign grace, you will arrive at the startling fact that every great period of spiritual awakening this world has ever known has come in connection with such preaching. Brethren, history and the **pale imitation** of revival present among us today, demand a re-study of and a return to the truth of grace in the hands of a Sovereign, whose exercise of mercy is optional within and to Himself.

The preaching of sovereign grace is not therefore the giving of undue prominence to any single doctrine of Scripture. It is rather the proclaiming of a sovereign God graciously dealing with sinners as it pleases Him. We are often and somewhat vociferously accused of being guilty of the first part of this statement. This writer would certainly join in condemning the same. It is quite true that there is danger here. Any doctrine isolated from the whole body of revealed truth becomes perverted doctrine.

The preaching of sovereign grace is **not** an enemy of true evangelism. Let me hasten to say that the preaching of sovereign grace will kill deader than a doornail the message and method of present-day evangelism! And some of us believe with a deadly intensity that the false message and method must be killed before the true message and method can become effective. We further believe that the only way this can be done is by the preaching of truth about God, the truth about man, and the truth about Christ who died and lives that **God might be just and justifier!** These lines will appeal to **no one** who is happy about the results of evangelism today, but should you be one of many who mourn here, you will join in the task of raising up again the standard of sovereign grace!

A sovereign Christ is almost unheard of in church circles today—a Christ into whose hands all things have been given, who has all authority, who gives life and quickens whom He will, who decides the destinies of all men, who is Lord over all flesh. Present-day evangelism, for the most part, poses to men the question, "What will you do with Jesus?" Bible or true evangelism poses the question, "What will the sovereign Christ do with me?" Present-day evangelism says to men, "Believe and be born again." Bible evangelism says to men, "Be born again so you can believe." The one makes the new birth depend on an act of men, the other an act of God. Present-day evangelism takes for granted God's mercy and grace, rather than marveling at them in adoration and worship.

Hear Paul say, **"I obtained mercy;"** hear Peter say, "to all who have **obtained** like precious faith." How I long to hear this note in the churches today! Salvation today is a physical rather than a spiritual matter. The preaching of sovereign grace is the need of the hour if we shall be true to God's Word and true to the souls of men.

After Rolfe Barnard developed a network of Sovereign Grace Conferences he was content to leave them in capable hands while he preferred to go and preach to the lost. He was a trailblazer rather than an ongoing leader of a movement. He was too catholic in spirit to be confined by one particular group. He preached for anyone with a heart for the lost and a love of God: he preached often in the churches of Presbyterians, Methodists, any who desired to see men saved and God receive glory. Oddly, the very movement he birthed he eventually viewed as a monster which he created; he was greatly disturbed over the churches within the grace community who had turned to a life of antinomianism and who treated the doctrines of grace more academically than preaching them practically to the salvation of souls.

One part of history that has been overlooked is Barnard's close friendship with Ernie Reisinger. This is unfortunate for they were both instrumental in the resurgence of Calvinism within Southern Baptist life. Geoffrey Thomas, in his excellent biography of Ernest Reisinger (Banner of Truth, 2002), failed to grasp the significant influence of Rolfe Barnard upon Ernest Reisinger. Thomas only mentions Barnard in passing on page 116 of his book. Actually, it was Rolfe Barnard's *mentoring* of Reisinger which so impacted Reisinger's influence among Reformed circles.

In fact, it was Reisinger who actively promoted Rolfe Barnard as an evangelist through hosting him at churches around the Carlisle area and distributing his sermons on reel to reel to ministers throughout the country! I have in my possession a "Welcome Card" with Barnard's photo on it which Ernie Reisinger had printed up to advertise Barnard in his home church. In addition to this, Reisinger was a regular contributor to Barnard's monthly publication *Redeemer's Witness* writing the following articles:

"Be Zealous!" issue November, 1964
"Be Zealous!" issue December, 1964
"Methods—Personal Evangelism—Invitations?" issue March, 1965
"Lawlessness" issue April, 1965
"Dangers of Our Day" issue May, 1965
"How God Calls Men" issue June/July, 1965
"How God Calls Men, cont." issue August/September, 1965
"More Than Knowledge" issue October, 1965
"The Law Is Holy, Just and Good" issue November/December, 1965
"Books to Fight Ignorance" issue January/February, 1966
"The Bible Is Clear" issue March/April, 1966
"Obedience: A Test of Love" issue May/June, 1966

It is important to make note of this powerful friendship between Barnard and Reisinger. Both men were dynamic forces for Calvinistic resurgence in America in the Twentieth Century.

Ten Classic Sermons

But thou, O man of God, flee these things; and follow after righteousness, godliness, faith, love, patience, meekness. Fight the good fight of faith, lay hold on eternal life, whereunto thou art also called, and hast professed a good profession before many witnesses. — 1 Timothy 6:11-12

It is fitting at this juncture to introduce sermonic material of Rolfe Barnard. It is by his preaching that we know him. I must emphasize the fact that merely reading his sermons *do not do him justice—he must be heard.* I therefore encourage you to listen to his many sermons available on the Internet. Many fruitful hours can be spent listening to Barnard preach!

To get a flavor of his preaching we present the ten carefully selected sermons in printed form. Some are transcribed from audio sermons, some already exist in print. His printed sermons can be purchased through Revival Literature (www.revivallit.org). Sixty-eight of these sermons were self published in three volumes by Eulala Bullock, a convert of Barnard. The following ten sermons are representative of Brother Barnard's preaching ministry. The first message is "classic Barnard" preached under a tent in the early 1950's in an evangelistic campaign in Natchez, Texas. You may wish to listen to this sermon online as well! The Rolfe Barnard Library at SermonAudio.com and SermonIndex.com provide all of Barnard's existing sermonic material.

SERMON 1: You Can't Resist the Holy Ghost and Get By

Next Sunday night we will bring in the best message that God has ever been pleased to give us, the only message that we preach in every campaign, the message that God has used to bring so many to the Lord. The subject will be: "The God of the Bible Kills People—Will He Kill You?"

You know this generation has built them a little god to suit themselves and the holy character of the Bible God is well nigh unknown. If this generation knew what kind of a person God would be, this generation would be afraid to flaunt their sinfulness in His holy nostrils. Now God never set out to save everybody. Before the foundation of the world, God looked down and saw everybody that He believes of His means to make willing to be saved on His terms. And He's going to save those people ... And God Almighty is going to do the job He started out to do. I'm glad for that, I'm certainly glad for that.

You know just a few people are going to be saved. Do you believe that? Jesus said so. We didn't come to Natchez especially that everybody in town would like our message. I do not believe any man can preach the truth now and get great crowds. I don't try to get great crowds but I want to get everybody we can. But most people will worship a god that will let them live like the devil and not bother them. And most people want a Jesus that won't interfere with their own way of living. And this generation has got to be challenged, Brother, and God's going to accomplish His purposes through preachers and churches that stay true to the Book and dispose of men, and press responsibilities upon man, hold them up before His character and His holiness and shut them up the best we can to the Lord Jesus Christ.

Today I received so many phone calls; I rejoice in them. There is hardly any rest because the phone is ringing but we thank God it rings that way! And I say to you, my friends, that in a little over a week of hard preaching four times a day and under the tent you can put it down that not everybody in Natchez is happy about the preacher. But God is saving sinners. They're being saved now as they listen to the radio, and we're grateful for it. A little woman came to me tonight and said, "God saved me last night and I never knew a person could be as happy as I am today and my husband will be here tomorrow night and the next and I want to see him saved too."

And another woman came last night and said she'd come to the service and her pastor was able to help her. Now of course, no God-called pastor will heal the wounds of a sinner slightly. We've not here to see that people don't have any burdens and to settle all their problems; we're not here to fix it so you can just rest your arms and coast, Brother! I want Christians to be knee deep in trouble all the time! Fighting the devil and resisting sin. But I do maintain it's the Christian's privilege to have peace of heart while you are in that battle and the darts are flying from every direction. The child of God can have a peace that the world cannot give and I thank God it cannot take away.

Now it's praying time in Natchez, folks, and we ask all of you to keep on praying and witnessing and I know that unless this generation sees some more real agonizing at the throne of God there that we haven't got a bit of a chance of revival in your day and mine. We might as well just face that. We cannot be spectators and have God give revival, He's not going to wish revival upon us. But people are being challenged and some are praying and some are being saved and the devil is fighting. We're bucking all the little league baseball and picture shows and the sinfulness of men and the work of the devil, but thank God, if you keep on praying.

Everywhere I go I drive my first crowd away. And then we pray and preach them back and then a lot of them go to getting saved! Did you know that? There has never been a revival any other way. You can't have revival and keep the devil in a good humor. You keep on praying, will you? Just keep on praying. I want to see sinners crying out to God and I thank God for the victory last night!

Now tonight, why you can revel in booze and lust, reject Jesus as Lord, resist the strivings and wooing of the Holy Spirit, why you can do all of that and not be cut off at once by a holy God and sent to hell? My friends, I'm not a pessimist. An optimist somebody says is a person who just has one eye open and a pessimist is a fellow that hasn't got any eyes open. But I'm not a pessimist nor am I an optimist, I try to be a realist. But, ladies and gentlemen, there never was a time when this world of sinners had as much light from an Almighty God about His character and His will and His provisions of grace and mercy today. And sin is measured in terms of light. My friends, listen, if that be true and it is every progression of knowledge and light brings responsibility. And when men sin against what they know to be wrong and right their responsibility is great. There isn't a man or woman in the city of Natchez hardly that isn't sinning against what he knows to be right. This generation of unsaved men and women weren't born in ignorance and heathenism. They were born in America in the shadow of gospel churches. Now God hasn't got a big preacher on the horizon today. There isn't a living preacher on the face of the earth that can get a crowd to hear him preach, that's so. But God's got hundreds and thousands of little peanut preachers, just little one gallon preachers, that are preaching the truth as it is in the Bible as it is in Christ Jesus. This is not the day when God's doing big things. This is the day when He's not using one man but He's using hundreds of little men. This is the day not when He's got a John Wesley, or a D. L. Moody, or a George Whitefield, or a Sam Jones, or a Charles Finney. This is the day when He's got hundreds of little preachers and churches that are standing on the street corners crying aloud, causing the people to hear about their transgressions, calling people to mourn and bewail their sins and afflict themselves and plough up the fallow ground of their hearts, and as the Scriptures say, convert themselves. The Scriptures say, sinner, save thyself. There is a responsibility upon the part of the sinner.

The old time preachers used to say that man is not on trial, he's on probation. Sometimes if you do not use that word probation in its right sense it might give the wrong impression. But rightly used, the old time preachers said, that it simply meant that mankind is not on trial, he's already tried, but he is on probation. God is letting him have some time to see whether or not that man in all his faculties and possession of his will power, his brain and his heart, hearing the truth, getting light from God, to see whether a man will apply himself to repentance toward God and a saving faith in Jesus Christ and the perseverance in holy living. But men and woman today, instead of spending their time seeking God, are spending their time seeking pleasure. This is a day when men revel in everything imaginable to satisfy their desires of their bodies and of their minds and of their sinful hearts. The words of most people today are, "Eat, drink, and be merry, for tomorrow we die." The devil, notwithstanding to the contrary, we've just got one life to live and we're going to have a good time in this life while we have it to live.

Never in the history of the world was so much booze being drunk, so much lust being indulged in, so many people going plumb dab crazy over some kind of silly pleasure. This is the day when the world has the Saturday night carnival spirit. Nobody ever stays at home at night, they're going out somewhere, they are too tired to go to church but they've got to go somewhere to have a good time. This is the day of "Eat, drink, and be merry!" And yet Almighty God doesn't take this pleasure-mad world and cut it off and send it to hell now. Tonight we want to ask in the Bible why this is a day when people thumb their noses at a holy God. Galatians chapter 6, verse 7, says, *"Be not deceived; God is not mocked: for whatsoever a man soweth, that shall he also reap."* The Greek is, "be not deceived, don't thumb your nose at God." And yet that's what people do today.

Let a preacher begin to draw the line and let him preach that the gospel is not less holy than the law of God, and let him preach that God's Son didn't come down here to die so that men could do as they please; but He came down here to die and endured the penalty that was our just due and the power of the Holy Spirit (no man is saved unless he's got the Spirit) the power of the Holy Spirit gives him that which God requires that we have not been able to perform and He gives us the ability to live as God would have us live and to please Him in our daily walk. And yet this is a day when men and women lawlessly cry, "Away with all restraint, and we'll sow to the wind, and we'll not hear anybody who tells us that if we sow to the wind we will reap the whirlwind!" And men thumb their noses at a holy God. And God doesn't cut them off and send them to hell. Why doesn't He? Why doesn't He? This is a day, preeminently the day, of rejection of Jesus as Lord.

My preacher brethren, you hear me! I will get on my back here and let you walk over me if you want to, if it will help you to preach as we ought to preach. And I will remind you that for two generations we have lost the Jesus of the Bible and we've preached a mutilated Jesus and a cut-in-half-two Jesus, and we've left out the fact that Jesus was declared by the resurrection to be Lord! As well as Savior. And that the lordship of Jesus Christ cannot be ignored by men and women and still get to heaven when they die.

Thank God, I had the privilege of going to Southwestern

Theological Seminary in Fort Worth, Texas. Dr. W. T. Conner, he's now gone to glory, was the teacher of systematic theology. And he used to drill us young preachers in the doctrine. He taught us what election means. He taught us predestination. He taught us adoption. He taught us justification. He taught us regeneration. He taught us sanctification. He taught us glorification. He taught us the doctrine of the fall. He taught us the doctrine of the cross. He taught us *all* the great doctrines of the Word of God. And he used to teach us that God Almighty demands as a condition of salvation on the part of the sinner repentance toward God. And he said that repentance toward God means that the love of sin must die! Must die in a man's soul! And when the love of sin has died the sinner must in his heart, he must renounce it and repudiate it and forsake it and turn from it—all of it! And cry to God for deliverance from its power. And then he said the other condition that God Almighty requires of sinful men is absolute saving faith and that saving faith means surrender to Jesus Christ as Lord! And trust in His atoning work as Savior.

And I say to you, that the lordship of Jesus Christ is the doorway to the kingdom of God. There is no other than that God requires *total submission to Jesus as Lord*, and He will take nobody who tries to get in the kingdom and denies the lordship of Christ in his life! Now everybody wants a Savior, you go to the jail and you can preach a half-gospel and present the Savior and all the folks are anxious to have a Savior—but don't any of them want a Lord. Don't any of them want a Lord! But I tell you, you can't have my Jesus as Savior if you deny Him the place as absolute King *and* Lord *and* Master *and* Ruler of your life! G. Campbell Morgan said, "Young preachers! Preach the lordship of Jesus Christ."

Since I've been in this town and over the radio, I have been preaching repentance. Repentance looks in this way towards the lordship of Jesus Christ. No man can have my Jesus as Savior until he mourns in his heart and absolutely repudiates the fact that he has placed self where Jesus Christ demands that He alone shall be. *Jesus must reign.* He's going to reign in this whole world and He's going to reign in your heart if He saves you. I believe in salvation by grace but not in salvation by *disgrace.* I believe in Romans 5:21, *"That as sin hath reigned unto death, even so might grace reign through righteousness unto eternal life by Jesus Christ our Lord."*

That means that salvation by grace is not something that God accomplishes and makes possible for you and does away with His righteous demands, but it means that God Almighty conquers your rebellion and establishes a new disposition in your soul that makes you want to do right. He puts up the white flag of peace and forgives you of your sins and constitutes you a citizen and member of His eternal kingdom.

This is the day of rejection of the Lord Jesus Christ. He's got a right to reign; He ought to reign. Oh and yet He doesn't. Still the cry of this generation is, *"We will not have this man to reign over us!"* And the tragedy of this hour is this is a day when people get them a preacher to insist that Christianity is Jesus as Savior and not Lord. They'll get a preacher to let them do as they please and lift up unholy hands on the Lord's Day and profane the temple of God and call it Christianity!

Rolfe Barnard doesn't know much; I don't know much. I want to learn; I study like a dog. I want to preach the truth. I wouldn't go up and down this country, these meetings *hit hard*. I tell you *they kill me!* I get so blue I want to die! And I just can't stand it and I have to go to the book of Revelation and go over there and see that God is going to gather a people redeemed out of every tongue and nation, and I dip my hands into the blood of my Lord, and I put it on my heart, on my lips and my eyes and my tired body, and I tell the devil to go on back to hell because I'm gonna go on preaching! I'm going to keep on preaching because I've got to stand before God at the judgment and I want to preach as a dying man to dying men! I haven't got any time to pat people on the head. Oh, my friends, I don't know how long I'll have to preach to you but get in this business of wholehearted obedience to Christ and surrender to Him and be saved! That's right.

I don't know the hearts of people. I'm not God Almighty, but I tell you that this generation denies my Jesus *the place He demands. He demands absolute lordship* in your life. My heart breaks within me; you say, "I don't think anything is wrong with this." Nobody asked you. Nobody asked me. Jesus must reign. You must bring every thought into captivity to Him. You must let Him control you. He must be Lord of all, or I insist He will not be Lord at all.

In a meeting where God was blessing, all hell was flying in my home city of Winston-Salem. A big worldly Baptist church was being shocked and God was saving, lives were being changed. And a broken-hearted woman cried out while I was preaching in the morning service, and she said, "Brother Barnard, I've been taught all my life that Christ ought to have first place in the life of His child." And I said, "That's not so, Sister. Christ does. Christ does. He won't have second place." He won't have second place, you can't crowd Him out. Oh, I know you talk about how you got saved and then you went back to the world and said, "goodbye" to Jesus; that is just sassafras, my friends. Oh, My sheep hear My voice and they follow Me. Oh they may make imperfect tracks like this old poor sinner, but my face is in the right direction! God bless your heart, they might fall but they won't stay. This is a lifelong pact and yet Jesus is denied today. His name is used to cuss with. His name is made to make whoopee with. His church is despised and His Spirit is rejected. And yet men are not cut off. How can men cry out lawlessly and say, "We will not have Him reign in our lives!" and not be cut off?

My friends, the character and program of a holy God demands that people like that shall in God's good time be cut off and sent to hell. The character and purpose of Almighty God and His program demands that in God's own good time, men who reject Jesus as Lord, men who thumb their noses in His face, men who live lives as if they had a body but no soul, and say, "No God for me!" The program, the purpose, and the character of a holy God demands that someday in God's time they shall be cut off and sent to hell. In the 13th chapter of Matthew I read, *"The Son of man shall send forth his angels, and they shall gather out of his kingdom all things that offend, and them which do iniquity."* You know that'll be fine. You may think I am crazy but I am not interested in cleaning up this town. I think the only hope for Natchez is the coming of Jesus Christ. I don't believe we will get it done any other way.

All I'm trying to do is to warn everybody I can. That's the reason we've gone into homes; we're glad we are spending $1,100 for the radio; this message will go out into multiplied thousands of homes, and when you get home tonight, people we couldn't drag or hog tie to get into this tent, and they will spend some part of this night in some sort of sin and they will listen to the radio and at the judgment we'll be glad! I want every child of God in this town to sacrifice something in this effort that requires time and effort and money. These days demand that all of us do it. But we didn't come to this town to clean up your city. God bless your heart, this whole world is gone. This whole world is thumbing its nose at Almighty God and it is sunken in sin! But one thing we can do is warn them and God Almighty is going to save some of them to the praise of the glory of His Name!

We are getting phone calls about people being changed. I'd rather have the phone calls I am getting now. I'd rather have a woman come and tell me how God saved her last night, and how happy she was. And how her husband was under conviction! And that she wanted us to pray that God Almighty would save him! That's what I'm giving my life for! That's what I'm preaching for! But I can't clean up this whole world. I've seen many dives in this town but I don't think you're going to get many of them cleaned up. Let me tell you, I preached for twenty-six months in the world's biggest oil town and for sixteen months I was the only preacher in a city of 50,000. I got the governor of the state of Texas to declare Marshall law. We closed up every dive in the whole outfit! We drove out of town 1,200 public women! And they let me lead the drive and told them not to come back. They let me light the match and we burned up 3,700 slot machines! And in a month's time it was just as bad as when we started. It's a hopeless task, my friend. Now don't misunderstand me. I'm in favor of giving them hell! I'm in favor of preaching, but let me tell you I'm in favor of hanging their hides up on every telephone post I can! This whole world is going to hell; but my job, my purpose is to save some people!

This church down here, come hell or high water, is going to do the job that Jesus empowered her to do with His Holy Spirit and made possible by His shed blood! Listen to me. Wouldn't it be wonderful if you were here every night? You know the day's coming when He's going to send His angels down here to Natchez and all these bootleggers, and black market outfits, and picture show operators, and your folks that run your houses of ill fame and the folks that patronize them, and the folks that run your big gambling establishments, and the folks that entertain your visitors with booze; God Almighty is going to send His angels and they are going to pick them up from Natchez and cast them into the lake of fire! That's right, Brother. But He hasn't done it yet.

I read in 2 Thessalonians, chapter 1:7, *"And to you who are troubled rest with us, when the Lord Jesus shall be revealed from heaven with his mighty angels, In flaming fire taking vengeance on them that know not God, and that obey not the gospel of our Lord Jesus Christ: Who shall be punished with everlasting destruction from the presence of the Lord, and from the glory of his power."* That time's coming! Why is it coming? Why justice demands it. Why is it coming? Why the character of God demands it. In the 13th chapter of the book of Luke, quoting the Lord Jesus, *"I tell you, Nay: but, except ye repent, ye shall all likewise perish."* He told them this parable: *"A certain man had a fig tree planted in his vineyard; and he came and sought fruit thereon, and found none. Then said he unto the dresser of his vineyard, Behold, these three years I come seeking fruit on this fig tree, and find none: cut it down; why cumbereth it the ground? And he answering said unto him, Lord, let it alone this year also, till I shall dig about it, and dung it: And if it bear fruit, well: and if not, then after that thou shalt cut it down."*

Why hasn't God already cut you down? Why don't He? I go to meetings in Chicago and years ago I went downtown to State Street, to the Pacific Garden Mission. About a block before I got to State Street during the depression, every Communist in America had him a soap box and was standing on the corners. And sometimes in New York City I tried to hold street meetings after the church in a city-wide meeting and they wouldn't let me. But the police let Communists stand on a street corner and the police would give them protection as the Communists cussed God! And I stood there and a Communist was just raising Cain. And oh boy, he's having him a time! And he's calling God every dirty unthinkable name he can think of. And finally he got so riled up that he began to shake his fists up toward heaven and he called God a lot of dirty names and said, "God, you are a dirty so-and-so, they say you're up there, I don't believe you are! And if you are up there and you don't like what I'm saying about you why don't you come down here and do something about it!" And God didn't do a thing. Why? Why? Why didn't God kill him? God had the power to. Listen to me, ladies and gentlemen, why hasn't God *killed you?* You're a haughty rebel. You won't let God run your life. You tell Jesus He cannot rule in your heart! When the Spirit knocks at your door you say, "Not tonight, I've got other fish to fry! I'm not willing to surrender to Jesus!" People tell me, "Brother Barnard, I don't want to be a Christian." The reason you don't want to be a Christian is you are afraid you might not hold out. You know that to be a Christian is to live a holy life and you see those people in the church and you see the dirty lives they live and you say they are not Christians—and chances are you're right, and you know that if the Lord ever becomes the absolute Lord of your life He will *demand perfect obedience and holiness* and heart obedience to Him. And you say, I don't want to, because I can't hold out. You are telling me a story, why don't God kill you right now? You're a haughty rebel! You despise His authority! I warn you, God's love is a holy love and the Scriptures say, *"Thou hatest all workers of iniquity."* Thou hatest all workers of iniquity. This is how he regards those who openly despise Him. Again and again the Bible makes known to us the solemn fact that God looks upon the wicked as cumbering the earth! Why don't He cut you down? They're repugnant to Him; He says, they're dross and not gold, they're vessels of dishonor, they're vessels of wrath!

Why doesn't God cut men off now? The fact is the reason they are not being cut off now leads men to presume and sin presumptuously and take advantage of the mercy and longsuffering of God. In Ecclesiastes 8:11 we read, *"Because sentence against an evil work is not executed speedily, therefore the heart of the sons of men is fully set in them to do evil."* Though a sinner, watch it! Listen, *"Though a sinner do evil an hundred times, and his days be prolonged, yet surely I know that it shall be well with them that fear God, which fear before him: But it shall not be well with the wicked, neither shall he prolong his days, which are as a shadow; because he feareth not before God."* Why doesn't God cut this generation off? The Day is coming when He is! The Day is coming when He's going to cut one generation off. The Day is coming when He's going to thrust in the sickle and the blood of men shall form a pool a hundred miles around. It's a terrible picture of carnage when pity is no more and the day of the visitation of His wrath comes.

He's sending His armies and takes the wicked and them that do iniquity and everything that offends and casts them into the lake of fire! And the lake of brimstone. Why don't He do it now? He doesn't do it, because Jesus Christ hung on Calvary's cross and came from God's throne, from a throne of judgment to a throne of grace and mercy; and grace now reigns and mercy is now extended and God delights in His mercy and judgment waits. And now men and women hear the wondrous story of the grace and the mercy of Almighty God.

The Scriptures say three things about God's mercy. Paul said, *"I obtained mercy." "I obtained mercy."* The Scriptures are very clear that men need mercy, not justice. Brother, if you get what's coming to you, you'll be sent to hell. Your heart is against God. Your feet are swift to shed blood. From the time of your mother's womb you go about speaking lies and hypocrisies. I'm quoting the Word of God, *"There is none that doeth good, no, not one." "There is none righteous." "For all have sinned, and come short of the glory of God."* Ohhh, my friends! We need mercy! And not justice!

When I was living in Oklahoma, a man by the name of Cunningham in Oklahoma City was arrested and accused of having murdered his wife. The police had found his wife's body cut in many little pieces and put in a tote sack and tied securely with some iron weights and it was thrown down into the bottom of the river that flows beside Oklahoma City. And they found evidence and arrested the husband. And they brought him to trial and tried him before twelve men and the jury said, he's guilty. And the judge pronounced that he should be hanged by the neck until he be dead. On a certain day they took him down to the McAlester Penitentiary and he was awaiting the time of the execution. He was a multi-millionaire and he used all of his money. He hired a set of brilliant lawyers and they circulated petitions all over Oklahoma and got tens of thousands of people to sign the petitions and urged the governor to commute his sentence to life in prison. They tried to get appeals and took it to a higher court and every time the court would say, Guilty! Guilty! Guilty! They influenced the newspapers and they worked for a solid year and got him stay after stay, and finally the governor of the state issued a statement. He said, "I've considered the evidence! I find that the evidence was properly handled and according to the evidence of the trial this man is guilty. And I cannot face my God and commute his sentence." And so this man had to go on and let them hang him by the neck until he was dead.

Oh, my friends! Ohhhh, if old Rolfe Barnard could do what's required of him and tell men of the strict justice of God and tell you that *every sin* is worthy of death! And that God by no means will clear the guilty. I try to get men to see their need of a Savior. I don't believe that anybody cares that Jesus did die until they *see* that they need Him to die in their stead! And that will break the heart of any old sinner in hell if he ever faces it! But I tell you, I get a kick out of going and trying to *get men lost* and get them to see they are guilty and try to get them to see they have no place without God and then tell them that in their stead, Jesus Christ, God's Almighty Son died on Calvary's cross for sinners! And there is wonder working power in the shed blood of Jesus Christ to cleanse a man's heart to get his sins UNDER THE BLOOD and get entrance into the kingdom of God.

But that's mercy, my friends, not justice. In the second place, the Bible says that God's got plenty of mercy. I sure am glad of that. God's not a pauper. Nobody's gonna exhaust the storehouse of mercy! Not many folks are ever gonna feel they want mercy; not many folks are every going to cry for mercy. Most men will pray, "I thank you, Lord, that I'm not like other men. I do this and I don't do that." Not many are ever going to smite themselves and refuse to look up and say, "God be merciful to me; I am the biggest sinner out of hell!" Ohh, not many will do it! Not many will do it. But everybody could, thank God! And if everybody could, God would have plenty to go around! God will have plenty to go around. Let me read it in God's Word: *"And you hath he quickened, who were dead in trespasses and sins; Wherein in time past ye walked according to the course of this world, according to the prince of the power of the air, the spirit that now worketh in children of disobedience"* I am reading your biography before you were saved. *"Among whom also we all had our conversation in times past in the lusts of our flesh, fulfilling the desires of the flesh and of the mind; and were by nature the children of wrath, even as others. But God,"* thank God! Those are the two biggest words I have ever found in the Bible! *"But God, who is RICH IN MERCY,"* thank God! Mercy that was great and grace was free! That was multiplied to me and my burdened soul found liberty at Calvary! God's got plenty of mercy for the vilest sinner that ever writhed and wiggled his way to an eternal hell, if he just applied the courts of heaven for mercy. My God's got plenty!

There is no sinner in this world too big for God. Ohhh no! No sinner in this world is too big for God! And the last thing the Scripture says about God's mercy is that He is rich in mercy to all who call upon Him. He's rich in mercy to *all* who call upon Him! The Scripture says, *"Whosoever shall call upon the name of the Lord shall be saved."* What does that mean, Preacher? Well, I don't know. It doesn't say call five minutes or two seconds, it just says, *"Whosoever shall call."* If I were you I'd call!

Old Bud Robinson said he called, and he called, and he cried and he waited on God and he said one time when he said that God would never have anything to do with him and thus came to the end of his own strength, he said a miracle happened. He said, "God dropped a chunk of glory in my soul and there has been no sin burden ever since." Do you believe that? John Wesley, I have his journal and every preacher in this world ought to read that journal. Poor old John Wesley said, "I preached at St. John's today and I'm told I'm not to preach there no more. The people were disturbed." The church in that day went to take communion and they didn't believe in inward experience. Wesley came to Georgia as a missionary and got in some Moravians and they kept telling him that salvation was inward. That it started inward and worked out. And that salvation demanded inward holiness. John Wesley didn't know everything but he knew one thing, he knew that something had to happen in here. Something's got to happen in here my folks! Something's got to happen in here! There has to be an operation of the Spirit! It will make you hungry and thirsty and pant after righteousness. And Wesley went to preaching after he got saved and the preachers hated him and cursed him and told all manners of lies—you read that journal! They dragged John Wesley off his horse and beat him and left him for dead. God worked a miracle and raised him up and he'd get back on his horse and go preach somewhere else.

Ohhh my! Listen to me! Whosoever shall call! Well, Brother, keep on calling! Keep on calling *until God makes Jesus real to you.* Don't let Rolfe Barnard convince you to know my Lord. Don't you do it. My Lord said, *"If any man THIRST, let him come unto me, and DRINK."* Stay in His presence until He does something for you! I tell people, I told a man last night, he's been making professions and he came again last night and he said, "There's no victory, there's no power, there's no desire to witness." I said, "Brother, don't let us talk you into anything." He said, "What should I do?" I said,

I'd camp on God's trail." I would! I'd call on Him. I'd search His Scriptures. I'd plow up my old broken heart. I'd afflict myself. I'd wait on God. Brother, I believe that salvation is *something my Lord does for you.* He does for you. One of the marks of a false preacher is that he heals the wounds of sinners slightly. Oh, don't be too quick, my brother, to dry that tear away. The tragedy of today is not people who have burdens, it's the people who don't have any. The tragedy of today is not people who do not have conflicts. Brother, I believe if you ever get saved the battle's gonna start. Hell is going to start poppin if you ever get saved. That's right, Brother. Somebody says, If you're saved you never have any doubt. No, that's not so. If you never doubted your salvation I'll tell you why, you don't have any to doubt. There is no such thing as perfect peace, my brother. You're not perfect yet. And, Brother, real faith and doubt go together. But chronic doubt is a sure sign you're lost.

Old Dr. B. H. Carroll, the greatest preacher this old country ever knew said, "Gentlemen! If you've been saved, one thing is dead certain, the gospel came to you one time in power and God singled you out. Maybe you was in a big crowd but you lost consciousness of everybody, it was just you and God." Before anybody ever gets saved that sinner and Almighty God get alone. It may be down under a sycamore tree, it may be in a crowded auditorium, but God will find you. He'll pick you out and the gospel will come not in words only but in POWER. He will make you a captive of my Lord and Savior Jesus Christ.

And I tell people keep on coming to my Lord, maybe next time you'll touch the hem of His garment and VIRTUE will go out unto you and HEALING WATERS will flow in your soul and you'll have the consciousness that you've TOUCHED GOD. That you've touched God. Mercy to all who call on Him, thank God! Do you know everybody is going to get to heaven who wants to go there. Everybody's gonna get saved that wants to be saved. Thank God! EVERYBODY THAT WANTS TO BE SAVED IS GONNA BE SAVED. Wicked old sinners will be saved.

I was holding a meeting in Detroit, Michigan; one Thursday after the benediction of the morning service, old freckled-face-red-headed Mister Childers came up to me. He worked in a Chevy factory in Detroit. He said, "Preacher, if I come get you tomorrow, I have planned it if you can, if you will I will lay off work." He said, "I'll come and get you, I couldn't tell you how to get there but I'll come the twenty miles across town and get you and take you. There is a man over in my neighborhood that is dying of cancer of the stomach. He drunk so much booze that it had rusted out his stomach and cancer set in. He's been down in the state of Georgia in a sanitarium and the doctors told him he's gonna die pretty soon and they couldn't do anything for him and asked him if he'd like to be sent somewhere to die. And he said, "Well, I've got no kin folk except my sister in Detroit and I'd be much obliged if you ship me there and let her take care of me and I'd like to die in my sister's home." And so they sent that man there. And this red-headed man Childers found out about him someway and he's been going to see him, trying to witness to him. And the man was awful wicked, and he said he would just cuss him as he witnessed to him and I never heard such wicked cuss words in all my life. I just sit there and cry as he cusses me and I can't get a word of the gospel over to him and when he is not full of dope he's just screaming in pain cause that cancer is just gnawing his insides out. And he said, "It looks to me a fellow in that shape wold be afraid to die and go to hell but I can't get a word in edgewise to him. Preacher, I've got a lot of confidence in you. I'll lay off tomorrow and I'll come and get you and take you over there if you'll go and talk to that fellow before he dies. I don't know if it will do any good or not but I sure love for you to have a shot at him before he dies."

I said, "You come and get me." That night came a blizzard, the next morning it was eleven below zero, snow and ice everywhere. Old Childers didn't give up, he chugged through the twenty miles of Detroit city traffic in the snow and the sleet and the ice. And he got to me and we got in his car and chugged back, we'd get stuck in the snow, it was awful, they hadn't got the streets cleaned, just a terrible blizzard, and finally we got over to where that fellow was. And we got out of the car and went up to the house on the porch and rang the doorbell, and his sister came and admitted us and Mr. Childers said, "I brought the preacher to talk to your brother." She said, "I'm awful sorry, Mr. Childers, the doctors just left and my brother's in such terrible pain they gave him a double shot of dope and he is sound asleep and can't be woke up for several hours."

Old red-headed Childers, he was a good conservative Baptist, but he slipped down on his knees and he began to pray, and I tell you it was a sight to listen to him pray! He said, "Lord, that man in there is dying and I've driven 20 miles and back in the snow, laid off from work, and this preacher's over here and I want this preacher to get to preach to this man one time before he dies." And he said, "Lord, *please wake him up. Amen.*" And the sister went in the room and in a minute she came back and said, "Praise the Lord, he's awake!"

I don't know, you can go on wondering about that tonight, but the God I worship ain't dead folks. He ain't dead! I ain't got no time for these quacks, these folks that claim they have power to heal. I've got no power but God has. God has. He don't heal a lot of folks but I have seen Him heal some. Not many, not many, most of the folks don't get healed. But God ain't dead, Brother! God ain't dead and I saw Him. You can't tell me that God didn't go in there and wake that guy up. God's merciful! We went in, I was a little younger than I am now, and I went at the old boy all wrong. I tried to tell him about the love of God and the gospel and I got started pretty good and he started cussing me. Oh he just cussed up a storm! And when he kind of wound down I did what I should have done to start with. Where should we start when we go to witnessing to men? Tell them Jesus loves them? No, no. No, no. Talk about sin. Talk about sin. That's where to start. That's where Jesus always started, sin. And Brother, I began to quote every Scripture I could think of about sin. I quoted them all then I got on hell and I quoted every verse I ever memorized and I just poured hell into that boy for about twenty minutes and he'd start to cuss and I'd talk louder and I'd drown him out and then I got on the judgment. I was absolutely without mercy! I went after him! And when I kind of wound down he was sobbing like his heart would break.

And finally he quit sobbing and he said, "Preacher, you are right. The reason I cuss this other fellow out and I cussed you so much is that it makes me feel a little better." He said, "Preacher, I'm dying! This old cancer is eating me up and it's my fault. The doctor sent me back here to die and I know I'll be in hell in a few days or maybe in a few hours and I'm scared to death and it just makes me feel a little better when I cuss."

I said, "Brother, if I was in your shape I wouldn't be cussing; it won't be long till you're in the hand of God." He said, "Preacher, there is no hope for me. I have been as low down and mean as I have been and God wouldn't save an old devil like me and there is nothing for Him to do but to send me to hell!"

Boy, I had my fish! I had my fish! Anytime I find somebody that's got that attitude I got GOOD NEWS for them! And I turned around and began to preach the gospel to him and pretty soon the Spirit of God was working in that old devil's heart and the GOSPEL MESSAGE SUNK in and God can bring a man to eternal life anytime if it is apprehended and accepted and believed. And then bless God, just like a fool woman when she's happy, he commenced to crying. And after he cried a little while old red-headed Childers, I looked at him and if he hadn't fallen on the floor by the bed just like a stuck pig, thanking God! Thanking God! Thanking God! And then he got up and he said, "Preacher, I told this fella that you sing sometimes. I wonder if you'd sing something for him." I said, "Well." I turned to the fella and he couldn't talk then but in a hoarse whisper, and I said, "Would you like me to pick the song?" He said, "Preacher, I hadn't been to church in about forty years but I was raised in a home where they went to church. And my mother used to sing a song, I have kinda forgotten some of it, but I remember a little bit of it and it was something about grace."

I said, "I wonder if it went something like this: Amazing grace how sweet the sound that saved a wretch like me. I once was lost but now I'm found. Was blind but now I see." He said, "That's it! That's it!" And I sang through the first three verses and he held up his hand and said, "Preacher, I remember the last verse. I'm gonna sing it with you." Then in an old broken voice we sang together, "When we've been there ten thousand years, bright shining is the sun. We've no less days to sing God's praise than we first begun."

And after a while we left. We bundled up and got in the car and we were chugging down the road and that car was just going that way and I looked over and old Childers' eyes filled with tears, his face bathed in tears. I said, "Pull over, you fool! You're gonna get us killed! What's the matter with you?" He said, "I'm just thanking and praising God. Ain't God merciful! I was the meanest lowest down devil that ever crawled on his belly and I satisfied the lust of the flesh and God conquered me and saved me! And now He just saved that old devil! He drank enough booze to rot out his stomach! And now HE CONQUERED HIM AND SAVED HIM AND PUT

A SONG IN HIS HEART. Ain't God merciful!" And then we sat there together in that car and we sang the hymn, "He Died at Calvary." We had a good time!

The next day my phone rang and the sister said, "Preacher, my brother's dying and he wonders if you can make it. Will you come? He wants you by his side when he dies." And I got in a taxi and we got through the city traffic but when I got there he had gone to the other side. The sister said, "Well, my brother said, 'The preacher's not going to get here. Tell him that God has shown mercy to another sinner.'"

Oh, my friend, judgment waits a little while. Mercy, mercy is yours if you want it. But it's mercy for *guilty sinners*. If you'll take your place as a guilty sinner, God will show mercy to you. Let us stand. God help us. I want you to sing the first verse of the song he sang, "On Calvary." Mercy there was great and grace was free ... on Calvary. God have mercy over the radio you're listening to me. Sinner, do you want the mercy of God? Will you humble yourself, come down off your high horse, plead guilty, and sue for mercy tonight. God will save sinners who plead guilty and plead the mercy of God. Bow your heads over the radio and cry to God. Every head here in the tent bowed. How many people here tonight will say, "Preacher, I'm a guilty sinner. I know I'm lost. I know I'm lost. I know God's not my Lord." I want to see if you're honest. How many here? Lift your hand, saying, "I'm not a Christian." Lift it high. Way up high. Way up high. Don't be ashamed of it. I want to see it. Way up high. God bless you all around. Now, what are you going to do about it? Stand there and take chances on the judgment of God? Or plead for mercy? Whosoever shall call upon the Name, whosoever, shall call upon the name of the Lord. He's rich to all who call. Surrender to Him as your Lord. The pastor and workers will be in the prayer room it is right here to my left. I want you to walk this aisle and come and seek my Lord tonight. Cry to Him. Don't stand there under His wrath until He cuts you off. While mercy is offered, men, young ladies, men and women all over this tent, God help you. Just as I am without one plea, but that thy blood was shed for me ... come on. Come on, sinner, and seek my Lord. Who will be the first one to step out, saying, "I'm a sinner seeking mercy and I'm gonna seek Him tonight. I'm gonna call on God for mercy tonight." Come on! While we sing.

SERMON 2: Calling Men to Come Clean with God

(Volume Two: Sermon 6, taken from his radio ministry)

Last Lord's Day we dwelt at length on the fact that Almighty God laid the axe at the root and that every tree that bringeth not forth good fruit was going to be hewn down and cast into the fire. I want to continue our study on the ministry of John the Baptist, "Calling Men to Come Clean with God" and to throw down theirs arms and to cease their willful violation of God's holy law and to submit their lives to the rule and the reign of the Lord Jesus Christ before it is everlasting too late.

John the Baptist laid the axe of God's coming judgment at the very root of the sinful condition of men and women, and we desperately need again and again all over this country men of the like, of the persuasion, and of the character of John the Baptist, the forerunner of the Lord Jesus Christ, to come and insist that men shall come clean with God. There is no excuse now; God Almighty will not accept any plea of ignorance. He commands all men everywhere to repent. John the Baptist said in Matthew 3:2, *"Repent ye: for the kingdom of heaven is at hand."* The Savior Himself says, *"Except ye repent, ye shall all likewise perish"* (Luke 13:5).

I've been amazed as I go up and down the country to find out how many preachers have found out that repentance is not to be preached to the Gentiles. We have Bible teachers who tell us the Jews were supposed to repent, but that all a sinner has to do now is simply receive Jesus Christ as his Savior by what they call simple faith, and they'll be saved. But the Scriptures nowhere separate repentance and faith. Sometimes repentance alone is mentioned, and it always supposes faith; and sometimes the way to God is faith, and it is just mentioned alone, but is always presupposes repentance. Somebody says, "Which comes first—repentance or faith?" I do not know, they come together, but you cannot have one without the other. We desperately need in these desperately wicked days the clarion call to go forth everywhere, for God commands all men everywhere to repent. To repent! That's the desperate need of this hour. Dr. Harry A. Ironside said, "Shallow preaching that does not grapple with the terrible fact of man's sinfulness and guilt—preaching that does not call on men everywhere to repent—that kind of preaching results in shallow conversions. And so we have myriads of glib-tongued professors today who give no evidence of regeneration whatsoever. They go about prating about being saved by grace, but they manifest no grace in their lives."

Dr. L. E. Maxwell of Prairie Bible Institute yonder in Canada in his great book, *Crowded to Christ*, tells of a young preacher who graduated from one of our Bible institutes and he went over yonder to India and preached the nice smooth gospel that he was taught in the Bible institute. The Bible teachers have the dispensations all arranged, and they've got everything fitted nicely into little pockets, you know— this is for that time, the other's for some other time. This young preacher had gone over there and preached his nice little easy believism over yonder in India, and everybody over there had believed. Why, sure! And they took Jesus as their Savior and put Him up on a shelf with the rest of their gods. And this young man went over there and built a great church membership of people who believed in Jesus, but as he continued to preach he noticed there was no fruit. There was no fruit, there was no zeal, there were no tears, there was no passion, there was no compassion. There was no "ache" to warn men everywhere, and finally in his desperate condition he came to the conclusion that led him to disband his congregation and start at the bottom and begin all over again. Then instead of preaching his easy believism, he began to preach the truth as it is in God's Word, that God Almighty demands that men come absolutely one hundred percent clean with Him and throw down their arms and put their shotgun down at the feet of the Lord Jesus Christ, throw up their hands in utter submission and quit rebelling against the rule of Christ in their lives, quit violating God's holy law in their daily walk!

And I wouldn't be surprised if that's not what this nation needs. We have thousands of people who attend some sort of church service this morning; some of you listening to me now—and the earlier it is the better. You'll go to some of these early morning services now so you'll have more time to feed the lusts of that old body and that old mind and that old flesh and that old carnality that's in you. And we're turning America into a Protestant Catholicism, where we go and pay our tribute to a holy God one hour on Sunday morning, and then we do as we please the rest of that day that God Almighty says is His day, and is to be kept for the glory of God and the rest of the body. I say to you, my friends, that there is no evidence of regeneration inside unless it is evidenced by the fruits of repentance, an obedient, abundant, abiding, victorious preserving faith in the Lord Jesus Christ in our daily lives!

I tell you now that in spite of the Bible teaching to the contrary notwithstanding, the preaching of repentance is the demand of Almighty God to all men everywhere. Calling on men to repent is not contrary to the preaching of the grace of a sovereign God, but the preaching of repentance prepares men and women to be interested in the gracious provision of God in Christ, wherein He imputes not the sin of the world to men, but puts it on Jesus Christ. We've got lots of people today, especially in the Piedmont section, who are mighty, mighty afraid lest the sinner will have something he can claim a part in and have merit in. But I tell you, there is no merit on the part of the sinner, for that sinner enabled by God's grace to recognize his desperate need.

The Scripture says, *"They that be whole need not a physician, but they that are sick."* A man who's covered with putrid sores from the soles of his feet to the top of his head, like the sinner described in Isaiah—the sooner he finds out that he is sick, the sooner he may be calling, screaming for Jesus Christ the Great Physician to put the healing balm of Gilead on his sin-sick soul and rescue him by His marvelous power. My friend, there isn't one bit of merit at all for a sick man to call for a doctor. There wasn't any merit in the prodigal son who left home and wound up in the hog pen; there was no merit for him to crawl and go back home and say, "Father, I have sinned!" He merited no pardon, but when he did go back and take his place in the dust of repentance, it did put him in a place to receive a pardon and salvation.

I tell you, there is no sinner who was ever saved apart from the grace of God. Know assuredly that a sinner can never receive the grace of God who does not recognize (watch it!) his need, and his need is for repentance, and this is not contrary to the grace of God, nor does it limit the grace of God, nor does it accrue merit to the repenting sinner—but it is God's way of *preparing* the sinner to hear with gladsome ear the good tidings that God was in Christ reconciling the world to Himself.

We desperately need what I am talking about this morning. Oh, my soul! Isn't it a tragedy that we try to soften the terms upon which God proffers Jesus Christ to men and women!

The terms are repentance toward God and faith in the Lord Jesus Christ, and you and I right here in this city are living in a day of lawlessness. Shameless impenitence marks the actions of this generation of people. You know there is some hope for people as long as the conscience pricks them, and their hearts bleed over their wrongdoing, but people today do as they please and say, "Phooey on God." If God gets in their way, they'll import them some Bible teachers to say, "Well, that's not for us today." Or they do something, and they'll say, "Well, I'm not concerned; I'm getting along fine, thank you!" I say that men are in desperate condition now because they are shamelessly propagandizing the fact that they don't give a whoop what God says in His Word about the way they do. They joined the church, took the preacher's hand, were sprinkled or dunked, they went to service once early on Sunday morning; and the priest in Protestant garb will put a little hypodermic needle in their arms and give them a little spiritual cocaine shot, and make them feel better so they can go out and sin some more!

We desperately need some John the Baptists to go up and down this land in our day in all the fury of Sinai's thunders and terrors and shout out again that the law of God has not been repealed, that God still demands men to repent, and that God still demands men to believe, and God still demands that men surrender to the lordship of Jesus Christ in all the avenues of their lives. We need men now to call men to repentance. We need desperately to read sermons like the Lord preached on the Mount. Now our nation is full of Bible teachers who tell us that the Sermon on the Mount is not for today; it's for the millennial age, they say, and it's universally ignored now, and they tell us the exalted demands of the Sermon on the Mount will be a lot more easily obeyed in the millennial age when the lion and the lamb shall lie down together and the knowledge of the Lord shall cover this old earth as the waters over the sea. But I look you in the face and tell you, my friends, that the Sermon on the Mount is for T-O-D-A-Y, today! And the ethical standards that we are told are too high, and that men cannot possibly live up to them now, are still God's measuring rod for the character of His citizens of the eternal kingdom both in time and in eternity.

Ah, they tell us, we couldn't turn another cheek when somebody slaps us, and when somebody steals our coat, we couldn't give them another, and we couldn't pray for those who spitefully use us and persecute us, and we couldn't do this and that and the other that the Scriptures tell us to do. Man's ethical standard today is not too high, and we go up and down the country and whittle down the claims of God Almighty's holy law, but I warn you now that A-L-L, all Christ's teachings are meant by Him on purpose to be unacceptable to this old carnal, godless, dirty, filthy flesh of Rolfe Barnard and everybody else.

You know, the early Christians who became martyrs (most of them) followed through what I'm preaching to you now. They could have muzzled an open confession of Christ until that command could have been more easily obeyed, but they didn't do it. Many of them paid with their lives, but they gained heaven and the glorious hope of Christ in eternity.

Walk the streets of this nation if you don't believe it—see the women sporting their bodies and showing their naked flesh. Watch them mowing their lawns with not enough clothes on to make a good sized handkerchief. Go all over this town and see church members telling God to go to hell; they'll pay no attention to what He's written in His holy Book. And I say to you, this lawless, lawless (God help us!) this lawless age in the churches and out calls for preaching like John the Baptist. Whether men hear or not, it must be done.

I wish God would raise up people to hear me. We are getting on other radio stations to get this message out. I wish God's people who hear me would pray for me. I want an old fashioned baptism of Holy Ghost power! I wish I could burn these warning messages into the hearts of these self-satisfied, God-dishonoring, Christ-rejecting, Holy Spirit-denying and despising, lawbreaking generation of men and women who are going to hell so fast they are kicking up the dust in the devil's eyes, and going to hell listening to us preach.

I tell you, John the Baptist, came and said, "God's laid the axe to the root," when men came to him and said, "We've been listening to you preach." As we learned last Lord's Day, they came with this one cry, "What must we do? It must be our move now." Oh, my soul! Oh, to hear men once again interested in what the holy claims of God Almighty are. And John the Baptist wielding the sword of truth in the Spirit crossed these people just where they lived in order that the one thing might bring them to the dust of death and the death of self, and therefore resurrection in the power of the Lord Jesus Christ.

The soldiers came and said, "What must we do?" And he crossed them on the thing nearest their heart. The publicans came and said, "What must we do?" And he told them to turn from the thing that was nearest their heart. The Pharisees came and he told them, "Ye generation of vipers! Who hath warned you!" And he told them to bring forth fruit worthy of repentance. Ladies and gentlemen, listen to me! All of man's rebellion is usually wrapped up, heads up, in *just one thing.* These publicans, their rebellion and their lawlessness came to a head (like a boil, you know) over their stealing money. And the same with the soldiers, and the same with the Pharisees. *God always crosses a man at the point of his rebellion.* And when God's will and man's will cross, something's got to give. If man's will prevails, he'll go to hell, but if God's will prevails He'll conquer that sinner. You know, my friend, it's obedience to the command of God—or it's death!

It's to be shut up with all our inability to face our responsibility, and to remember that God before He raises anybody first *kills him,* and that God *demands unconditional surrender to the lordship of His blessed Son in your life and mine.* My soul! I wonder where your rebellion is headed up. I wonder just what one thing comes up before you every time the claims of Christ are pressed upon you. You are willing to give up everything except one thing, and I tell you that that'll go, that'll be cast at the feet of Jesus Christ! You are going to turn in abhorrence and hatred of that, you're going to pull it out of your life and cast it at the feet of the Lord Jesus Christ, or you are going to eternal hell. That's right, my friend.

How about you, sinner? Your rebellion and violation heads up in one place, and you want to go to heaven but you won't drop the sin, and you don't want to go to hell, but you won't drop the sin. I tell you, God Almighty demands that you drop it and throw it at the feet of Jesus Christ and come clean with Him, or you are going to be sent to burn in eternity forever and ever by a God who loved this world enough to give His Son to die for sinners, but doesn't love it enough to send men to heaven who love sin and hate God. May God help us today, is my prayer.

SERMON 3: Evangelism Inside the Church Membership

(Volume Two: 21)

The other day I received a call from a pastor from whom I had not heard for years. A long time ago the sovereign Lord performed a major operation upon a congregation of which he was pastor and I was the evangelist. Now he is in another state and pastor of another congregation. He said that the people of his congregation needed to be plowed up, busted right down the middle, and brought to an awareness of the gospel of God's glory. He asked that I come to be used, if it should please the Lord, to perform that operation. His call reminded me of a situation that I have to wrestle with each time I go for a "revival meeting." Shall I aim at the condition within the church that prevents it from truly representing Christ or just seek to pull some precious souls from the fire, as if by fire?

Increasingly it is, at least in my limited experience, becoming harder each day to do the latter. Evangelism which seeks to reach men for Christ, who are outside our churches, is essential, but I am persuaded that what is more critical in our time is evangelism *inside the membership of our churches.* This seems to be the imperative for our time. Nearly everyone is a member of somebody's church. I am far from being a loner in this regard. There are two questions that are pressing for answers now and pressing more people than at any time in memory. They are, first, are we the church of Jesus Christ that we claim to be? Secondly, are we the ministry of Jesus Christ that we claim to be? We need desperately to ask and answer these questions. I believe that self-criticism lies at the very heart of a biblical ministry and church. It is not cause for satisfaction that at present in this country we are still strong on confidence and weak in self-criticism. We ought to face the fact that the very existence of most churches is under serious attack, not simply whether they shall continue but whether they should continue!

The ability to see any line of distinction between the Christian faith that has it origin in the person of Jesus Christ, and the forms of today's respectable religion that stop short of an unconditional relationship with God in Christ and stop short of an unconditional commitment to Christ, has largely been lost. One could almost say that church membership is fast becoming the best place to hide from God.

When we turn from the gospel to the situation today, we are met by the fact that congregations have made decisions for Christ, they believe the Bible, they meet once a week for a period of "worship," and for the hearing of a sermon. Occasionally they call in a visiting preacher and hold a revival meeting, employing techniques and pressure to manipulate other human beings (for their own good, of course) to "decide for Christ." When one plays with this sort of thing, one should know that he is walking on the edge of the pit of hell.

It is still true that membership in the church is meant to be the outer symbol of inner commitment to Jesus Christ. But churches today are loaded with nominal members, at peace with the status quo. That's Latin for "the mess we are in." They are nice, quiet, friendly folks who are totally ignorant of the Word of God but quite devoted to the traditions of their fathers. They yearn for institutional security, rather than adventures of Christian freedom, come weal or woe. Their preachers have sold their evangelical birthright for a mess of pot-bellied respectability.

Back after all this to my opening remarks. Can we afford to ignore and religiously refuse to open the awful sore of powerless, popular Sunday morning religion? Shall we allow church members to go to hell unwarned or shall we set our faces toward God and cry, *"Revive thy work in the midst of the years."*

We won't make much headway in finding a solution if we do not understand the problem. A cure is not likely to be found if we have no knowledge of the disease. In the matter of salvation the problem is man's sin; the solution is God's grace. The disease is moral depravity and spiritual inability; the remedy is God's mercy in Christ.

If a man is near-sighted, he only needs corrective glasses but if he is blind, he needs the miracle of sight! If a man is sick, he only needs medical aid, but if he is dead, he needs the miracle of life! If man has only strayed from the way, he needs directions, but if he is completely lost, he needs to be found!

Here is the question to be settled by preachers and people,"What happened in the garden?" When one feels obliged to come to some conclusions on the subjects of the election, irresistible grace and particular redemption, it would be wise for him to first determine the condition of the sinner who is to be saved. If man was only wounded by the fall he needs assistance; if he is dead in sins, he needs to be resurrected and that by the purpose and power of the God of life. If fallen man still has his moral ability and power of choice, then let us wait for him to choose and seek God, but if he loves darkness and will not come to Christ then Christ must love and come to him.

SERMON 4: Turn or Burn
(Volume Two: 8)

We bring you today the fourth and last in the series of messages on the general subject, "John the Baptist Comes to Town";—repentance, God's requirement, the chief duty of all men everywhere and the gift of God to believing sinners. We have been trying in these last three messages to press the demand of a sovereign God as it came through the lips of John the Baptist. That demand was: REPENT! You know, my friends, God Almighty has nothing else to say to an eternity-bound soul. You need not bring your problems or your alibis or your theology, or anything else, to try to have a Bible conference with a holy God. He's got just one thing to say to a sinner: "Stack arms, sinner! Throw down that shotgun! Yield yourself to My claims." Plant, by the grace of God, the flag of King Jesus in your life, then the Lord God will put up the white flag of peace, and you will know the peace that this old world didn't give, and therefore cannot take away. *"Therefore being justified by faith, we have peace with God through our Lord Jesus Christ."*

And now with your Bibles open, I want to speak to you on the subject, "Turn or Burn." John the Baptist says, "Repent, or else." It is repent or hell. There are no if's and and's about it. That is the only command that God has for the sinner. If you ignore that, He won't do business with you on any other ground. That is the only place that God will deal with a sinner, the place of repentance. You have no time to argue about being a special creation of Adam's ruined and lost race; He just looks every human being in the face now and says, "You are all cut out of the same cloth, and you've got to repent." John the Baptist evidently knew by heart Psalm 7:11-12, where the Psalmist speaking of God says, *"God judgeth the righteous, and God is angry with the wicked every day. If he turn not, he will whet his sword; he hath bent his bow, and made it ready."* Turn or burn!

Richard Baxter went down to England years ago saying, "Sinner, turn or burn." The gifted and sainted and lamented Spurgeon had a sermon, "Turn or Burn." And that is just what it is. Our text here, from which I think John the Baptist drank deeply, simply puts it on the line—if you don't turn, God will whet His sword! He has got it ready. He has prepared the instruments of death, and you have made a pit and you have dug it; then you have fallen into the ditch you made. It is turn or burn. God has a sword, and God *will punish sin.* The old-time preachers believed this. They went up and down the land and copied or republished God's demands, saying, "Turn, sinner, turn!" There is no time to argue. There is not time to delay. There is no time for a conference. Turn! Throw down your arms. It is turn or burn!

The heart of the gospel is that God in His marvelous grace said, "Sinner, the way has been prepared so that, as you throw down your arms, peace and pardon may be yours." And that way is through the Lord Jesus in His precious life and His death and His present reign, and because of who He is and what He does now, God Almighty is able and willing (Praise God!) to promise (imagine God promising an old sinner anything, but He does—isn't that grace?)—to promise that the vilest sinner out of hell, if he repents toward God and believes in Christ, that pardon will be his! He will be set free. Thank God! Isn't that grace? Isn't that great!

You know, my friends, universally almost all preachers used to preach against sin. Now it's unpopular to even mention any kind of sin. We hear a lot now about "God is love," but also according to the Bible *He is Judge.* In the Bible, line upon line, precept upon precept, and plain text upon text says, *"The wicked shall [SHALL] be turned into hell, and all the nations that forget God"* (Psalm 9:17). I wonder how many preachers, I am preaching to you now who are afraid to speak out here. I warn you, my friends, that you are preaching to a generation that is wicked, and because they are wicked, they have had a conference and abolished hell, and they think that deciding they don't like hell has done away with it! And because this is a hypocritical generation, it will have the same punishment.

Now we invent all sorts of doctrines and movements and isms to get out of facing the plain facts that *it is repent or it is hell.* You are living in a day, my friends, when men have endeavored to prove that God will clear the guilty. He says in the Bible that He won't. You are living in a day when men and women are endeavoring to prove that He will by some kind of means refrain from punishing sin, when He says He won't. Two hundred years ago the predominant strain of the pulpits all over England and America was one of terror and justice, and that kind of preaching produced a breed of God-fearing men and women who made our nation possible. Now we lap up a soft gospel of easy-believes, and we have a soft-generation of so-called Christians. God help us to come back to the plain preaching of the Word of God.

You know, my friends, people sneered at Noah when he preached righteousness. No wonder the people didn't pay much attention to him. Imagine old Noah coming back to America and walking down the streets and seeing the parade of naked flesh and all the out-right flagrant disobedience of God's plain teaching. Men and women doubling their fists at God, snubbing theirs noses at Him, and blowing the smoke of their absolute impenitent attitude in the holy nostrils of God! Imagine Noah coming and preaching righteousness. No wonder they didn't get in the ark! No wonder they didn't pay any attention to his preaching! Perhaps they made fun of Noah. But the day came when the flood was there and they came to appreciate the old man after it was too late.

I tell you over this radio station, someday you will know I am telling you the truth. I am not here to flatter you—I am here to warn you, and I tell you that God Almighty says, "If the sinner turns not, he will burn in hell." God will whet His sword. You know, John the Baptist was sent to tell men just that. He said, "It is repenting time now." He said, "No time to argue now." God help us! I think I have had hundreds come to me, and if you would listen to their talk, they are cut out of a little different cloth from anybody else, and I tell them that it is high time that they just came on down and join the human race! We are all in the same boat, sinner. He just says, "Sinner, throw down your arms. Repent—right now. Right now!" That is the only message He has for a sinner.

He won't talk to you. You say, "Brother Barnard, you don't understand my case." God does and He says, "I have just one thing to say to you; you have pointed your shotgun at Me as long as you need to, and I haven't cut off your neck yet, and I have been patient and longsuffering, and you have been shooting at every claim of a holy God and I have been patient—but I have just one thing to say to you sinner, and that is: You come on down here and take your place and repent. Repent! Repent!"

You can't make a Bible conferee out of a holy God. You can't make out like you are different from everybody else. God commands all men everywhere to repent. He won't even talk to you. He won't do business with you at all on any other plane. He won't just let you pour out your sob stories and then say, "Well, I understand now, you are a different person from most folks, and I will have to get a brand new scheme of dealing with you." He is not going to do it, sinner. He will just look you in the face and say, "Repent, or else!" It's repent or else. Luke 13:5: *"Except ye repent, ye shall all likewise perish."*

You are just bringing all your alibis but all the time you are talking about you're this and you're that, and about this and that and the other. You have the shotgun of your hatred of God's holiness and your unwillingness to bow to God's rule pointed right straight at the heart of God. And you are just like your great, great granddaddy, old Adam—you are trying to reach up and with your filthy hands snatch God off the throne and sit there yourself! God says, "Sinner, I will just tell you right now, I have got nothing else to say to you. You just turn or you are going to burn." That's pretty plain, isn't it? But that is the God's truth!

It is time we quit this nice little dealing, trying to slip up on the blind side of God and making out like we are just not double-barreled, hell-deserving sinners. Why, that is what we are! Why, if we had our way, we would have pushed God off the throne a long time ago. If we had been there in person, we would have driven the nails in the hands and feet of the Lord Jesus Christ, and our voices would have drowned out everybody else's when they cried, "Away with Him. Away with Him! Crucify Him and release unto us Barabbas." That is the kind of folks we are. Those people did exactly what you would have done if you had been there in person, and old Adam did exactly what you would have done if you had been there in person. I am telling you, if what I am saying to you is so, God Almighty couldn't be holy and deal with us and talk over conditions and try to work out something that would be mutually satisfactory to both of us. God Almighty, if He is God at all, has just one thing to say to rebellious sinners, "Sinner, repent! Repent!"

What kind of turning is God talking about? What kind of turning is necessary? Well, bless your dear heart, it is an ACTUAL turning. A lot of people are always talking to me about they want to turn. Well, you are going to go to hell *wanting to turn*. *Repentance is an actual turning.* It is not simply wanting to—it is not simply trying to find out how to. It is an *actual turning from sin.* It is to see your face in the mirror of God's holy law and get a glimpse of yourself and see yourself as *God sees you.* I tell you, any form of repentance is worse than nothing if it attempts to deceive God and lie about your condition. I tell you, your darling sins must be turned from! One leak in the ship is enough to sink that ship. And I tell you, God Almighty declares it necessary that you have repentance after the order of *giving up all of your sins.* That is what He is talking about. If you don't, it is no Christ. The gates of heaven are barred against any human being who thinks that you can enter that straight gate with all of your idols hugged to your own bosom and all of your rebellion still carried in your arms.

Oh, my friends, God Almighty demands an ACTUAL turning. John says, "Do it! Do it!" They came to him and said, "What must we do? We've been listening to you preach; evidently it's our move now." And John says, "You are dead right, Bud. You quit doing that, and you do this, that and the other." Somebody says, "That is legal." I warn you, my friends, that no sinner ever has come to real repentance, which is a reliance on Jesus Christ, without facing the way it is done and who he is. And legally, or any other way you want to, that is the way of real repentance. A man has got to actually turn on himself, *take sides with God against himself.*

Now, Bud, that is hard to do, because your mamma don't want you to do that. Your mamma swears that you are a sweet little boy, and your wife will say, "Brother Barnard, I want you to pray for my husband; he is such a good man." But *God says that his old heart is as vile as the pit of hell itself!* But Mother says, "My boy is a good boy," and the wife says, "My husband is a good husband, he has just one bad habit." But you listen to me now. Listen to me now! It has got to be an actual turning. You've got to take sides with God against yourself. That is hard to do, isn't it? Now it is easy to quit a few little things you do, but, oh, my soul, to take sides with God and say, "God, that is right." That is what confession is, "You're right, God.

I agree with You, God. You are telling me the truth and I will hide it and disguise it no longer." That is what confession is; it's this actual taking sides against yourself, your old nature, that is who you are, that part of you that makes you do what you do, that thing that makes you tick. *Repentance is taking sides against and abhorring yourself and the way you do; this actually has to take place.*

And then the repentance that God Almighty demands is ENTIRE, no reservation. You can't hug something. You can't fool God. You can't keep any rebellion. I know that this matter of laying down your arms will have to be done all over again and again and again and again. There is nothing in the Bible about a repentance that you did thirty years ago and that wound it up. No! No! No! No man can have any evidence that he is born from above except there is some fruit, and the *fruit of the new birth is repentance and faith.* It is an everyday position, but it has got to start sometime. A man has got to bring everything that he knows anything about, every rebellion of which he is conscious, and lay those things and that rebellion down, and take sides against himself—and no reservations, please! No holding one hand behind your back, please! No sir! The rich young ruler couldn't get in except he did that. I tell you what is a fact, my friends, *a pig will always be a pig* I don't care how you clean him up, and a *sinner will always be an old wicked sinner* unless he comes to the place of repentance where God Almighty will do business with him.

Now that is hard to do, isn't it? That is hard to do. And Bud, you are not going to do it if you can help it. You would rather go to hell, some of you, than have this operation. Oh, my soul, to come laying every ambition and every desire and every well devised plan of your whole life and say, "Lord, it is all dross in my sight; I turn it over to You." That's hard to do. As a matter of fact, no man can do that just by deciding that he will do it. *No man will ever do that apart from the goodness and grace and mercy of God.* That is the reason those of you who listen to my voice now who have the slightest evidence that you have been able to repent, you thank God that He has enabled you to come to the place, instead of congratulating yourself and alibiing yourself, that you took sides with God against yourself and repented!

What kind of turning is demanded by a holy God? Well, bless your heart, it is IMMEDIATE. The longer I preach the more this thing makes the hair stand up on my head. God commands all men to repent—when? Well, every time that word occurs in the New Testament it says it is in the imperative mood, "RIGHT NOW!" Right now! I have known some people throughout my ministry, and up and down the land, who talk to me about how they want to go to heaven when they die, and they don't want to go to hell, and yet they sleep well and they eat well. They make a good living, and they are nice sociable people; they are good citizens; they listen to you preach and never bat an eyelash, and are perfectly unaware of the fact that every time they draw breath that was given to them by a holy sovereign God, against whose reign and whose will they are absolutely sinning every day of their lives!

Here is this old wicked world, and just like a revolution yonder in Cuba or somewhere else, the rebels are out in the hills and the mountains and every time they see a soldier they take a shot at him because they are aiming to overthrow the dictator or the king or whoever it may be. This old world is seeing where two people claim to be sovereign—Satan and the Lord. Some people say, "Well, I am not such a bad fellow, Brother Preacher. I do this and I do that." I know, but *you are a member of the rebel army; you are a shotgun carrier for the enemies of King Jesus,* and if your side wins, God will be put out of business.

God Almighty has sent forth the proclamation and said, "Rebel! Lay down your arms. Do it right now! And I promise pardon." But you say, "Well, I will do it when I get ready." Men walk the streets and breathe God's air, eat God's food and drink God's water, and enjoy God's blessings and continue with the shotgun of their wills pointed at the very heart of God. *God Almighty demands immediate repentance.* Not tomorrow, not next day, but NOW! God doesn't say, "It is all right, you just keep on. You just keep on being on the enemy's side. You just keep on." Every dime he makes, God gave him power to make that dime. Every ounce of food he consumes, God Almighty produced that food. Try to make a crop yourself without God's help. Every bit of the water that refreshes your old tired body came from a well that God Almighty provided. That is right. Every breath of air you take is God's air, and you breathe God's air and shoot at God at the same time. You eat God's food and use it to give strength to your resistance to the demands of the sovereign Christ. I tell you, my friends,

God couldn't be God—God wouldn't be God—God would be a disgrace if He allowed sinners to take their time about what they are going to do about ceasing their resistance against His rule. That is the reason that in the Bible, God says, "Repent right now!"

God doesn't like it, Brother. God doesn't think it is nice for you to be shooting at Him. God doesn't like that at all. "God is angry with the wicked every day!" The Word of God says that *the sinner is under the wrath of God* right now, and that wrath abides on him continually. That is the reason that God Almighty demands immediate repentance. Immediate repentance! Hear me, my friends, it is turn or burn! It was so in John the Baptist's day—it is so for now. It will always be so. *The only hope for a sinner is to turn from his rebellion, out of which nest grows all his lawlessness, and turn himself over to the Lord Jesus Christ.*

SERMON 5: How to Prepare Your Heart to Receive God's Truth

(Volume Two: 15)

There is so much in the Bible, I hope that what I decided on is the mind of the Lord. I want to speak as carefully as I can tonight on the subject of preparing one's heart to receive God's truth. Preparing your own heart to receive the engrafted Word, which is able to save the soul. James 1:16-22: *"Do not err, my beloved brethren. Every good gift and every perfect gift is from above, and cometh down from the Father of lights, with whom is no variableness, neither shadow of turning. Of his own will begat he us with the word of truth, that we should be a kind of firstfruits of his creatures. Wherefore, my beloved brethren, let every man be swift to hear, slow to speak, slow to wrath: For the wrath of man worketh not the righteousness of God. Wherefore lay apart all filthiness and superfluity of naughtiness, and receive with meekness the engrafted word, which is able to save your souls. But be doers of the word, and not hearers only, deceiving your own selves."*

We notice here that James is writing to somebody he loved; he called them "beloved brethren." In these words that James wrote in verses 19-22, we find some excellent advice to anyone who is not yet united to the Lord Jesus. By way of advice, here are three things in these verses that are addressed to unsaved men and women who would prepare their hearts to receive the engrafted Word. He says of this engrafted Word that it is able to save your soul. Now it may seem strange that the preacher would say that if anybody wishes to become vitally united to Christ—not just stand afar off and claim to believe in His work of atonement, but to be united to Christ—for we definitely hold that you cannot separate Him from what He did. We believe with all of our heart that multitudes of people honestly and earnestly are doing what they say "trusting in the shed blood of Christ," but they *are not saved.* Because we do not believe that you can participate in the merits of the death of the Lord Jesus Christ, unless you are regenerated.

Thus we say to men and women that if you would in these days of religious confusion where everybody has a gospel, and everybody has a doctrine and everybody has six interpretations of those doctrines, and what I say is just what I say, and there is not much respect for what anybody says. But if you value your souls' welfare, you will take seriously the words of the apostle James here, to prepare your heart, for unless your heart is prepared by you, you will never receive the Word savingly. Did you get it? You will spend all the days of your life, talking about how you believe the Word and how you are trusting in the blood, but an unprepared heart cannot receive the Word of truth. The only way to be born of the Spirit is by the incorruptible Word of the living God.

That introduces me to the biggest tragedy of my ministry as I go from place to place; I wonder if anybody gets saved, because nobody has got time to prepare his heart. You didn't prepare your heart for whatever message the Lord has for you, because you didn't have time, did you? So it will just bounce off of you and it will go in one ear and out the other. It won't be my fault and it won't be the fault of the Word. Your heart cannot receive truth unless it has been prepared, do you see it? Even if you are a Christian, you won't get anything out of anybody's divine service, unless you prepare your own heart. We must plow our own heart and prepare it, so if the seed would drop, it would fall on good ground.

Proverbs 16:1: *"The preparations of the heart in man, and the answer of the tongue, is from the LORD."* Hosea 10:12: *"Sow to yourselves in righteousness, reap in mercy; break up your fallow ground: for it is time to seek the LORD, till he come and rain righteousness upon you."* Any spiritual truth that falls on bad ground doesn't bear fruit. Matthew 13:8-9: *"But other fell into good ground, and brought forth fruit, some an hundredfold, some sixtyfold, some thirtyfold. Who hath ears to hear, let him hear."* We are told plainly in those different parables that He went out and sowed seed, and the seed was good; there was nothing wrong with the seed or the sowing of the seed. The trouble was that He sowed it on four kinds of ground, and only one ground was prepared.

So the seed fell on some ground and the fellow was converted. You remember how old Bill got gloriously converted, and he shouted, and he went down on the streets and told how God had saved him. And two weeks later he'd folded up his tent, taken down the flag, and took off! You see, the Scriptures say there was no root there. He flourished for a little while, but because the seed didn't take root, the first time a little wind storm of adversity came, he played out. Matthew 13:5-6: *"Some fell upon stony places, where they had not much earth: and forthwith they sprung up, because they had no deepness of earth: And when the sun was up, they were scorched; and because they had no root, they withered away."*

But there was one type of ground, and only one, that had been thoroughly prepared. Matthew 13:8-9: *"But other fell into good ground, and brought forth fruit, some an hundredfold, some sixtyfold, some thirtyfold. Who hath ears to hear, let him hear."*

This is interesting in view of the fact that James is giving some advice about how men and women ought to hear the Word of God. This is excellent advice in Hosea 10:12: *"Sow to yourselves in righteousness, reap in mercy; break up your fallow ground: for it is time to seek the LORD, till he come and rain righteousness upon you."* Somebody said, "Well, I don't understand that." Well, that makes two of us. There is very little in the Bible that we can understand, but thank God, we can believe. Now if any kind of spiritual truth comes your way, unless your heart has been prepared to receive truth, you can't receive it; the truth will just bounce off.

I was talking to a preacher the other day and he said, "Brother Barnard, I can't understand. I went through a Baptist college. I went through the seminary three years. I taught in one of our Baptist schools. I pastored in our Baptist churches and I held evangelistic campaigns all over the West. And until two years ago, I had never seen anything in the Word of God about salvation by grace." He said, "Now I pick up my Bible and it's on so many, many pages. But until two years ago, I would read the verses and what the verses said just went in one ear and out the other." Even that preacher was not able to receive the truth until God had brought this thing and the other thing on his life, until he had a prepared heart. Now that is true of any unsaved person.

In James 1:19-21, he lays down three things that those who are interested in plowing their hearts, so they can receive the engrafted Word or the rooted Word, must do. The seed is sown and it takes root. If you plant a little tree, it has to go down and take root before it grows up. That is true in salvation; sinners are not saved accidentally. A preacher tells sinners he can't save himself and that is right; a sinner is helpless. That's right, he cannot move into the spiritual, because he is dead in trespasses and sins. But there are some things a lost man can do; he could look at himself through God's law. A sinner could buy himself a Bible and he could read carefully what God says about him. Then he needs to start plowing his own heart—nothing to keep a sinner from doing that, is there? Now that wouldn't save him, but unless the sinner's heart becomes so that the seed will take root—he may make a profession, he may have some kind of experience, but unless the seed of the gospel takes root, it will not bear fruit. And if you are not bearing fruit, you are not God's child. Is that all right?

James says there are three things that a sinner ought to do if he is interested in having a heart that can receive truth. A sinner must cease from rebellion against the Word of truth. Look again at James 1:18: *"Of his own will begat he us with the word of truth, that we should be a kind of firstfruits of his creatures."* Wherefore, in view of the fact that men are born again by the Holy Spirit with the use of the truth of the gospel, verse 19 says, *"Wherefore, my beloved brethren, let every man be swift to hear, slow to speak, slow to wrath."* You must cut out all of this business of bucking the truth. When the gospel is preached, there are those who do not make an effort to hear; the reason you don't hear is because you don't want to. This Word must be heard, and not bucked, and it must be received until it takes root. If it doesn't, you will just make a profession and go on to hell. It has got to take root. People are swift to mouth their ignorant nothings against the truth of God, and they do it with some enmity.

In Texas a lady rushed up to me and said, "Brother Preacher, I am just torn all to pieces; you are tearing everything up that I ever heard. All I ever heard is against what you are preaching." I said, "I am sorry to hear that. What was it about the message tonight that disturbed you?" She said, "Well, this morning and tonight. I have just walked the floor all day since the morning service; I never heard anything like that." She was in a desperate condition. I said, "Tell me what it is. Maybe I am wrong. I'll listen." And she said so-and-so, and I said, "You didn't quote all the verse." She said, "Well, what is it?" I said, "You are the one that started it, you quote it for me." She said, "I don't know. I don't even know where it is found in the Bible." She was awfully well informed to be so torn up and be dead certain that what she was hearing was not so! She came prepared not to believe anything she heard. She had been warned not to come and hear me. If there is a person that wants to be dead certain to go to hell, you keep on closing your mind and refusing to be swift to hear the truth of God. The woman could quote part of a Scripture, but I said, "You didn't quote all of it." Then we would turn to it and read it, and she said, "Well, I never saw that." Then she said, "But some of the things you said ..." I said, "Do I have Scripture for it?" I said, "Let's turn to some of those Scriptures and reread them and you tell me if you find fault with what the Scripture says." We turned and read some of them and she said, "I had never seen them in the Scriptures." Don't be in such a hurry, but be swift to hear and slow to rebel. James says, *"Wherefore, my beloved brethren, let every man be swift to hear,"* and that in view of verse 18, *"Of his own will begat he us with the word of truth."*

Now I want to mention five great teachings of the Word of God about which men rebel. Unsaved men will rebel against all five of these things, or they will rebel against any of them. Unless your heart has been prepared. Only a prepared heart can take these five Bible teachings: First, you will rebel about what kind of a person the Bible says you are. Look at your Bible and find out what it says about you and me. Romans 3:10-18: *"As it is written, There is none righteous, no, not one: There is none that understandeth, there is none that seeketh after God. They are all gone out of the way, they are together become unprofitable; there is none that doeth good, no, not one. Their throat is an open sepulchre; with their tongues they have used deceit; the poison of asps is under their lips: Whose mouth is full of cursing and bitterness: Their feet are swift to shed blood: Destruction and misery are in their ways: And the way of peace have they not known: There is no fear of God before their eyes."* And Psalm 58:3-5: *"The wicked are estranged from the womb: they go astray as soon as they be born, speaking lies. Their poison is like the poison of a serpent: they are like the deaf adder that stoppeth her ear; Which will not hearken to the voice of charmers, charming never so wisely.* Listen to Isaiah 1:3-6: *"The ox knoweth his owner, and the ass his master's crib: but Israel doth not know, my people doth not consider. Ah sinful nation, a people laden with iniquity, a seed of evildoers, children that are corrupters: they have forsaken the LORD, they have provoked the Holy One of Israel unto anger, they are gone away backward. Why should ye be stricken any more? ye will revolt more and more: the whole head is sick, and the whole heart faint. From the sole of the foot even unto the head there is no soundness in it; but wounds, and bruises, and putrifying sores: they have not been closed, neither bound up, neither mollified with ointment."*

The Bible says some terrible things about us, folks. And you can't take it, you rebel against it, and you are going to keep on rebelling against it until you end up in hell, unless you make up your mind that you value your eternity-bound soul and you start preparing your heart and asking God to enable some of the truth about yourself to sink in there and take root. And you get desperate to find whether there is any hope for a person that is a big sinner like you are. You just can't take that apart from a prepared heart. God says your best righteousness is as filthy rags. You drink iniquity like water; you just lap it up. Your very plowing is sin; your imaginations are evil. The thoughts of your heart are rotten, and if we could open you up, out of it would come all these filthy things.

The Bible talks that way about men. Genesis 6:5: *"And GOD saw that the wickedness of man was great in the earth, and that every imagination of the thoughts of his heart was only evil continually."* And Job says, *"How much more abominable and filthy is man, which drinketh iniquity like water?"* An unprepared heart will buck that and yet you will never be saved unless it is brought home to you what kind of a person you are! Because you will never be interested in getting to Christ until you see how awfully sinful you are. Be swift to hear what God says about you!

If I were preaching to nice people it would be different, but I am not. I am preaching to people who are born in sin, conceived in iniquity, and you are a cesspool and hotbed of rebellion against God. You hate everything that is high and holy and if it were not for the restraining power of the Spirit of God and the influences of the gospel in this world, this would be only a madhouse here. You are not nice people—*you are a ruined people*. You are a rebellious people, you are a stiffnecked people, and you don't like to be told that! And you are going to hell fighting it, unless your heart is prepared to receive God's truth about yourself.

Then there is another teaching in the Word of God that is wrapped up in this business of the need of a prepared heart. Men do not get saved apart from being confronted with the strictness and the severity of God's holy law. Where no law is preached, there is no gospel preached because the gospel can be only preached in the context of the holy law of God. And where men and women are not awakened by the utter strictness and the terrible severity of God's holy law, they will never be interested really in having a part in the merits of the shed blood of the Redeemer dying on the cross. I know that's so. And yet all I've got to do to an unsaved man, in the name of God, is tell him not to do something and he will be sure to do it. That is his nature. They hate law and restrictions. And yet unless a man is confronted with and becomes swift to hear how terribly strict God's holy law is and how unutterable, how horribly severe His law is, they will never be interested in the Lord Jesus Christ and only a prepared heart can receive the truth. It will just bounce off of you. It bounced off of me and I had sinful flesh just like you have.

You have got to face it. You better become swift to hear how strict and severe God's law is. It is as strict as the Bible says it is, you dead-sure need a Savior. If it's as severe as the Bible says it is, my, how terrible it will be to go out and meet God in Whose hands will be the penalty, and *He will punish them in hell and in all eternity.*

Matthew 13:41-42: *"The Son of man shall send forth his angels, and they shall gather out of his kingdom all things that offend, and them which do iniquity; And shall cast them into a furnace of fire: there shall be wailing and gnashing of teeth."*

Listen to Luke 12:5: *But I will forewarn you whom ye shall fear: Fear him, which after he hath killed hath power to cast into hell; yea, I say unto you, Fear him."*

There is a third Bible truth that cannot be received except by a prepared heart and that is the *absoluteness of the sovereignty of God.* I don't mean the sovereignty of God—lots of people believe that—but the absoluteness of it. We are living in a day now when most people accept the Lord, some of the wicked people will brag on the Lord. Multitudes accept the Lord, but the Lord they accepted has been stripped of His glory. If you take Christ out of His office, people will take Him as their buddy-buddy; even the Hollywood actors are buddy-buddy with this little lord that everybody likes today; but it is the Lord stripped of the absoluteness of His sovereignty. And you can't take it. I don't care how big a profession you make, you will buck it, you will rebel against the utter absoluteness, the totalitarian rule and reign and claims of King Jesus! You can't take it except with a prepared heart.

It wouldn't be a bit of trouble in getting most people converted in America if everybody in this country would do like most preachers have done—preach a Jesus who has been stripped of His glory. There is no trouble in getting people to accept Jesus, this nice little jesus that buddy-buddies with people and lets people go on and live as they please. But the difference is, this Jesus Christ has no rivals. He is absolute. He has the reigns of every man's heart in His hands and He exercises those reigns.

If I am speaking to somebody that doesn't know my Lord, you had better take this seriously. You will never get saved if you don't get serious about this. The Word of the truth of the gospel has got to take root and it will take root in your heart only as your heart has been able to thrust out the rebellion that is in it. You were born with it, born with rebellion against these great truths.

There is another truth that men cannot take unless it is with a prepared heart. That the *way of salvation is in the shed blood of the Lord Jesus Christ.* Self-righteous people will go to hell saying, "I think I am as good as the other fellow. I think if he makes it I'll make it. I am not such a bad fellow." You will keep talking that way and you will never care anything about the blood of Christ. You will never have any interest in the truth that you are in such a desperate condition that Another (and that One is the Son of God) had to die or you would go to hell. This truth is going to have to take root, your heart needs to take root, your heart needs to be prepared.

Now as I have been preaching these thirty-eight years, I have found out that some people, at least in their heads, will say, Well, Brother Barnard, I can take the strictness and severity of God's law, and I can take the fact that the only way I can be saved is by Jesus dying, and I can take the sovereignty of the Lord. But when I come to this last truth of the Bible that involves this matter of salvation: that saving faith is not simply the act of the will of the natural man, it is not moral persuasion but is a grace of an inward and spiritual view of Christ in His sweetness and glory. And that while you have to exercise faith, *God has to work it in you before you can work it out.* That is the most offensive thing in the Bible, that is what stirs up people in my meetings more than anything else. They have heard all their lives, "Now sinner, if you just take Jesus as your Savior, he will save you." That would be fine, if you could do it and unless you do it, you are going to hell. But the most offensive thing in the teachings of the Word of God is: God requires faith, and you ain't got it, unless *He is pleased to give it to you. "For by grace are ye saved through faith."*

You can make all the decisions you want to but you will never be joined to Christ by making a decision. We are all eternity-bound men and women and unless God Almighty is pleased to perform a miracle in you and reveal Christ in you, you are doomed to hell. Now that is offensive, isn't it? And if you don't quit rebelling against it and start preparing your heart to ask God to break up your old heart and help you to throw your rebellion down, and become swift to hear a person praying that the truth may be buried in there and rooted in there, for we are born by the will of God through the Word of truth. Men just can't take that and therefore it is left out of what is called preaching today. Your heart needs to be prepared and unless it is you will rebel in every one of these five things. You just can't take them with a heart that hasn't been plowed. James says, "You be swift to hear."

I want to mention two other things that James says, *"Lay aside sin in your life."* Who is to do this? The man who wants a prepared heart, the man that wants to be saved. James says, "I'll tell you what to do: (1) Be swift to hear, cease your rebellion against truth; (2) You lay aside sin. James is not teaching that a man must be sinless and perfect in order to be saved, for if that was true nobody would be saved. But what James is saying here, you have the heart and mind and be willing to lay aside any and all sin which keeps you from receiving God's truth. God commands you through James that you had better not keep on hugging sin, you better lay it aside. You say, "Will that save me?" No, it is a matter of heart preparation. What saves you is the truth taking root in there, but it is not going to take root in there as long as there is sin you cling to. You say, "That's hard to do." Yes, that's right. That is the reason this matter of salvation is an agony. Acts tells us (14:22) this: *"Confirming the souls of the disciples, and exhorting them to continue in the faith, and that we must through much tribulation enter into the kingdom of God."* I don't know your heart but if there is anything keeping you from becoming a devoted disciple of my Lord, please lay it aside. That won't save you, but it is heart preparation and it is going to take place before God saves you and you are to do that. Lay it aside.

Then James says, *"Receive with meekness the engrafted word, which is able to save your souls."* The trouble is not that you don't understand; the trouble is sin, SIN. You are not going to hell because you don't understand the doctrines of the Bible, you are going to hell to pay for your sins. You lay aside anything in your life that is keeping you from receiving God's truth. And then just like a little child, God says it, you just believe it. Amen! You are liable to come to the assurance of God's wonderful salvation if you keep on just believing what God tells you. James would say, "Take time to prepare your heart by being swift to hear and slow to rebel, by laying aside sin and with meekness receive the engrafted Word which is able to save your soul."

SERMON 6: Six Things We Face in Preaching the Gospel
(SermonIndex)

In the month of July, 1954, on a Sunday evening, I began a series of meetings with Brother E. W. Johnson down in Pine Bluff, Arkansas. I brought a message that night and ten years later I was through Pine Bluff and Brother Johnson told me that that message had split his church wide open. Just one message, he said the people went out of the service that evening about evenly divided. They didn't come to a vote for eight years, but he said that his church was already split of course, but that one message was the *meat axe* and it took eight years under his quiet way for it to come to its climax and then the people demanded the right to vote on it; he said it all came to a climax in one service.

I asked him I said, "Brother Johnson, was I in the flesh?" I had been that way a lot of times; was I wrong? He said, "No. I believe one time you were in the Spirit." But he said the people went away believing in two different Gods. Half of them believed in a God who is God. We preachers call it a sovereign God, that simply means very God. And the others went away with the god of 20ᵗʰ century Christianity, a god who would like to do well but he is unable to do so. Well, that's pretty well the message tonight.

In 1954 I scribbled down on a envelope six issues that seem to be worth facing and seem to carry within them what all of his controversy is about. Tonight, the only time I ever got an invitation in my life to come hold a meeting and the preacher dictated my sermon is this one. And I'm glad to come. How many folks were in the Park Meeting in 1952 or 1951? He wanted me to bring this message and those of you who remember it, I dead sure don't. I haven't touched this since 1954 but when he wrote me the letter I knew I had outlined my sermons, and I began to dig and I came up upon that old envelope. I still have it and here goes!

Now of course, no man ever repeated sermons; no man ever preached from the same text the same way—the Scriptures' too deep for that—but I appreciate this privilege and the confidence and the honor the dear pastor's paid me and it's like coming home. And I just want to talk tonight, it is prayer meeting night, on six issues that still face us and we have to take sides as individuals, as congregations, as public preachers, anybody that names the name of Jesus Christ living in this day. You've been living in a day when these six issues have wrapped up the controversy about what Christianity is all about in your day and mine.

I bring you glad tidings of great joy; hell is just a poppin everywhere, doors are opening, preachers are seeking the truth of God's grace as I have never seen it, and I rejoice and especially with you people who have been in the battle and have stood by me and made my little ministry possible.

There are six basic issues that I bring you again tonight that we have to take sides upon and these issues will determine our gospel. The other day I heard a godly man, Brother James Stewart, down in Houston, Texas speaking to about sixty Baptist pastors, and he said that he longed in his heart that true evangelism would make its appearance once again in America. He said the evangelism that depends upon the sovereign Holy Spirit to bring men to Christ. And they had such a prayer meeting as you wouldn't think would be possible today as that dear man has long lifted up his voice against the shallowness of what we call evangelism in America. And those preachers got on their faces and sobbed out their sins and their confessions to God. They were all Southern Baptist preachers. But they didn't fight the man's message; fifteen years ago they would have. But they are coming up to the lick log now and the message and methods that looked like it was getting such wonderful results, they're not getting the results now. And this generation of people in our churches and in our pulpits is open now to hear from God like I've never seen. And I rejoice.

If I had a text tonight I would take that text in John chapter 3 verse 8, which reads like this: *"The wind bloweth where it listeth, and thou hearest the sound thereof, but canst not tell whence it cometh, and whither it goeth: so is every one that is born of the Spirit."* When the last word's been said, evangelism that can get people saved without the blowing of the Spirit who blows when He wills and nobody can explain it, or the evangelism that is absolutely helpless unless the wind blows, that pretty well sums up the whole shooting match.

I was reading one of the old Puritans the other day. God shut him up in a little village with two hundred people for about thirty-seven years, and he preached for thirty-three years and never had a convert and then the wind began to blow. I feel sorry for the brother; wouldn't it have been wonderful if he'd lived in our day when we can get people converted *without the Holy Ghost?* But he couldn't. The poor old man didn't know that there was any way on earth for men to be born into the kingdom of God except that there is a holy wind that opens their hearts and applies the truths. And all he knew to do was keep on ploughing and breathing a prayer, "Oh, Thou sovereign Spirit, we cannot command You, but we plead for Thy presence and we long for Your blessing."

The six issues that I bring again tonight, but first we have to take sides, not in our heads but in our hearts over this proposition that man was utterly ruined in the garden of Eden or that he *was somewhat injured.* Those of you heard me preach a great deal know that I have tried, as I get older, to shy away from man's terminology. I do not know if this will strike you right or not but I quit using the adjectives on what they call the "five points." I no longer use the term "total depravity" because it takes three hours and a half to explain what we do not mean by the word "total." But that does not mean that I do not take sides, and this is the starting point! That we deal with men and women who haven't been injured they were *ruined.* When in the loins of Adam they willfully reached up and sought to pull God off the throne and sit there themselves! And the penalty was DEATH. Not injury but DEATH. And there is where the whole thing starts.

I remember 1950 in July after I had been here, I came to a parting of ways with a man rebuking me that man was somewhat injured in the fall. Of course, he had to take that position in order to preach what he believes is so, that God has done His part toward the salvation of men, now it's up to men. If man has some ability, all right. If he has no ability, all right. But I learned long since that what we call the doctrines of election and predestination and those terms—that isn't what offends people. What offends people is to rob them of that thing they've been using to get multitudes of people thinking they're saved and appealing to the big wills of men and women who have nothing but *perverted wills.* I heard a radio preacher who used to believe the gospel and tried to preach it but the pressure of the hour got him. I heard him in Winston-Salem the other day; he preached for fifteen minutes to prove beyond a shadow of a doubt that God's done everything He can do and now it's up to the sinner.

Now the so-called gospel on which modern day churches in America was built has been built on a gospel that teaches that men got a pretty bad blow but they weren't ruined, and that therefore salvation is God taking the first step and man taking the rest. We have to make up our minds there. When I brought this message in 1954, we hadn't heard that the first eleven chapters of Genesis ain't so! Course we had to find that out in your day and mine. But if it ain't so, then there is no salvation. For if we weren't ruined in Adam, Christ can't do a thing on God's earth for us, so until further notice we'll still take the position, and stay with it, and fight for it, if we must, that we belong to a race that was *utterly ruined*. Not in need of a shove but, oh God, in need of a Savior. Utterly lost and utterly ruined and utterly unable to lift ourselves by our own bootstraps—we will stay by that.

I watched this thing grow from 1950 for this section east of the Mississippi River what happened at Pollard Baptist Church had ramifications all over the South. Out of it came your blessed young preacher. I've watched them as they have stumbled, I've prayed for them when I thought they were going wrong, and rejoiced when God was blessing. It's been a struggle. And we're not out of the woods yet but anybody that's had a better time than I've had I couldn't imagine it! I've seen it as it just started, and now its breaking out all over the world. And I'm almost persuaded I may live to see the time when the gospel will be returned to the churches of America. Wouldn't that be wonderful!

The second issue that we have to take sides on is simply this: that's salvation is utterly of the Lord or only partially. Utterly of the Lord or only partially. If salvation is up to man we need not bother God! We just get down on our knees and say, "Save yourself!" This is the battleground. Some don't pray at all; some have taken this doctrine and become what we call "hardshells"; there is always that danger. There is a thin line between truth and error. And there is nothing as dangerous as something that has a lot of truth in it and a lot of error. But the battleground is still being fought, and with all of the conflicts and with all of the mistakes and all of the bone-headed things we have done, it has still been a pleasure to insist, in spite of everything, that SALVATION IS GOD'S WORK FIRST, LAST AND ALL THE TIME. Salvation is either altogether of the Lord or it is just part of the Lord and part of men. Now the popular gospel is still that in salvation God had something to do in it and man casts the deciding vote, but it is not so. Not so. Wouldn't it be wonderful—this is worth praying for, this is what we are slaving for, this is what we're groaning for, this is what we mean by the word "sacrificing"—if we knew that the gospel would be returned to our churches and that a sinner couldn't run from one church and have his wounds healed by going somewhere else, by preaching this damnable doctrine that God has done part of it and now He's *hoping* that man will do the rest. No, you have to take sides. Salvation is either all of the Lord or it's just part of Him. And that's an issue.

I don't want to stay to midnight so I will just mention these tonight: 167 times in the New Testament, the word "kaleo" or its equivalent, it means "call." There 167 times in the New Testament. I have been going up and down the land awhile subject to pastors; you are looking at a miracle! How in the name of heaven I have stayed in the ministry beats me. Beats me. I tried to PREACH THAT! TO A CHURCH WORLD THAT IS STILL ABSOLUTELY IGNORING THE FACT THAT SALVATION 167 TIMES IN THE NEW TESTAMENT IS AT THE END OF GOD'S CALL. How on earth we could have built all our mission programs and all our big churches and all our denominations and LEAVE OUT THE FACT THAT MEN ARE DEAD IN THEIR SPIRITUAL GRAVES AND THERE IS ONLY ONE VOICE THAT'S GOT AUTHORITY TO SPEAK AND GIVE DEAD MEN LIFE. But the whole outfit is built on it. God didn't put one word in the New Testament 167 times to be written off. Men are still saved utterly by hearing in the gospel, *as the Holy Ghost makes it effective,* A VOICE THAT HAS IN IT AUTHORITY TO GIVE LIFE TO DEAD MEN. That is the only way anybody ever did get saved.

The other day down in Houston, a young lady broke up the service and she came running down the front and said, "I heard Him!" Why sure she heard Him. SHE HEARD THROUGH MY VOICE, SHE HEARD HIS VOICE, AND CHRIST WAS MADE ALIVE BY THE HOLY GHOST, AND SHE HEARD HIM SPEAK! Not with these ears but with a ear of faith, just as plainly as is He'd said, *"Lazarus, come forth."* That girl heard it. That's the way people are saved. *Salvation is God saving dead men.* And He saves men by the Word, as He does everything else and men hear. And they are saved!

The third issue that we face is that salvation is a gift and not an offer. The old Puritans used to use the expression Christ is freely offered in the gospel, which is so. But it's meaningless. It's that same proposition as the Scripture "whosoever will may come"; the Scripture does not say that. But it is so that whosoever will may come, but that's meaningless because *nobody will.* Nobody will. Somebody says, "Well, I believe whosoever will may come!" I do too. But nobody will, so why fuss about it? Why fuss about it? They tell me, "Well, I believe Christ is freely offered in the gospel." I do too. *But nobody's interested.* So why fuss about it? But ohhh, it's a little deeper than that. Salvation is not an offer for men to decide what they'll do about it. Salvation is a gift. And you better listen to me! You don't turn down a gift cause nobody ever offers a gift to anybody until they are dead sure it will be appreciated. You better get that. That's right, this is back on this same issue. Sure, my Lord Jesus was dealing with the woman of Samaria and He said unto her, *"If thou knewest [the what?] the gift of God."* That brings us back to the same thing the heart has to be prepared or the gift will not be offered. My Lord didn't put Himself up for barter. The most damnable thing that has perverted the gospel of Christ all the days of our years has been this stuff about, "You dear people, you make up your mind what you'll do with Christ." It's not given you to make that disposition of Christ; *you are commanded to repent toward God. You are commanded to believe the gospel but you are never given a choice.* You are just faced with a duty! Isn't that right? Listen to me! I have had a burden in my heart to all the people I go to over America; if there is anybody on God's topside of God's earth that ought to have tender hearts, ought to be able to weep in here, it's men and women who received the gift! You received a gift. If God Almighty would give you Christ surely no sinner on God's earth could be as bad as you. I wish I could wrap up everybody in America who claims to believe in the grace of God that's lost joy, that still isn't in amazement for the unspeakable gift. He gives it to prepared hearts. To prepared hearts.

Shackled with a load of guilt burdened clear up to the hilt but He touched me. Oh, He touched me! And oh, the joy that filled my soul, something happened, He touched me, and made me whole. Salvation isn't an offer to be considered. Salvation is God's gift to men. Thanks be unto God! The apostle Paul says, for the *unspeakable gift!* The gift goes back to the heart of God! Thanks be unto God! Not that we consider the matter and use our little ole brain, but in HIS ALL CONQUERING GRACE HE GIVES ETERNAL LIFE TO MEN AND WOMEN. Salvation is a gift, it is not an offer.

And then, of course, the fourth issue is that salvation comes by revelation, not by *decision.* Boy, we've had some scraps here! Mr. Spurgeon, used to say, "Surely you must decide for Jesus Christ." But for a *revealed Christ.* A revealed Christ. A young preacher in Winston-Salem came to see me last fall, the time I was home. He and his wife like to come over and talk to me. He said, "Brother Barnard, I sure wish I could have you in my church but I can't. The first time you told my crowd that unless God worked a miracle in their lives they're gonna split hell right open." He said, "That would scare my people to death." I said, "Isn't that so?" He said, "Yeah. But my people never heard it." I said, "What do you preach?" I knew what he preached. He preached that a man gets saved when he decides to believe on Jesus whom he knows nothing about! That man's a fool to trust a hole in the wall. Oh yes, salvation comes not by Rolfe Barnard making up his mind but by the Spirit of God making Jesus Christ, who's alive, *real to a man*. So if everybody in the world got shot before sunrise and you were the only one left and if somebody asked you if Christ was alive, you'd say, "Yes sir. Yes sir. I met Him. I walk with Him. He's real to me. Salvation comes by God working a miracle. Wouldn't it be wonderful if in our day, I near would jump out of my skin, if the gospel was preached that faith is Christ made real inside, would be returned to America.

I've got five brothers and sisters still living, they're all church workers, and only one of them would be comfortable if you talked about Christ. They are Sunday school teachers and deacons and this that and the other; they don't know a thing on God's earth ABOUT A LIVING LORD! I never get to see them. They are caught up in this generation, they made their "decisions," and they are doing their best to keep out of jail and get to heaven when they die. And I long for them to be shut up in their Sunday schools and in their pulpits and over the radio, but they'll never be shut up to the fact that you can't get saved without getting in touch by faith with a *living Lord* who died; salvation comes by revelation and not by decision.

The fifth issue that we still face is put in words like this: salvation is made effective in a man's life by God bringing a man to repentance and faith or if men themselves will repent and believe. People say, "Well, I believe God can save anybody if a man will repent toward God and believe in Jesus Christ." So would I. But ain't nobody gonna do it! So why fuss about it? If that's all there is to why tell them about hell? But thank God, the Scriptures teach more than that. They teach that God Almighty has sent a man, the man Christ Jesus with the prints of the nails in His hands and the prints of the crown of thorns on His head! And He's sitting on a throne. God put

Him there and gave Him one task among others, to grant repentance and forgiveness of sin. Bless God, that's a white horse of a different color. I shut men up as I go all over the country and I say, "Sinner, why don't you repent? The best way to find out you can't is to start trying! Just start trying to abhor yourself, you can quit your cussing out the mule but you can't do a great deal about *what's inside.* Go on, sinner! Believe these preachers and make up your mind what you're gonna do and you'll find out it won't work. But thank God, we've got good news! On the cross the Lord Jesus Christ bought the right to give repentance and faith and He's in that business! Praise God! We've got hope there.

The sixth issue, Moffatt translates Romans 11:29, "God never goes back on His call." The King James says, *"For the gifts and calling of God are without repentance."* I like Moffatt's translation. "God never goes back on His call." He never does. There are several things wrapped up in this: I'll just mention them and I'll quit. Believers are going to persevere in holiness because that is what they were chosen for. They were chosen in Him that they might be holy. It's settled. But they must persevere in holiness. Believers are gonna be conformed to the image of Christ, but they must be conformed to the image of Christ. I've studied the Puritans and I've studied John Calvin and I've studied everybody I could get books or borrow from. I differ with the Puritans, I differ with Brother Calvin. I believe the warnings in the book of Hebrews are not the people who almost got saved but didn't. I wish I could believe when he talks about people who have tasted and been illuminated, tasted the power; they didn't get almost saved—I believe they got saved. Now if you're going to throw me out, I believe that New Testament salvation calls for you to spit on your hands and roll up your sleeves and see to it that these terrible warnings never take place in your life. That's what I believe. You say, "Brother Barnard, what are you trying to do, tear up our Baptist doctrine of the eternal security of the believer?" I don't know what to do about it, but I'm going to look you in the face and tell you now, that the Scriptures talk about crucifying afresh the Son of God and he's talking to God's people! It talks about putting Him to open shame and it's talking to saved people.

And I used an expression one time that liked to shock me. I believe that hell is hot on your trail tonight. I believe the devil gets you if he can. I believe that God's people better quit getting their doctrine out of books and they better face the fact that salvation isn't something you can put in a tin can. It's a daily relationship. And if there ever was a generation of church people this side of hell that needs to be shocked out of this damnable, carnal idea that the security of the believer is to live like hell and go to heaven when you die. No! Oh no. Our forefathers thought they needed what they call the means of grace. There is a cocksureness today that is gonna fill hell full of church members if we don't watch out. I don't know how to handle those passages in Hebrews—they just scare the living daylights out of me. If we sin willfully, that's talking to Christian people. How shall we escape if we treat lightly so great salvation? That's talking to Christian people. You say, "Brother Barnard, you trying to scare us into doing right?" The book of Hebrews will if you will read it. It dead sure will! Oh, it is impossible to renew them to repentance. That scares me. That scares me. But the gifts and callings of God are without repentance. He never goes back on His call. Therefore brethren, beloved, we are persuaded that there are better things for you. And I close with this description of salvation. The Lord knoweth them that put their trust in Him and let everyone that nameth the name of the Lord depart from iniquity. Run from it. Run from it! The child of God will be conformed to the image of Christ but he must put on the whole armor of God. Dig in. Dig in.

SERMON 7: Election

(Volume Two: 18)

Matthew 15:22-28: *"And, behold, a woman of Canaan came out of the same coasts, and cried unto him, saying, Have mercy on me, O Lord, thou Son of David; my daughter is grievously vexed with a devil. But he answered her not a word. And his disciples came and besought him, saying, Send her away; for she crieth after us. But he answered and said, I am not sent but unto the lost sheep of the house of Israel. Then came she and worshipped him, saying, Lord, help me. But he answered and said, It is not meet to take the children's bread, and to cast it to dogs. And she said, Truth, Lord: yet the dogs eat of the crumbs which fall from their masters' table. Then Jesus answered and said unto her, O woman, great is thy faith: be it unto thee even as thou wilt. And her daughter was made whole from that very hour."*

In this Scripture, we have the story of a Gentile woman approaching our Lord and at first He didn't say anything to her and when He does say something, He brings up the doctrine of national election. But instead of that stopping her, she came and worshipped Him, saying, "Lord, help me!" The doctrine of election did not discourage her and it *does not discourage any person who is seeking help from the Lord.*

I read a sermon by Mr. Spurgeon about this story. He suggested perhaps one reason the Lord confronted this woman with a very stern doctrine, it looks like is to discourage her, but He just wanted her to get the truth about the matter before she heard it misrepresented, as she later would. Somebody was bound to tell this seeking woman that our Lord's ministry was confined exclusively for a while to the Jewish people and He wasn't looking for Gentiles. And they'd tell it in a way to make error out of truth and discourage a woman who needed encouragement.

One of the things that I hear so many times each week—it seems that religious people, including preachers, are making a terrible bugaboo out of the fact that the little new church we are trying to start believes in the doctrine of election, national election for the Jews, and individual election for the Christian believer. And I hear all manner of things about this terrible truth. Now and then I feel impressed of the Spirit to address myself to any who are present who are in earnest about your soul's relationship to God and to say a helpful word.

We want to encourage you not to join the ranks of people who are ashamed of what is in the Bible, but also to encourage you that it is not simply this truth, but it is every truth in the Bible that you must approach as a little child willing to be taught. And your conception of any teaching in the Word of God will be guided by your conception of the God of the Word. If you've got a *little* God that you can comprehend, that you can understand, then you will expect to understand His teachings.

The apostle Paul, of all the writers of the New Testament, is the one who devotes more time than anybody, except our Lord, to what we call the doctrines of grace. And the apostle Paul is in agreement with what Christ taught—he didn't learn something our Lord didn't know. But Paul is responsible for setting forth the doctrines of grace, and when he gets on these things he has a word for us that would be very helpful if we paid attention to him.

Every great truth in the Bible is subject to faith but none of them to understanding. There is no man living that can explain how God is one yet three—He is Father, Son and Holy Ghost. There is no man living who can explain that the Lord Jesus Christ is one and yet two—He is God and He is man. There is no man living that can understand a single basic teaching of the Word of God. The Holy Ghost led Paul to bring out election and the sovereignty of God in Romans chapters 9,10, and 11. And Paul has a word of caution for us; this should be our reaction to these great truths as given in Romans 11:33-36: *"O the depth of the riches both of the wisdom and knowledge of God! how unsearchable are his judgments, and his ways past finding out! For who hath known the mind of the Lord? or who hath been his counsellor? Or who hath first given to him, and it shall be recompensed unto him again? For of him, and through him, and to him, are all things: to whom be glory for ever. Amen."* Now this is a good place to camp and I use this before coming to the text. These wonderful truths are too deep for you to fully understand.

I like the words of Barnhouse, that good teacher of God's Word, that while we cannot understand, while we wait for more light, *we can worship.* That's sounds like a Christian; that sounds like somebody who has some conception of the majesty and the glory of the Lord. *"For who hath known the mind of the Lord?"*

The apostle Paul was a graduate of the greatest university of his day. As a young man he was a member of the Sanhedrin and you had to know something to be in that body! He was a student of the greatest teacher of the day. And after he was saved, he went to school to Jesus Christ personally by the Spirit down in Arabia for three years. And after Paul had expounded all its richness and fullness of these great truths, he threw up his hands and worshiped a God whose ways are so far above our ways, that it behooves us children of the dust to shut our mouths, quit criticizing God and worship. Quit trying to reason out the great truths of the Bible in such detail that we would dishonor God and make our wisdom to equal His.

"For of him, and through him, and to him, are all things: to whom be glory for ever. Amen." Every truth in the Bible is going

to bring glory to God, and every truth in this Bible is going to bring glory to God by being a blessing to mankind. When God says He does all things to promote His glory, He is not pulling His rank like they do in the Army. He chooses to promote His glory by promoting the good of men. 1 Corinthians 2:7: *"But we speak the wisdom of God in a mystery, even the hidden wisdom, which God ordained before the world unto our glory."*

Now with this word of caution I want to approach the subject of election and be like a teacher. There is such a vast ignorance as to what the doctrine of election is. My God, isn't it awful to take a doctrine, even take it in its truth and use it to discourage men and women from seeking with their whole hearts to know Christ as Lord and Savior?

The first time the glory of God is mentioned as a truth in the Bible, we find in Exodus 33 that God promotes His glory. Moses asked the Lord, *"Shew me thy glory,"* and God said in verse 19, *"I will make all my goodness pass before thee, and I will proclaim the name of the LORD before thee; and will be gracious to whom I will be gracious, and will shew mercy on whom I will shew mercy."* Now that blessed truth is being used today to discourage and deceive people. I've been in Baptist churches where the very mention of it caused confusion, for people who say they know the Lord immediately begin to accuse God of being a devil and accuse God of being a monster! I hear this precious doctrine that is a blessed doctrine in the sight of God, that was used by my Lord as a source of encouragement when He faced people, I hear it so misrepresented today. If we believed what God says instead of some of these preachers, we wouldn't have all this confusion about the doctrine of election. I say to you the way back to the power of God is not by letting these who pervert the truth have all the say! We must come to the Lord and find the truth!

I say it again, that God Almighty is sovereign; He is sovereign in creation. *"For by him were all things created, that are in heaven, and that are in earth, visible and invisible, whether they be thrones, or dominions, or principalities, or powers: all things were created by him, and for him: And he is before all things, and by him all things consist"* (Colossians 1:16-17).

He is sovereign in providence. He handles the nations as seemeth good in His sight. Psalm 22:28 reads, *"For the kingdom is the LORD'S: and he is the governor among the nations."*

Our Lord is sovereign in salvation. Paul states in Romans, *"Therefore hath he mercy on whom he will have mercy, and whom he will he hardeneth."* He is gracious to whom He will be gracious. He shows mercy to whom He will show mercy. God Almighty has a right to do that very thing and whether you believe it or not, it is so! I do not apologize for the glorious doctrine that God sovereignly and according to His own will chooses those whom He will save. I am not ready to apologize for that!

This truth instead of being jeered at, this truth instead of being ignored, this truth instead of being used as a club to discourage people who are seeking the way—this is the grandest truth of all! For the wisest person in all of creation is Almighty God and I'm glad that the One in whom is all wisdom is running everything! I am glad that God is sovereign but if He were not supreme I believe the wisest men on earth would hold a meeting and elect Him to be sovereign. We've got to have God as sovereign or the Devil as sovereign and I had rather have God, wouldn't you?

God is perfect in wisdom and it is a disgrace to call anything that He says He does a "damnable doctrine," when God Almighty is full of wisdom. And anybody that would talk that way is showing more than his ignorance, he is showing that he isn't acquainted with God. For anybody that wants to have a saving relationship with the God and Father of our Lord Jesus Christ will bow and say, "Lord, Thou are all-wise, whatever You do!" *"As for God, his way is perfect: the word of the LORD is tried: he is a buckler to all those that trust in him."* Praise God for it! Thank the Lord, for He giveth and He taketh away, and blessed be the name of the Lord. He is all-wise.

The God of the Bible is represented as having the name Holy. Note in Isaiah 57:15: *"For thus saith the high and lofty One that inhabiteth eternity, whose name is Holy; I dwell in the high and holy place, with him also that is of a contrite and humble spirit, to revive the spirit of the humble, and to revive the heart of the contrite ones."* Then He is perfect in holiness. He is so perfect in wisdom that He cannot do wrong. He is so perfect in holiness that He will not do wrong. He is too wise to make a mistake and too good to do wrong.

The essence of the God of the Bible is, "God is love."

The old-time theologians were right when they said that every attribute of God streamed from His love. God is holy, but God Almighty is love. Everything that God does has the basis of His doing it: LOVE, love. If He damns a man, sends him to hell, He does it out of the basis of love—for there is no such thing as perfect love that just loves everything. You may say you love your wife with a perfect love but if there is no difference between your love of a pure woman and your hatred of a wicked woman, then there is nothing to your hatred and there is nothing to your love. God has His essence in love and being LOVE, bless God, He is fit to do as He pleases!

God is sovereign in the dispensation of His grace. Our Lord Jesus Christ tells us in Luke 4:25-26: *"But I tell you of a truth, many widows were in Israel in the days of Elias, when the heaven was shut up three years and six months, when great famine was throughout all the land; But unto none of them was Elias sent, save unto Sarepta, a city of Sidon, unto a woman that was a widow."* This was a Gentile heathen woman! And in verse 27 our Lord said, *"And many lepers were in Israel in the time of Eliseus the prophet; and none of them was cleansed, saving Naaman the Syrian."* God went and picked out Naaman, the Hitler of his day, and a Gentile, but God picked him and sovereignly saved him!

Our Bible is clear about one thing—that God has made sovereign choices between men and angels. The angels that left their first estate, from that day until now, God has not made one move to save them or make salvation possible to them. *"For if God spared not the angels that sinned, but cast them down to hell, and delivered them into chains of darkness, to be reserved unto judgment."* says Peter.

You say you don't believe that God is sovereign in His choice. Well, I tell you that He dead sure is, and for reasons that He hasn't explained to us He chose to allow the angels to sin and be cast out and He has never made one move to effect their salvation. He is sovereign between angels and mankind. Do you think there was anything in Zacchaeus that was good and appealed to Christ? No, he was a sinner and a thief. It was the sovereign choice of a sovereign God, who acts as He pleases. *"And Jesus said unto him, This day is salvation come to this house, forasmuch as he also is a son of Abraham. For the Son of man is come to seek and to save that which was lost"* Luke 19:9-10.

Do you mean to tell me that as old Saul went down that road to Damascus to kill some more Christians, that the Lord looked down and saw that Saul was a nice sort of fellow and if He could just get him saved he would do a lot for God! No sir! God didn't say, "I'll save him so he will serve Me." There was no reason on earth why Jesus Christ was pleased to reveal Himself to Saul, except that God Almighty had set His love upon him and went there and struck him blind and saved him by His wonderful grace! Read that story in Acts 9, verses 1-6.

Go with me yonder to Jacob's well and tell me what you see in the life and heart of that harlot woman who had five living ex-husbands and was then living with a sixth. As she comes there to draw water at Jacob's well, tell me what our blessed Lord saw inside of that wicked harlot woman that cause Him to save her. You can't do it! Listen! If anybody gets Saul saved, it will have to be God! If anybody gets that old harlot woman saved, the Lord will have to do it! If anybody saved a thief like Zacchaeus, God will have to do it! No need to talk about cooperating with God here. Zacchaeus was stealing, Saul was killing Christians, the woman at the well was committing adultery. AND YET GOD IN HIS SOVEREIGN MERCY ARRESTED THEM, STOPPED THEM, CROSSED THEIR PATHS AND SAVED THEM BY HIS MARVELOUS GRACE.

Sinner, you are not to be occupied with God's secret decrees. You can study them from now till you are blue in the face and you'll never know anything about God's electing grace until He is pleased to reveal it to you. That will be after He saves you. As far as you are concerned, it doesn't come under the head of your immediate business. Your business now is to face your lost and ruined condition and *look to the crucified and risen Christ.* We are not trying to get any sinner to believe any doctrine. We are trying to get you to *surrender to the glorious person of the Lord Jesus Christ.* The doctrine of election has been abused in this country. *Your duty is to obey the revealed will of God.* The Lord has told you to *repent.* My Lord has told you to *believe.* That's your duty; you better start facing it. Jesus said in Mark 1:15: *"The kingdom of God is at hand: repent ye, and believe the gospel."* And in Acts we are told, *"That they should repent and turn to God, and do works meet for repentance."* Your duty is to repent of your sins and turn to God. That is as plain as it can be.

The only evidence anybody has that he is one of those that God chose in Christ before the foundation of the world, is that the gospel came and made a change in his life. It came to you in power. You just forgot about God's secret decrees and began to pay attention to what He tells you in His blessed Word. God commandeth all men everywhere to repent—to repent now. Have you repented? He doesn't tell you to take your time about it. In the words of Christ Jesus or Paul, they always tell you to *repent right now.* Do you mean to tell me you are willing to continue living in open rebellion to God Almighty's command for you to repent toward God now? Are you not afraid to go to sleep another night without repenting? Only God can wake you up in the morning and you might wake up in hell!

If you can plow through the many church members who are making fun of these great truths, you might come to the real truth. Many of them disturb you because they are using these great truths to hide their unwillingness to come clean with God. All this fuss about this being a "damnable doctrine" is not coming from honest hearts. It comes from hearts that are using what they think it teaches as an excuse for their unbelief and failure to bow to the Lord Jesus Christ.

Just listen how this blessed truth of election is misrepresented. Somebody says, "Preacher, don't you think that if a father had two sons and he was good to one of them but he was mean to the other one—he just blessed one of them and cursed the other one—don't you think that would be terrible?" Certainly I do. But that isn't the way it is with God and man. It is not a great loving Father being nice to one son and being wicked and mean to another son. It is a holy God and a just God dealing not with sons but with *criminals— criminals who have broken His holy law and are subject to nothing but the judgment of a holy God!*

A man said to me, "You can't tell me something like this, that God would make a man and then send him to hell." Leave out one thing and you've got it right! Ladies and gentlemen, if God made you in the shape you are now in, and then sent you to hell He is a monster. If you could prove to me that God is responsible for that old wicked heart of yours, and for that old wicked body of yours and you could prove to me that you are in the shape God made you in, that would be different. But you love sin, *you drink iniquity like it is water,* you are prone to do evil and adverse to do good. But you can't prove that God made you like that. According to the Bible God made man upright. Ecclesiastes 7:28 and Genesis 1:27 says, God created you in the very image of God. By your own sin you changed that image and it is now marred.

But now God is not dealing with men and women as His erring sons but He deals with them as criminals against His holy law. Oh, it behooves this generation to be silent in the presence of that! The only claim that any sinner this side of hell has, and can stand up and say, "God, I demand what's coming to me," is hell. All on earth that any of the sons of Adam has coming to him is exactly what God promised us in Genesis 2:17: *"In the day that thou eatest thereof thou shalt surely die."* The only demand that anybody has on God is "Kill me and send me to hell." And if you are not willing to do that, lost man, don't join this gang of unsaved church members who are telling God how to run His business and who refuse to believe the Bible because it's too deep for their puny little minds!

This world is a giant prison house full of people, not on probation, full of people that have been brought into God's courtroom, been tried, and they've been found guilty! They have been sentenced to eternal death. Unless God will grant them a pardon, this whole world will go to hell!

Thank the Lord for the glorious truth that God does the saving. He does it because he purposed to do it. That truth is precious and it does not oppose any other truth in the Bible. I've heard so much the last ten years about the goodness of God. They say, "Brother Barnard, the kind of God you preach isn't good. I believe in a good God." So do I. You say, "Brother Barnard, I believe God is good to everybody." I do too. If He hadn't been good to you, you would have been in hell a long time ago! He tells us how good He is in Matthew 5:45: *"He maketh his sun to rise on the evil and on the good, and sendeth rain on the just and on the unjust."*

Oh, how longsuffering God is to all mankind! I believe that in virtue of the death of my blessed Lord, the throne of grace and judgment is stayed. A man gets out on the street tomorrow, opens his mouth and with the breath that God gave him blasphemes the holy name of God and the earth doesn't open and he doesn't drop into hell. Why? The goodness of God.

This generation is going to hell trusting in the goodness of God apart from being *vitally joined to Christ.* I believe in the goodness of God, sending His blessing on all mankind, but you will go to hell if you don't find out that trusting in the goodness of God apart from vital connection with Christ is not enough. There is no salvation in the fact that God is so good He sends rain on the just and unjust! The only salvation is in the fact that God is in Christ saving sinners. God is good, yes. He is too good to be unjust to anybody, but He is so holy and so just that unless you come to terms with the terms of His gospel—and unless you *come in full surrender to Christ as He is freely offered in the gospel*—goodness or no goodness, hell is your doom!

And the doctrine of election simply agrees with that. The doctrine of election hems you up so that there is salvation only in Christ. Salvation is not in the fact that God deals in mercy toward all mankind. Salvation is not in the fact that God is longsuffering. *Salvation is in Jesus Christ, the well-beloved Son of the living God.* And goodness or no goodness, there isn't any salvation anywhere else! The doctrine of election that they make fun of us for believing is simply this: That *God does what He does in Christ.* I am so glad there are two ways to spell elect. One is E-L-E-C-T, and the other is B-E-L-I-E-V-E, believe in Christ.

I am glad the gospel is the story of Jesus Christ purchasing the salvation of everybody that God chose in Christ. I am also glad that the gospel is a blessed story of Christ hanging on a cross and being raised from a glorious grave, that everybody who believes on Him shall be saved. Everybody that God chose in Christ is going to get saved—I'm glad. But nobody is going to get saved out of Christ! Everybody that gets saved will get saved as he is vitally joined to Christ.

Most of the church members will talk about how good God is, but the doctrine of election tells us this is how good God is: *He is good enough to save every vile sinner that gets to Christ!* This is a hopeful doctrine. How it does give hope, *"For whosoever shall call upon the name of the Lord shall be saved"* (Romans 10:13).

Somebody said, "We believe in praying." So do I. I don't believe a sinner is saved by doing like the evangelists tell them now: "If you walk down this aisle and get down on your knees and pray the sinner's prayer, God will save you." No.

No, that's not true! It's a lie of hell to deceive people. I forbid no sinner to pray; I keep saying, "Go home and get alone with God and cry to Him for a new heart. Cry to Him for the grace of repentance." Yes, keep on praying. You're not going to hurt anything by praying.

The Bible doesn't say that God told the sons of Jacob to seek Him in vain. We want to look at Romans 10:13-15: *"For whosoever shall call upon the name of the Lord shall be saved. How then shall they call on him in whom they have not believed? and how shall they believe in him of whom they have not heard? and how shall they hear without a preacher? And how shall they preach, except they be sent? as it is written, How beautiful are the feet of them that preach the gospel of peace, and bring glad tidings of good things!"* Notice verse 17: *"So then faith cometh by hearing, and hearing by the word of God."* Praise the Lord for these words of our Lord Jesus Christ. I believe the man who prays was given a desire to pray and God gave it. So I say, "Pray on, sinner. Seek on, sinner!" The doctrine of election doesn't speak against that. I believe that God chooses those who are saved. I also believe what Matthew 7:7 says: *"Ask, and it shall be given you; seek, and ye shall find; knock, and it shall be opened unto you."* I am dead certain that if you ever start seeking the Lord, it proves what I am preaching! Before you ever started seeking Him, He was seeking you!

This blessed doctrine of election certainly does not oppose the invitations of the gospel. Oh my, wouldn't it be awful if we couldn't quote such Scriptures as Revelation 22:17: *"And the Spirit and the bride say, Come. And let him that heareth say, Come. And let him that is athirst come. And whosoever will, let him take the water of life freely."* Or Isaiah, 55:1: *Ho, every one that thirsteth, come ye to the waters, and he that hath no money; come ye, buy, and eat; yea, come, buy wine and milk without money and without price."* Or Matthew 11:28-29: *"Come unto me, all ye that labour and are heavy laden, and I will give you rest. Take my yoke upon you, and learn of me; for I am meek and lowly in heart: and ye shall find rest unto your souls."* What wonderful invitations! These invitations are as wide as the thirst of mankind, they are as wide as the need of mankind, and they are as wide as the guilt of mankind. Oh, the glory of the gospel invitations. God is sincere and I believe them.

But I am not going to get you to thinking that coming to Christ can be done with your feet or your hands or your lips. Coming to Christ is not walking down an aisle; it is not a physical matter. *It is a spiritual matter.* All the light that you will ever have is what is revealed in the gospel and you will have to *come to Him believing what the gospel says about Him.* You are not going to receive a revelation of some light shining. I believe that Christ must be revealed to your heart, but He will be revealed to your heart as you by faith act upon the gospel. This is according to the Scriptures in John 17:3: *"And this is life eternal, that they might know thee the only true God, and Jesus Christ, whom thou hast sent."* And Luke 10:22: *No man knoweth who the Son is, but the Father; and who the Father is, but the Son, and he to whom the Son will reveal him."*

No invitations of the Bible are opposed to this glorious truth of election. What is the gospel? *Christ is the gospel and the gospel is Christ.* What is the gospel message to anybody? *"Believe on the Lord Jesus Christ, and thou shalt be saved."* *"Verily, verily, I say unto you, He that believeth on me hath everlasting life."* Just as clear as it can be. Listen: election or no election, if you can believe on Christ, you're saved!

This great but perverted truth has a marvelous effect on people who do not know Christ. The old time theologians always divided their congregations of sinners into two groups: the awakened sinners and the ones who were still asleep. The awakened fellow is the one who says, "Oh, I wish I could be saved. I wish I could know the Lord!" Something has happened to that fellow. Probably a year ago he walked the streets and whistled by the cemetery of his sins. But something happened: he's awakened now, he's worried, he's afraid, he's interested, he's meek, he's seeing the Lord.

Nobody will ever be saved apart from that. Oh, my soul! Hell is going to be filled up not with sinners who were trying to be saved but with sinners who were sleeping the sleep of death!

This blessed truth of God's sovereign election has a marvelous blessed effect on the awakened sinner. In the first place, it is used in the hands of the Holy Ghost to strike to death all your self-effort. Listen sinner, if you don't quit listening to the preachers of this day, you are going to hell working as hard as you can to do something yourself to be saved! The Arminian preacher stirs up your flesh with "You do this" and "You do that." Then we come along and say, "You will never be saved until you quit doing something." Salvation is of the Lord!

I am trying to get you to look to Christ. God says in Isaiah 45:22: *"Look unto me, and be ye saved, all the ends of the earth: for I am God, and there is none else."* Get you to repent yourself? No! *Get you to look to Him to grant repentance!* Get you to think that in your own strength you can get to Christ? No! Get you to quit in your own strength and just fall prostrate in the arms of Him who is mighty to save! We tell you, if you are ever saved, it is because God will save you. Everything you need is in Christ. God has nothing for you except in Christ. You have just one need out of self into Christ! Look to Him. If I can get a sinner to where he is dead to all self-effort, I've got him half saved; the battle is almost won.

Election is a very blessed truth because it brings hope to the hopeless. Here is this prison house full of criminals. The doctrine of election comes along and says, "If any will save you, it must be God. But oh, that is His business!" And there is rejoicing in heaven, according to Luke 15:10: *"over one sinner that repenteth."* And just think—all without money or any price! Just think how many souls He has saved. Was there such a man as Saul of Tarsus, breathing out threatening and slaughter against the disciples of the Lord, yet God saved him! Oh, my! That's hope, that's hope to the vilest. If he saved a man like that, why won't He save me? I'll tell you what I'm going to do, sink or swim, live or die, survive or perish, salvation or damnation, I'll cast myself at the feet of the Lord. Here I am. If I go to hell, I'll go to hell depending on You, Lord. If you go to hell with that attitude you will be the first one that ever did.

Oh, what hope! This blessed doctrine brings a wonderful word to a sinner that is interested and awakened to his need. You say, "Preacher, I wish I could be saved." This glorious doctrine that we preach, the foundation of the gospel, comes to tell you about Somebody that will get to you, for you can't get to Him. Well, fall where you are. He will get to you. You can't make it yourself, so surrender right there. His everlasting arms will pick you up. Bless God, that's right! Then this truth has a word for you sleepy sinners. You are just getting along all right. You say, "Preacher, I don't intend to go to hell; some of these days I'm going to repent and get to God." Listen! You are *in the prison house; you are condemned already.* You are in the hands of Almighty God. If you get out of that prison, He has got to get you out. If you get saved, *God must do it.* God must do it! Salvation is of the Lord. Well, I am encouraged again at the vast numbers through the ages that He has been pleased to save. As wicked as I am, the Lord had mercy on me and saved me by His marvelous grace. Are you saved?

SERMON 8: What It Means to Be Lost
(SermonAudio Sermon, Rolfe Barnard Library)

I am being more and more shut up to God who gives the Holy Spirit to men who obey Him and I am laboring under the same difficulty that every child of God labors under now and I want to obey the Lord. People say, "Is there any hope for us?" We must bestir ourselves that we not be fighting dead issues or spreading our shots too widely but have some consciousness of obeying God. If America ever experiences another visitation from God it will not be apart from the obedience of His people.

Now tonight I am about preached out but I want to speak to this congregation as if you were what every church ought to be, a training school, Bible institute, Christian college. In the morning we have been addressing ourselves to the youngsters who have come from far and near to get training for what we call the public ministry—my heart goes out to them for I believe that unless we do have a visitation from Almighty God in this country in another few years, that the day of the public preacher is almost on the way out. And I don't know if that's bad, it is my own conviction that we are being shut up to what we should have been doing all the time where the church is not only a bunch of worshiping people but a bunch of people under strict discipline learning how to fight the war. I hope I am over-pessimistic but I think you have to be crazy to ever expect that a gospel preacher will ever get a hearing in this country again unless God does mightily intervene.

I go to place to place and sometimes I go to where they haven't heard any truth in forty years and I get a big harvest, but today folks just are not interested in hearing anybody expound the Word of God. Now we can get the blues about that or we can restudy the book of Acts which is the textbook for methods and preaching and the message of every church. I want to teach y'all tonight, don't go to sleep on me, but I believe that we must, as we've never been taught to do, we must *all* become proclaimers of the gospel. I believe that's exactly what revival would be. We keep talking that we want revival. In Acts they did not go around saying, "will you except Jesus?" No sir. They went and preached and they preached the gospel. There is a passage of Scripture in one of the Epistles and it talks about some folks who have learned but never having come to the knowledge of the truth. And I believe that our methods, how ever blest they may have been, I believe they are utterly unfit for the anti-Christian spirit we are living in today.

And I think that this church must not depend upon the Texas School of Theology all together to prepare people to preach; I believe that every member of this church must be saturated with God's message and God's methods so that when you do ring the doorbell and get inside you can do more than you have been able to do under this *spectator-type of Christianity* that you all have been raised under to where the preacher does the preaching and we do the listening. We've got to do what they did in the Bible. When God sent Peter to preach to Cornelius, he didn't try to get Cornelius to do anything, he just went down there to preach the gospel to him. And while he yet spake the Word, the Holy Ghost fell on them that heard it.

Now we have got to become thoroughly disciplined people. We've got to folks! Now don't get mad at me but we need to stop being so pious and religious and go to being *obedient.* We've got to become training institutes with sharp weapons if we are going to obey God in this day. Now we say we've got to have revival. I've been here now in my fourth so-called revival meeting and every day the pastor's heart breaks and he says, we've got to have revival. Well, what on God's earth would that be? Well, it would be men and women full of the gospel, preaching it where folks are and they are not in our houses of worship! Huh? We've got to learn how to be skillful wielders of the Word of God.

You get in a home now and under God if there is anybody in Africa any more heathen and pagan and ignorant of the very simple foundational truths of Christianity than they are right here in Houston, you couldn't find anybody more pagan in their attitudes and more ignorant of the simplest tenets of the Christian faith. This thing will get next to you. There is not a great use of us fighting over some terms now; folks wouldn't know what on earth we were talking about if we did! We've got to learn how to be skillful as the old Quaker's truism becomes more and more appropriate for us, "The service begins when the meeting ends."

Out here in these homes is the darkest sort of paganism. There couldn't be more of a pagan philosophy in the days of the apostles than we have to deal with now. Remember that in the days of the beginnings of Christianity the planting of churches were Jews getting converted or proselytes and they had some foundation, there was some form of contact between the apostles and the people who listened. But there isn't today. A woman was in our services Sunday morning and something was said about, "Have you ever made a profession of faith?" She was reared in a Protestant church, her father was a preacher, and she didn't have the slightest idea of what you are talking about of a "profession of faith." We little dream how the bottom has completely fallen out! And we've got to start all over again. I will meet you dear ones at the judgment. And I will haunt you with this Bible study tonight.

In the Gospel of Luke, chapter 19 and verse 10, the verse starts by explaining something that has gone on before. And here it says, *"For the Son of man is come to seek and to save that which was lost."* And the word *"lost"* there has to be interpreted in the context of the nine verses above it. And the word "lost" there doesn't mean what we call lost. The "lost" there means a man who is conscious of his need. The "lost" there means one who was given to Abraham in what we call the Abrahamic Covenant. And the statement is made there that Jesus Christ came down here not to make an effort to seek but to seek, and not to make an effort to save but to save, and not make salvation a possibility but to *accomplish it.* Everybody who is lost, in the sense of this context, is going to be saved. Our business today then is become skillful wielders of the Word of God, crying in our hearts, for the confirmation of God in the ministry of the Holy Spirit.

I'm known as a Calvinist; I don't know what that means. I know John Calvin wouldn't claim kin to us! But if you're gonna call yourself a Calvinist remember that Calvinism in its essence is simply this: not predestination, it's not election, it's not irresistible grace, it's not those terms. Calvinism, the contribution of Mr. Calvin was simply this: that the gospel has to be interpreted and applied by the Holy Spirit. Now I'll fight you for that; I won't fight you over those other terms. I don't use them myself—you can if you want to. You don't understand them and if you don't understand them you shouldn't get mad at folks you're trying to pop them into because they don't either! But the heart of this thing is that America is a pagan nation calling itself Christian! Because it has had a gospel that men can accept and believe and lay hold of *apart from the Holy Spirit.*

Now that's the issue of this hour. It wouldn't do folks a bit of good on God's earth for you to get them to believe what you call your "five points of Calvinism"; that's not the issue today. They would probably be *just a little deader than they are now if they switched their terminology.* But the issue that we've got to get excited about is that the gospel itself is a mystery and that nobody can understand it and nobody can accept it and nobody can believe it *except in the power of the Holy Spirit.* Isn't that right? And that's the only gospel that is the power of God unto salvation.

If there is any group under heaven I am going to touch the heartbreak of my ministry—the sovereign grace preachers that can't have a prayer meeting in their church! The sovereign grace churches! That are thrice dead and they couldn't weep over a sinner for five seconds! Brother, they are all over America! And they have missed it a million miles! What you talking about, Brother Barnard? I'm saying THAT THE ISSUE OF THE HOUR IS THE GOSPEL OF THE GRACE OF GOD WHICH MEN NATURALLY HATE BECAUSE IT ANNIHILATES PRIDE. And especially in our day where we trust in our own efforts in building the New Jerusalem on this earth. I want you to get the real truth of the grace of God and not some trend! AND HERE IT IS: THE GRACE OF GOD UTTERLY ROBS MAN AND PUTS THE CROWN ON GOD'S HEAD. Grace simply means *divine initiative*; that God's in the business of GETTING MEN LOST. And God saves every human being who He *can get in a lost position.*

And if we are going to faithfully ring doorbells and if you don't you have no right to call yourself Christians! If the manhood and womanhood and young men and women of this church do not tote their end of the blanket that every Christian is a missionary, *you are a disgrace to the name of Christ.* You've got to remember, to remember that that pagan attitude, that self-complacency you find in ninety-nine and nine tenths of every home you get into or wherever you speak, didn't get that way all of a sudden; they got that way because what has passed for gospel message and gospel methods in your day and mine is *more Pelagian than old Pelagius ever was!* This generation has been made Christian by a gospel that does nothing short of saying, "Sinner, save yourself!"

I want us to get excited and skillful in wielding the sword of God in obedience for He's not going to bring revival with the kind of preaching methods we've had! He'd have to resign as God if He did! I want us to get in our hearts not as a matter of theological argument that everything that matters starts with Almighty God! There is just three things that spell Christianity: faith, repentance, and prayer. No man can know he's been born of the Spirit except from the fruits that come from new birth. And they are simply just repentance and faith. You're saying you are a Christian cause you wept a little bit and had what you call A GLORIOUS FEELING; the devil can give you that! But the devil can't give you repentance and a daily faith— that's the fruit of the new birth. And of course, the heart of what being a Christian is the matter of prayer. Everyone of them come from God. Everyone of them has to start with God. What may appear to be our human virtues are really God's gifts. The very passion and hunger for God has to come from God. *God creates the hunger and the thirst so He can satisfy.*

Any man who is too proud to be infinitely in debt to Him will never be a Christian. If God Almighty can't get a man to see struggling to merit salvation, get a man to bow head and heart just to receive a gift—that's our problem. Our job is to be instruments of God, in your day and mine, in getting people L-O-S-T. Lost. So lost, that they'll receive a gift. Whooo! So lost, that they'll receive a gift. And that old pride of yours is going to take a beating if you ever get to where you are humble enough and enough of a beggar and desperate enough to take even a gift from Almighty God.

I want you to know I was born with a nature that don't want to be dependent on God and that's the truth. How does God get people lost? He's not going to get anybody lost in your day and mine unless He can get the church members to where they are skillfully wielding the Word of truth where they've got a chance that is used in the hands of the Holy Spirit to *rob man of all hope and make him where somebody's definition of evangelism would be apropos of one beggar telling another beggar where he got bread.* That's pretty good! I'll tell you that's where I got that which satisfies my hunger and that's pretty good!

Now brethren, members of this church, you're known all over the country already as being people who have gone to seed, on what they call the doctrines of grace. They say of all us folks, we cant' pray, we don't care if anybody gets saved or not, that's what people think about us. Huh? That's what they tell. Huh? How much truth is in it? Huh? How much truth is in it? How many substitute a little knowledge for truth, just enough to make fools out of us? Huh? How guilty are we of all these things we say are lies. This bothers me. Members of this church, while you are soaking your souls in these great truths that must be taught *pour a little of David Brainerd's spirit on it while your soaking it.* Huh? Poor a little of holy McCheyne. God help us as people to hear in our little prayer room, "I'm not going out there unless You go with me"; "I'm not going to ring on that doorbell unless You go with me." Ohhh, this is it.

Jonathan Edwards said the greatest privilege he thought that ever came this way in his life, was the privilege of have David Brainerd die in his home. Just to listen to him die. Jonathan Edwards said that the gift that God gives to the church every one hundred years is like David Brainerd to study him. Oh, cry in your heart that He will give you something of what it means to be like David Brainerd. That He will give you something of what He did to holy McCheyne. David Brainerd didn't get to where he could leave the snow saturated with his blood all over northern New York as he agonized over the salvation of those heathen Indians; he didn't get that way by switching his chewing gum from one jaw to the other and accepting Jesus. He got that way by getting acquainted with the holy requirements of a thrice holy God and the awful condition of himself. Here's a man who entered in to that which my Lord said, "You want to go to heaven? Then agonize to enter in. At the straight gate." And he faced some things that we have evaded.

How shall we obey God in our day? We must get it in our heads that the grace of God doesn't turn out cacklers, it turns out mighty saints. What we need is some godly people. And the reason why your testimony and mine included doesn't get any higher than the ceiling is because of the unholiness of our character. Listen to David Brainerd, instead of evading things he faced them. He got to the place where he became a seeker; he wanted to get to the place where he could claim an interest in the merits of the shed blood of Jesus Christ. And I quote from him in his struggle, he searched and he searched and he said, "I found in me great struggles of heart rising and enmity against God." Imagine that. If you ever faced the holy requirements of God, if you faced them I think you'd get mad too. And I would love to see some people get mad enough at God that they'd either get them a shotgun and try to put Him out of business or they'd fall at His feet a *helpless beggar.*

Brainerd said, "I often quarreled with God." Us little folks we wouldn't do that! He said, "I often quarreled with God for laying the sin of Adam against me." He said, "I wish God had left me alone to stand for myself and not punish me at that rate by accusing me by what another man had done." He may not have understood original sin but he grappled with it. Huh? We don't even have the power of the Spirit, we just step over Him and say, "Won't you take Jesus?" And we did and are still going to hell! Listen to me, Brainerd said, "I charged God with cruelty!" He took it seriously. Scores of times Brainerd said he wished there was no God and I quote him, he said, "I longed to pull the eternal God out of His throne and stamp Him under my feet and have revenge on Him more than any man in my life." Brainerd was enraged at the idea of God's sovereignty and the injustice of God making creatures and then subjecting them to everlasting punishment.

And the point I'm making is Brainerd looked at these bone crushing, flesh killing things in the Word of God and he looked at them and he didn't have any faith yet, and he didn't have the Holy Spirit yet, to interpret it, and he looked at them as they are naked as they are in the Bible and if you would look at them YOU'D GET MAD TOO! The reason you never get mad is that you never saw the kind of God who is in the Bible and His holy requirements. You never would dare to do like David Brainerd said, and reach up and pull God off His throne! And get rid of Him! But he did. He did. He did. My, I don't know. This is SOME CALVINISM I WANT! Something that will lead me to the very valley of death and hell itself and he gets up on the other side of the Jordan rejoicing! This is what I'm talking about, *until a man gets a picture of the snakes and demons and the filth which is himself, he will never get over the wonder of sins forgiven.* We've got to come back to it!

And the four truths of the Word of God that God always has and still uses to get men plum lost, are the truths that David Brainerd didn't wink at and we are going to look at them tonight. First, **the strictness and severity of Almighty God's holy law.** You'll have to start there if you are going to get to the place of starting, is the strictness and the awful severity of the holy law of God. The holy law of God demands nothing short of outward and inward perfection! And the holy law of God is as plain as a wart on a dog's nose that anything short of perfection will incur the damnation of hell and the wrath of God! That's right. And Brainerd kept looking at that holy law of God and he said, "God Almighty ain't got no right! To create me, and demand PERFECTION. When I can't deliver!" That's one reason a fella's lost! For he's got to be perfect and he can't. Huh? He's got to be perfect and he can't. Now if that ain't so we might as well quit! But this business of God demands perfection. I can't get no comfort out of saying, Well, I expect I'm as good as you are. Huh? Well, that's exactly what the holy law of God demands. And God has to repeal His law and He hasn't done it, He's got to step down and He never will, or He's got to punish everything that falls short of absolute perfection in the keeping of His holy law.

I tell you right now if you'd ever face that you'd either get mad or saved one! That's the reason we're in the mess we are in now, we have ignored this impossible-to-be-kept holy law. We've got to become skillful *in getting people lost*. And a man ain't fixing to realize his terrible condition until *we face him with the absolute requirement of God that nobody will walk the streets of glory unless he is as holy as God and as good as Jesus Christ.* Whoo! That's right. And unless there's an imputation of *Somebody else's righteousness to me* I'm gonna split hell wide open! *And so are you.*

And then David Brainerd faced the second problem of truth that God Almighty always has been pleased to show men the truth about their lost condition. And Brainerd faced the fact that **God requires faith and He won't settle for anything else and he didn't have none.** And he couldn't find any place to buy it! And he couldn't WORK IT UP! I'm telling you, ladies and gentlemen, you have to face this now! IF YOU DO NOT REPENT TOWARD GOD BY YOUR OWN ACT AND BELIEVE IN THE LORD JESUS CHRIST, THERE'S NO HOPE FOR YOU. But the reason you are in the awful mess you are in and plum lost, is that what God Almighty absolutely demands and commands and requires you to do *you are utterly unable to perform.* I've been preaching for the last forty years and I'm not going to fight over some term whether election is this or that or the other or something like that; you can if you want to. You want the real fight, get in on this, Brother! This is worth dying for!

HEAR ME! No wonder nobody needs to become a seeker of the Lord who's been exalted and put on a throne, *who gives repentance and forgiveness of sins*; well honey, they've been taught for the last sixty years by what we call FUNDAMENTAL PREACHERS IN AMERICA *that they don't need God in this business of salvation; they can do it themselves.* That's right! And you think this world is mad at us because we believe in election and predestination, they don't even know how to spell those words! But I know what the war is getting hot about, its whether or not, is the reason that men and women are screaming to God for mercy now, is that they believe what they've been preached and they think that they can *produce repentance anytime they want to.* If that's so, a man may be in pretty bad condition but he ain't lost. Long as there is anything on God's green earth you can do to make a contribution to salvation you may be pretty badly whipped but you're not *lost.* You're not lost. You've got to become skillful in getting people lost. Lost. Lost.

And then David Brainerd faced the third thing, and this war gets hotter all the time! And he didn't evade it. And thank God, there wasn't no preacher around there to tell him that he can just forget about all those things you know and just take Jesus. He found out that *not only* that he had to be as holy as God and as good as Jesus Christ or he was going to be sent to hell. **He found out he had to produce repentance and faith that was his own act—God's not going to repent for you—and He's not going to believe for you but you can't do it yourself!** Whoo! You see what we call the gospel gets people to accept Jesus but the Bible gospel *gets men to be seekers of the Lord to do for them what they cannot do for themselves.* And that's the difference. We used to talk about old grandpa who lived in a day when people sought the Lord. Ain't nobody got time now to seek Him, they get saved before they ever seek Him! I've been in hundreds of Baptist churches, you want to have a little fight? I don't invite you to go with me now but I did see a few where this is where we kinda got in a little scrap! Is it so? Or are we gonna keep on using the old methods that have got us in the mess we are in now? Got us a generation of church members *that are as pagan as all get out.*

Are we willing to be Noahs, if that's God's will, for us to be in our day preachers of what? Righteousness. Huh? No one will be righteous on the basis of faith unless they've been *held over the hot coals of the utterly righteous demands of a holy righteous God.* You better start pleading with God to grant repentance to you. You gonna accept Jesus, are you! You better start seeking the Lord who purchased those rights by His precious blood. This is the heart of the controversy.

It becomes deeper when we face the third thing, David Brainerd kept crying to God, fighting mad at Him, arguing with Him, in controversy with Him, but he didn't take out because he wanted to get to the place where he could claim an interest in the merits of the shed blood of Christ. And he ran smack dab into the truth of God's Word that is the *most humbling and the most pride killing and the most flesh slaying thing I ever faced!* **He found out that God Almighty has the right to give or withhold faith. And under God that He exercises that right!** Whoo! Now you want to have a fight? Is that what you want to get into? Is that your Calvinism, honey? You better just stay on some terms you know without getting involved in this but this is what this church has got to invade this city with! *This is how God gets men plum lost. That God Almighty has a right and He exercises it, to give or withhold repentance and faith.* Got any Scripture for it? Of course I have. Sixth chapter of John, He gives life to whom He will. Whew! You mean to tell me I got no way I can come to God? Say, "Now here Lord, let's just do some business here, I've got a right, you've got to give me faith." You can't do that. He don't have to do it! HE DON'T HAVE TO DO IT! Now if you ever face this you'll get about as mad at God as David Brainerd did! Or you might *become a beggar.* Oh, Lord, if you pretty please, I sure would be much obliged! If You fix me so I can turn on myself and in dust and ashes abhor myself and spend the rest of my life standing in the need of mercy.

And then David Brainerd of course faced the last thing. And it is in the Word of God, **that God could save him or damn him and be just and get glory to Himself!** Whew! I will call attention in this pulpit before you forgot it and under God I believe we're gonna have to come back to it. Not many more than a hundred years ago, you walked down the aisle of a little Baptist church house or any other major denomination in America at that time, and say, "I've been saved and I want to be baptized and I want to join this church!" Some of the old brethren back then would say, "All right! We'll hear your *experience of grace*!" And if it suited them, they'd take you, if it didn't they'd say, "We will have to deal with you a little more, Brother." It's been an awful long time since anybody said, "We will have to talk to you a little more," you know! We don't do much of that now. And if he passed that test they would then ask him this, and if you want to get to the heart of Brother Calvin's theology, and Brother Luther, here it is: John Calvin said, "Nobody will walk the streets of glory who hadn't been made willing *to go to hell.*" Whew! And you say you're a Calvinist? Can you take that? That's what he taught. And a Baptist preacher a hundred years ago, if your experience of grace sounded all right, he'd say, "My brother or sister, are you willing to be damned *for the glory of God?*

Now I don't know if any of us here tonight, preacher included, know anything about faith or not. But that's what *it is.* Roman Catholicism in their day said faith was a mental ascent. The Reformers said, "It's a trust; not a bargain but a trust. Here I am. You're worthy of my surrender. You're worthy of my trust whatever You do with me." Whew! They said this was God-centered faith. You mean to tell me old Rolfe Barnard wouldn't just turn myself over, lock stock and barrel to Almighty Jesus Christ, leave it up to Him to what He does with me. That's trust. God Almighty help us grasp trust. And it leaves just one safe spot for Rolfe Barnard to call on God like that leper following Jesus Christ, when He was here in the days of His flesh; saying, *"Lord, if thou wilt, thou canst make me clean!"* When a fella's in that shape and he hears the gospel, oh that's awful good news! And in the next verse, the Lord Jesus Christ said, "I will." That's good news, Brother! That's good news.

I believe the Holy Spirit will be given to those who obey. Let's get us a Bible and start loving men and women enough to tell them the truth. Get them lost! Hum? Plum lost! Lost. Can't get out, locked up in God's prison house. Under God's condemnation. Sentence already passed. Door to the prison cell locked. And I haven't got a key. Somebody comes along, that's got the key! *That Somebody is the living Lord.* Somebody that is exalted and made a Sovereign and a Savior. For the expressed purpose that He can unlock the cell door and enable men and women to walk forth free!

You want revival? Let's start shutting men up to God. That salvation is of the Lord. Not a doctrine of the head but robbing men of all faith in everything they've ever done or ever will do. Some people are gonna become seekers of the Lord. Amen! Yes sir. That's my message. The reason I just use one invitation hymn is I believe it's true that I try to preach, we're gonna sing it as they softly play, "Pass Me Not O Gentle Savior." Here I am. Locked up in the prison house of the damned. I haven't got a key. No use to tell me to "walk out," I can't *get the door unlocked. Ohh I need a Savior! I need Somebody to tell me where I am and get me out of this jail. Amen!*

SERMON 9: Five Marks of a False Prophet
(Volume One: 14)

Matthew chapter 7 and verses 13-20 read: *"Enter ye in at the strait gate: for wide is the gate, and broad is the way, that leadeth to destruction, and many there be which go in thereat: Because strait is the gate, and narrow is the way, which leadeth unto life, and few there be that find it. Beware of false prophets, which come to you in sheep's clothing, but inwardly they are ravening wolves. Ye shall know them by their fruits. Do men gather grapes of thorns, or figs of thistles? Even so every good tree bringeth forth good fruit; but a corrupt tree bringeth forth evil fruit. A good tree cannot bring forth evil fruit, neither can a corrupt tree bring forth good fruit. Every tree that bringeth not forth good fruit is hewn down, and cast into the fire. Wherefore by their fruits ye shall know them."*

It is my conviction, not mine alone, that our task these days is three-fold in the public proclamation of the Word: *(1) We must proclaim and enforce God's holy law; (2) we must proclaim God's holy gospel in all of its purity and in its proper order; and (3) we must lift up our voices and call to the people's attention the Savior's plain admonition: "to beware of false prophets."*

Let me call your attention one more time that a false prophet is not necessarily an evil prophet. In the Old Testament, and sometimes in the New, there are evil prophets. They are malicious; they are satanically inspired. But a false prophet could be a fine fellow. He comes to you in sheep's clothing. But the fact that he is such a nice fellow, he is so earnest and he's so sincere, he seems to have such a passion for souls, and he seems to want to see people saved so intensely; *which makes him all the more dangerous* because the people will hear him as he preaches a message that doesn't bear good fruit. I don't care how nice a man is, if his message doesn't produce good fruit, he is a false prophet. And the Lord tells us to beware of false prophets and He tells us how we can tell false prophets by their fruits that result from the ministry of that fellow that preaches on the street, or over the radio, or from the pulpit stand or wherever he may preach. If his converts are not good, if his converts do not spend the rest of their lives as callers and seekers of the Lord, if his converts go to hell because they are depending on some physical act they performed or some prayer that they said or something like that, then *"beware of false prophets."*

I heard a preacher over the radio today telling the sinners to pray the sinner's prayer and he guaranteed that they would be saved. *Now that is a lie of hell and it came from the lips of a false prophet.* He may be a nice fellow and be very sincere but he knows nothing about the way God brings sinners to Himself. The reason he doesn't know is *because he doesn't know the Lord and has never been brought to salvation in Christ.* "If sin is damning its thousands, religion today is damning its tens of thousands."

And it is time now, in the battle of words and in the conflict of doctrine, and especially since you and I have lived all the days of our lives when the fruit has not been very good. And we have to dig ourselves considerably to find the slightest evidence that we have a saving interest in the blood of Christ and that we are *truly united to the Lord Jesus Christ.* The Scripture tells us that we are a branch if we are a child of God and the sap, the juice, the power and the life comes from the Vine. And we look at ourselves in these days, when we can almost hear the death rattle of real Christianity and it is hard for us to see that we have the slightest evidence in ourselves that there is any power flowing to us from the Vine, and then through us to lost mankind.

This is desperate language and certainly this is the time

for us to prick up our ears and beware of false prophets. To search our own experience and our own convictions and our own standing and condition to see whether or not we are on this broad road that is the road of religious profession where everybody on it calls Jesus "Lord." Where even some on it do some tremendous mighty acts, cast out demons and so forth. And where now we are living in a time when so many people are discovering that they had a strong faith, but they had their faith in the wrong person or the wrong thing. Where the winds from a thousand directions are blowing and the confidences and assurances of multitudes of people that thought they were built on a rock is long since gone since they found out their whole spiritual structure is blown away and here we are. "Beware of false prophets!"

Now this is not to be sneered at, since our Lord has so seriously warned us and admonished us to strive to enter in at the strait gate and thus walk the narrow way. And He also told us that there is a wide gate that leads to a broad way which leads to eternal destruction. The strait gate leads to a narrow way and that narrow way alone leads to life. It is not to be just passed over that in verse 15, God says, *"Beware of false prophets, which come to you in sheep's clothing, but inwardly they are ravening wolves."* Verse 16, *"Ye shall know them by their fruits."* He wants us to be keenly alert to see to it whether we believe a lie or whether we believe the truth, for if you believe the devil's lie you cannot be saved. And if you do not prick up your ears and cry to God to give you discernment, you will be like the folks who listen to the radio today: they believe everything they hear and thus they believe nothing. Oh, beware of false prophets! We need to heed that warning, especially today when we live in a day of mighty low ebb of spiritual power and very little truth is preached. We are in a desperate state and the preacher knows it and feels it and would do you good if he could.

Some people do not even bring their Bibles when they come to preaching. What do they expect? What on earth has happened to us? The people in Berea were wise. Acts 17:11: *"These were more noble than those in Thessalonica, in that they received the word with all readiness of mind, and searched the scriptures daily, whether those things were so."* If the Scriptures are true where my Lord said, *"My sheep hear my voice ... and they follow me,"* then when we don't use our

Bibles that is a mark of something that is terribly bad. I wish you had more interest in your soul. I wish I could jar you out of this state of death that we all seem to be in and I wish the Holy Spirit would spur somebody to the danger of not absolutely measuring everything you hear, not by what Rolfe Barnard says, but by what the Word of God says, because there is truth and I wish we believed it.

Beware of false prophets! We cannot ignore this. The Lord wants us to wake up to the fact that the way people get on this broad way is because they listen to false prophets, not bad men, but men who did not preach the truth, or they preached a half-truth and that is worse than a whole error, because people will believe it quicker when it is a half-truth.

I want to mention from the Word of God five marks of false preaching that are peculiar to the hour in which we live. And these marks by which men and women who really have an interest in eternity and has some belief that out yonder there is another life, and that what happens these days down here will determine what will happen out yonder. I believe these five things are worthy of our close attention. I do not take the time to mention many of the marks of a false prophet that we find in the Old Testament and the New. But I pick out five that seems to me to be peculiar to the preaching of this age that has got us in this awful deathlike state we are in where it seems that we are powerless to pray and we have no hunger for the Word of God. It seems that we are just about half-dead, dragging along and hoping for the best.

The Lord says we can tell these false prophets by their fruits. And as I look about the fruit of our ministry for these forty or fifty years, the fruit is getting worse all the time. The standards are going down all the time. The marks of death are growing all the while and the marks of life seem to be almost disappearing. I think these five things really make a picture of the type of preaching that we've had these many years and it has got the multitudes on this broad way, and it is leading multitudes of people who are sincere. They are dead but they are sincere. They are lifeless but they have believed what they have been told. But they are on the broad way and they think they are all right. And only an awakening of the Holy Ghost will ever awaken them and unless this happens they will go to hell and will be greatly surprised because they thought they were all right.

The first of these marks is that a *false preacher will speak peace to a sinner when God hasn't spoken peace.* The Old Testament talks about men who speak peace when there is no peace. One preacher said, "I have a deep conviction that we've made decisions for multitudes of people these days. We have filled our churches and many of them are going to hell who have accepted a proposition and know not our Lord."

How many of you have accepted a proposition instead of *surrendering to the Lord Jesus Christ? We are all eternity-bound men and women and unless God is pleased to perform a miracle in you and reveal Christ in you, you are doomed to hell.*

We have literally substituted the winsomeness of our personality and the power of our appeal for the only thing that has got any power in it. The gospel of Christ is the power of God unto salvation to everyone that believeth. Let me give you an illustration: God had to come to the apostle Peter and nearly kill him before he could get rid of his tradition and his Jewish prejudice and finally He sent Peter down to Cornelius who was down there praying and worshiping God the best he knew how. He was just hoping that somebody would come and speak to him the words of salvation. The apostle Peter went down there and knocked on the door: "Come in."

"I'm the apostle Peter. Are you Cornelius?"

"Yes."

"Well, I want to know, Cornelius, if you want to accept Jesus as your personal Savior?"

No, he didn't do any such thing! There is *no power in your little old invitation and there is not a bit of power in any man's decision. But there is power in the gospel of Christ.* Do you know what Peter did? He preached the gospel to him.

I'm telling you, for the last forty or sixty years, church members did not know the gospel themselves and when they went out and did personal work they did not give the sinners a bit of truth! They just stuck out their hand and said, "Won't you accept Jesus as your personal Savior?" And they did and *went on to hell.*

But listen, there isn't any power except in the gospel and if you get a chance to witness to a person, what are you going to tell him? Please do like Peter did. Give him the truth of God in Jesus Christ. And the Scriptures tell us in Acts 10:44: *"While Peter yet spake these words, the Holy Ghost fell on all them which heard the word."* They can't get saved by your little old invitation; that isn't worth a dime. They just accept a proposition and go on to hell believing they are all right! And these false preachers have spoken peace when there was no peace. The gospel of Christ is the power of God unto salvation. I am pleading that we quit all this foolishness and get us a Bible and go out here and represent Christ instead of disgracing Him. And when we witness to a sinner, do what they did in Bible times. Give him the Word and if the Holy Ghost falls on it, he will get saved while he is listening. *But he won't get saved by you just asking him, "Don't you want to accept Jesus?"*

Most of you folks are going to hell because all you got was a proposition you just accepted that somebody made— but there is no salvation in a proposition. The gospel of Christ is the power of God unto salvation. Repent and believe the gospel. Repent or perish.

These young preachers say, "Do you mean to tell me when we go out to do personal work, we ought to just give them the Word of God?" That is exactly right, and pray that the Holy Ghost will fall on them while they listen, and they will be saved if He does. You can't improve on this. When you go out to do a little personal work, you didn't give them the gospel; you just gave them your little invitation, and all they did was accept your invitation, and you told them that they were all right. You spoke peace when there wasn't any peace.

Hear Brother Barnard one more time between eternity, between heaven and hell; *there is only one Voice that has been given the authority, the power and the ability to speak peace to a troubled soul, and that is the Voice of God.* If that old sinner has to have you convince him that he is saved, you are *deceiving him. Only the Holy Ghost can comfort a sinner.* And if He comforts you and gives you peace, that is fine. Romans 5:1 says, *"Therefore being justified by faith, we have peace with God through our Lord Jesus Christ."* But if you got your hope of going to heaven because you accepted my proposition or somebody else's plea to accept Christ, I am afraid that your hope is false and you are deceived, and you are walking on the broad way that leads to destruction.

Another mark of a false prophet that is closely akin to this one is in the Old Testament which speaks of men healing the wounds of people slightly. I go from place to place and one time see glorious things another time deadness. I can't do it myself, so I just keep on and keep on. But I refuse to compromise. I have seen multitudes make a profession, but I won't know if any of them got saved or not till I get to the judgment. I hope many of them did, but I've never done one thing, and so help me God, I never will. I will never stoop to these underhanded methods to get people to say they accept Jesus, if they do not want Him mighty bad. I'm telling you what's the truth, these dry-eyed professors who say they got saved and continue on in their sins—I've actually seen men claim they got converted in the service at the old mourner's bench, and go right back out and light a cigarette. Why, there is no more salvation to that than there is in a monkey and you know it! Their salvation didn't even clean up the outside! That's no good and you know it's no good. Oh! Healing the wounds slightly.

With the exception of John the Baptist, who was filled with the Holy Ghost in his mother's womb, and Jeremiah likewise, I'm on pretty safe ground when I tell you that in order to save a human being, the lovely Lord *has to wound you*. And a preacher who will heal the wounds of a sinner is a false preacher. We have a generation of people now who say they have peace but they *never knew bitterness* and they scare me. My lovely Lord, *in order to conquer an old rebel, He crushes him to where he will bow to His blessed rule!* My Lord is kind enough to wound sinners, humble them, and break them! Let God give them joy. He is the only One who can give them joy and peace in Jesus Christ our Lord.

In times when I have seen just a little of what we call revival, I have thought sometimes that my old heart would break as I have seen men and women suffering under the wounds of Him who loves sinners enough, that rather than see them go to hell, He will wound them and He will wound them deeply. If He doesn't, they won't ever call on Him. We do not believe it, but it is so; a sinner will never call on the Lord if he can help it. *God has to crush him and wound him.* Don't heal the wounds of sinners slightly, don't do it. Let the One who inflicts the wound. And if the Lord doesn't wound you, you are going to hell, I tell you that. The wounds of my blessed Lord go mighty deep. He has to wound you or you will go to hell. Don't speak peace, let God speak peace; don't tell a man what God has done for him, *let the man tell you what*

God has done. You can't beat the Holy Spirit for doing what God Almighty gave Him to do.

In the third place, false prophets make the gate a lot *easier to get in than the Lord did.* It is so hard to get in this strait gate. My Lord said, *"Strive to enter in at the strait gate: for many, I say unto you, will seek to enter in, and shall not be able."* Oh, my soul! How easy it is made now, but it is only deception. But my Lord said, "You are dead in trespasses and sins, you have a heart of stone, you must be made a new creature in Christ or go to hell." *The Lord must make you willing to bow to His rule and reign. That old wicked hostility in your heart has got to come out and you have got to be made a willing captive of bloodstained Jesus, with His will central in your life, and nothing but an operation of the Holy Ghost in the power of the blood of Christ, the risen Lord, is sufficient for your need.* We know this is the truth according to the Scriptures. So what in the name of God will this generation of easy-going, sinful living men and women, claiming to be children of God, how will they fare when they stand at the judgment, having ignored this admonition of the Lord?

"Strive to enter in at the strait gate." It is so difficult. *You can't have this world and Christ too. One of them has got to go!* You can't have the spirit of this age and Christ too; one has got to go. You can't have all of this and heaven too; one of them has got to go. He told the truth. And I say to you that a false prophet who will preach this little easy gospel, that you can *keep your sins and do as you please* and every once in a while you can get up in the church and say, "Now I am saved, but I haven't been living right," and that will make you feel better for a couple of weeks, and after awhile you will die and go on to hell! Ladies and gentlemen, this is serious. This strait gate is difficult and the false prophet will tell you it is *easy.*

What are the marks of a false prophet? In this day, they make a way a whole lot broader than Jesus makes it. I know that this generation has not been told the truth. When I keep hearing people tell me, "I know I am saved but I am not living for the Lord," there is something wrong. This narrow way hasn't got room on it for men and women in rebellion against Christ! Hear me! This narrow way is a Christ-disciplined way. I tell you now that I would do you good and not evil at all. You had better bring your habits, your thoughts, your work, your body, your home and everything there is about you to

Christ, and *put them under His discipline.* Too long we've had a generation of church people that decide what they will do and what they will not do. I tell you now that I would do you good. It is not given us to walk this narrow way except under the discipline of the Lord of glory, and that will call for daily repentance and daily exercise of faith and daily surrender and commitment, and that will call for daily getting your orders from the Commander and Chief, the Lord Jesus Christ!

We don't know much about what I am talking about now. My heart leaps within me lest we've missed Christ altogether. This disciplined road is not disciplined by what we claim, but by what we do. Jesus states in Matthew: *"Not every one that saith unto me, Lord, Lord, shall enter into the kingdom of heaven; but he that doeth the will of my Father which is in heaven."* Not the person who says he is saved, but is not living right, but the Lord says, *"he that doeth the will of my Father which is in heaven."* The child of God *wants to do the will of God,* that is the desire of his soul. He is not in the broad way, he is in the narrow way because *he is under the strict discipline of Jesus Christ,* who earned the right to demand of us that we bring our very thoughts into captivity under Him. *"Bringing into captivity every thought to the obedience of Christ."* That is a job.

But the false prophet, his converts say, "Oh, I am saved," but the will of God is not the central thing in their lives and there is no salvation there. A false prophet speaks peace where there is no peace and heals the wounds of men slightly. He also makes the gate easy to enter instead of difficult and the way broad instead of narrow. He not only does this but *he offers salvation on cheaper terms than God does.* The terms have never been changed: any person who is able to repent—but repentance is not a once-for-all act. It goes on as long as you live. Anybody that can meet the terms of salvation, that is repentance and faith, he will be saved, thank God! *"For godly sorrow worketh repentance to salvation not to be repented of: but the sorrow of the world worketh death."*

But they will not be lowered and they cannot be cheapened and repentance is nothing more or less than *the dethronement of you and the enthronement of God's Son in here. And faith is utter confidence in and absolute obedience to the Lord Jesus Christ. Almighty God has to perform a miracle: He quickens you and shows you how sinful you are by His holy law. And as you cry unto Him for mercy He draws you to Christ and reveals to you who He is and makes you a new creature in Christ! He gives you the faith of the Son of God so you can believe to the saving of your soul and He also grants repentance. "Salvation is of the Lord."*

But what we've known all the days that I've been preaching, you just go through some motions one time and the preacher tells you that you are saved, and you go on to hell comfortable in your sins, believing that you are all right. No! Every commitment between you and God needs to be made time after time. The Scriptures say, *"he that believeth,"* he just keeps on believing. *"He that endureth,"* he doesn't play out; it's *"he that abideth"* ... he that drinketh ... he that obeyed. We walk by faith. Every day calls for new commitment to the *utter lordship of the Lord Jesus Christ,* utter dependence on His saving blood to wipe out the penalty of sin that God Almighty demands. And to make it cheaper than that is the mark of a false prophet. *Utter dethronement of self, utter enthronement of Christ; Christ where you have been, Christ giving the orders, Christ in command. That's repentance.*

I am going to look you in the face now. I will meet you at the judgment. Anybody on earth that will take the Bible and face it and find out what is in it *will be faced with the absolute claims of God for His Son in your life!* Anybody who will do that will either curse God and hope to die or it will bring you in deep repentance every day of your life. For the best saint that ever lived, when he is faced with all the claims and commands of God for His Son, will have to continually face the fact that you are far off, so far short. *His demands and His claims of His rule in our daily living, if it doesn't cause you to have tremendous experiences of repentance and crying to God for forgiveness and confession of sin, it is because you know nothing of Christ, you are a stranger to the Son of God.*

McCheyne said, "Christ's war is to be preferred to the devil's peace." And if Christ is in here, he will disturb you until the day you die. If He is not in there, if He is just a profession to you, if He is just somebody you hope will keep you out of hell and leave you alone while you live, you will never know anything about what I am talking about. But if Christ is in you, He is holy and He will disturb you and you will know to cry for forgiveness every day. You will know what it is to pour out your heart about your sins. *The reason you don't think that you are a big sinner is because Christ isn't in there.*

What is the awful price you pay for listening to false preachers? It will show up at the judgment. Listen, *"Many will say to me in that day, Lord, Lord, have we not prophesied in thy name? and in thy name have cast out devils? and in thy name done many wonderful works?"* That is the price people will pay for listening to false preachers, going through a wide gate of easy believism, walking on the broad way that doesn't bring you under Christ's discipline ever blessed day of your life. That is the price that the youngsters writing notes while the preacher is preaching will pay at the judgment. God will say, *"I never knew you: depart from me, ye that work iniquity."*

My Lord said, *"Beware of false prophets."* Beware! Beware!

SERMON 10: Casting Pearls Before Swine
(Volume Three: 23)

It says in Matthew 7:6, *"Give not that which is holy unto the dogs, neither cast ye your pearls before swine, lest they trample them under their feet, and turn again and rend you."*

Holy things, precious things, pearls of great price are reserved only for *prepared hearts.* If salvation were an offer it would be different, but *salvation is a gift.* It is true that in the language of some confessions of faith, Christ is freely offered to all men, but in the language of the Bible, salvation is the gift of God. And Christ is that gift. And it is the principle of the Word of God, and God never varies from it, that *He does not offer a gift to somebody who isn't prepared to accept it.* You can turn down an offer, but you don't turn down a gift or reject it.

Now it is true that men reject everything they know about Christ and despise it. In John 4:10: *"Jesus answered and said unto her, If thou knewest the gift of God, and who it is that saith to thee, Give me to drink; thou wouldest have asked of him, and he would have given thee living water."* The Lord plainly told the woman at the well that it is the gift of God. My Lord bought the right to give eternal life to as many as the Father hath given Him, according to John 17:2: *"As thou hast given him power over all flesh, that he should give eternal life to as many as thou hast given him."* He has the right to deal with all men for in that sense He has bought all men and He owns them. Because of His creation and purchase price, He has the right to deal with every individual of mankind.

The gospel is a *covenant arranged in the Godhead* whereby the Lord would give eternal life to those people chosen in Christ before the foundation of the world, according to Ephesians 1:4: *"According as he hath chosen us in him before the foundation of the world, that we should be holy and without blame before him in love."* 2 Thessalonians 2:13: *"But we are bound to give thanks alway to God for you, brethren beloved of the Lord, because God hath from the beginning chosen you to salvation through sanctification of the Spirit and belief of the truth."* And the Lord will dispose of the rest as seemeth good in His sight. God doesn't give His gift to people who will despise it. He doesn't say, "Here is eternal life, and I want you to make up your mind whether you will take it or reject it." No, salvation is Christ's precious gift! And He has the right, and He exercises the right to give His gift to people who would not trample it but would be glad to receive it. This is the principle upon which God works now, whether we can swallow it or not.

We are butchers of souls if we ignore the plain teaching of the Old Testament that the human heart must be plowed, the ground must be harrowed. Jeremiah 4:3: *"For thus saith the LORD to the men of Judah and Jerusalem, Break up your fallow ground, and sow not among thorns."* Listen to Hosea in 10:12, *"Sow to yourselves in righteousness, reap in mercy; break up your fallow ground: for it is time to seek the LORD, till he come and rain righteousness upon you."* And it is downright disobedience to the principle upon which God works to attempt to sow among thorns and expect a harvest!

It is true in the New Testament and in the Old Testament that the spiritual laws of harvest are exactly like the farmer. The farmer goes out and first plows deeply, then he harrows it, and at a certain time he sows the seed. The rain comes and the sun shines and after a while he goes and looks for a harvest. But he doesn't look for the harvest *before the plowing has been done*, and he doesn't sow the seed before the harrowing has been done. And neither does God! This is the law of God that cannot be ignored, unless you wish to become a butcher of your own soul and a butcher of every soul you touch. For it is eternally true that they only get God's best who sincerely want it and long for it and who are capable of appreciating it. If God were going around offering it and leaving it up to man as to whether he would accept it or reject it, that would be one thing—but that isn't what God does. *Salvation is a gift from God.* Salvation is the blessed boon from heaven and it comes as a gift of God, for Christ is salvation and salvation is Christ.

Now God doesn't simply pass His blessings out indiscriminately, He gives them *only to those who are prepared to receive them.* If you ever receive this precious gift from God and you start tracing back how it happened, you will be like the sainted Spurgeon—everything will go right back to God!

You won't know it beforehand but afterward you will find out that the reason you sought the Lord is because He first sought you. And you will find out the reason you love the Lord is because *He first loved you.* Now you may not know this beforehand—don't try to be a theologian, just try to get to Christ. Then after you get to Christ you can trace it back, and you will find that every blessing flows from God.

The mysteries of the soul's converse with God are not to be lightly made known in common talk. Such language as Song of Solomon 6:3: *"I am my beloved's, and my beloved is mine"* is not for public conversation. The apostle Paul had an experience where he was caught up into the third heaven, whatever that means, and he saw things and he heard things that he said he couldn't talk about. He didn't even tell he had such an experience for fourteen years, and he never did tell what it was.

The deep things that go on between a child and its parents or the husband and the wife are not for the marketplace; they are for the inner circle of the home. And so be it with the deep things that go on between a person and Almighty God. Oh, the easy familiarity—it well nigh assumes a position of blasphemy today in our stuff we call salvation. And we are on such good terms with *the King of Glory* until we've lost all sense of the wonder of being invited to come into His courts and sit at His feet and to be in His presence.

These are precious words in Malachi 3:16-17: *"Then they that feared the LORD spake often one to another: and the LORD hearkened, and heard it, and a book of remembrance was written before him for them that feared the LORD, and that thought upon his name. And they shall be mine, saith the LORD of hosts, in that day when I make up my jewels; and I will spare them, as a man spareth his own son that serveth him."*

When we try to stuff precious jewels down the throats of

the unprepared, all they will do is turn against us and rend us to pieces. Let me illustrate it: you get hold of a precious truth in the Bible after you have studied for twenty years— then like a flash you see it! It is a revelation, an illumination, for all truth comes this way. You have read a text a lot of times and it never meant anything to you, then you read it and it is revealed to you. Why hadn't you seen it before? You had not been prepared for it, your heart wasn't prepared for it, so it just bounced off; it just went in one ear and out the other.

I have had that experience and I know you have if you are a child of God. God's providence hemmed us in from many directions and we weren't aware of it. He had prepared us so that *word* was God's Word at that time; it came just like a flash. You said, "Oh, my, isn't that wonderful? I never saw that before!" And you are telling the truth. You hadn't been hemmed up where that Scripture could be made flesh to you, just in the same proportion that the Son of God was made flesh in the incarnation.

If you try to stuff spiritual truths down the throats of unprepared people, you are doing them harm, beloved. We must be patient as the farmer is in trying to raise a crop. Revealed truth must be revealed; you don't learn revealed truth, you experience revealed truth. All spiritual truth is spiritually discerned and it comes by revelation, a flash, an illumination. Beloved, one of our greatest obstacles is that, while we received truth by revelation, we get mad when somebody else won't receive it because we told them. And we do great harm in this and we shut the door and we ignore a precious truth—that the blessed things from God are received only by people who are prepared.

When trying to witness to a blind, devil-blinded sinner we can see this necessity. It is not that they are any worse than we were, it is just that they are still blind; that is where we once were blinded by the god of this age. They are smart as whips in lots of respects but they are just blind in one thing. The average lost person will agree with us on most truths in the Bible, but the difference is *they see no beauty in Christ. They say they believe in Jesus but they don't see any glory in Him.* There is nothing about Him that attracts them. Why? The sun is shining but they have no eyes to see, they are blind. Revelation 3:17: *"Because thou sayest, I am rich, and increased with goods, and have need of nothing; and knowest not that thou art wretched, and miserable, and poor, and blind, and naked."* People are in a terrible condition—they are blind on one thing—they don't see *the glory of God in the glorious gospel of Jesus Christ.* That's how Satan keeps people. He doesn't lead people into immorality; that is the work of the flesh, the old sinful nature. Satan works to keep people blinded to the glory of God in the face of Jesus Christ. In 2 Corinthians 4:6 we see, *"For God, who commanded the light to shine out of darkness, hath shined in our hearts, to give the light of the knowledge of the glory of God in the face of Jesus Christ."* If he can just keep sinners blinded to the glory of Christ, Satan has them, no matter what other truth they may see!

If we have to come to know Christ by a divine revelation it is glorious to us. And if you had similar experience in this respect as mine, when you came to see Him for the first time and tasted of Him, you couldn't understand how all those years you spent in darkness. Now with some impatience you approach a sinner, thinking you can cram the glory of Christ into an unprepared heart, but you can't. Let's be willing to be patient (as God is) to have that heart plowed and have it prepared. *Only prepared hearts can work through the veil of mystery and come to saving faith.*

Let me illustrate it one more way: everybody I deal with has some sort of faith in Christ. The Mohammedans believe in Christ; they will tell you that He is almost as good a prophet as Mohammed. The orthodox Jew will tell you he believes in Christ; some of them say that he is as great a prophet as Moses. The modernists believe very deeply and they have great faith in Christ, but there is a difference in that and *saving faith.* We ought not to be blinded for we are living in a heathen land when nearly everybody has a Bible and swears that he believes every word in it. They have never read it but they "believe" it. Nearly everybody in America "believes" in Christ (that's so), but only the prepared heart can receive Christ.

The Christ of the Bible is never offered to any except those who are prepared to receive Him. We can't wish Christ off on people, as much as we would like to. Now if you rob Him of His glory and rob Him of the awful scandal of His cross, you will have no difficulty getting people to accept that kind of a Jesus. But if you refuse to strip Him of *His absolute glory and sovereignty sitting on the throne with the reins of every human being in His hands, controlling the destiny of everything,* then they rebel against Him.

If you rob Christ of His absoluteness in the work of the cross, and His ministry on the throne, people will receive Him. An unprepared heart doesn't want to go to hell, if there is a hell, but *only a prepared heart wants King Jesus to be the absolute ruler of his life!* Hearts must be prepared. Give not holy things unto dogs. Don't cast your pearls before swine. If you do, they will just trample them under their feet; then they will turn and rend you. That is about the best picture in the New Testament of the average church now. They are just going through the motions and they will rend you.

Now the greatest task facing the churches of America is that they need to be evangelized themselves. They are such a hotbed of rebellion against the holy claims of Christ inside, they can't press those claims on anybody outside. Hearts have not been prepared.

John the Baptist was sent to prepare the way, to make a people ready; that was his job. The Lord organized His disciples two by two and sent them ahead to every village that Christ was to come. He sent two disciples to prepare the way. And they were given instructions that if they were not received to shake the dust of that city off their feet. Jesus withdrew Himself in such circumstances. It is recorded in Matthew 13:58: *"And he did not many mighty works there because of their unbelief."*

We need to remember afresh that there is no gospel, and there is no good news for the impenitent sinner, nor the uninterested sinner. The gospel is not for secure people. *The gospel is for people who are uneasy, weary, hungry, thirsty, and burdened with a load of sin. The law is to be preached to secure people and the gospel to people who are lost.*

Let me make three applications before I quit. God deals with a church after this principle, and a church that is willing to settle for less than best will get less than the best. Is there any hope in our day for a congregation of people that will not be satisfied with things as they are?

Mr. Spurgeon said, "Give me hungry people, give me broken people who will not rest as long as the crown rights of King Jesus are ignored by the multitudes." Have we come to the point as church people that we say, "We can't have anything better"? God deals with churches after this principle: we do not have the best because our hearts will accept less. And He doesn't give His best to churches unless those churches are prepared to appreciate it and cherish it. I believe that will all my heart.

It is still true that God gives bread to the hungry and He exalts the lowly and humbles the high and mighty. Listen to what it says in Isaiah 57:15: *"For thus saith the high and lofty One that inhabiteth eternity, whose name is Holy; I dwell in the high and holy place, with him also that is of a contrite and humble spirit, to revive the spirit of the humble, and to revive the heart of the contrite ones."* I have never been able to handle these words in Isaiah 66:8: *"For as soon as Zion travailed, she brought forth her children."* What do we desire as brothers and sisters in a local congregation? Do we want a deep moving of the Holy Spirit?

For nearly thirty-eight years I have been trying to preach a gospel that can be believed but not understood, shutting men up to abandonment of all hope in themselves and casting them utterly on God. The thing that hurts me so is the prayerlessness of our congregations. I do not know of a church that is a praying church, do you? I mean a praying people. Oh, it is hopeless to hope that the Spirit of grace and supplications would come on a local congregation and you would have a church in prayer? People who dare to believe that only the Holy Spirit can open a man's blind eyes. He uses means, but He is the only One that can do it, I can't. Trying to preach a gospel under which you won't see a person shed a tear unless the Holy Spirit takes charge.

Salvation by grace is too deep for the wisest man that ever lived to understand. No wonder the unsaved man says, "I wonder what on God's earth those people are talking about!" The Scripture says in 1 Corinthians 2:14: *"But the natural man receiveth not the things of the Spirit of God: for they are foolishness unto him: neither can he know them, because they are spiritually discerned."* The cross that breaks my heart even tonight is these young preachers and Sunday school teachers and whole churches coming together all over this country in Bible conferences. Their numbers are getting to be legion now. They think we can preach this message without being baptized with tears of real intercessory prayer and see results. *You can't preach what you call a Calvinist approach to the gospel of Christ and get results unless it is bathed in prayer. That is God's truth.*

How much longer are we going to think that truth in itself will get the job done? It will not. Mr. Spurgeon was about as good a preacher as I am, but poor little fellow was so weak that three hundred of his choicest men never did get to hear him preach. They were underneath the pulpit down in the basement of the tabernacle on their knees praying together every time he preached. We talk about the great numbers of souls that were ushered into the kingdom under Mr. Spurgeon's ministry. But you listen: He had three hundred men on their knees *praying for the gospel to "run well," praying for the progress of the gospel,* as it was being preached upstairs. That was the secret of his success.

I wish we would quit quoting his theology so much and face the fact that Spurgeon didn't believe what he preached would get the job done, *unless the Holy Spirit took charge.* And although he couldn't explain it—neither can I, neither can you—prayer has something to do with the *outpouring of the Spirit of God.*

Do we want the glory of God in our midst? We heard a tape by J. I. Packer and he called attention to 1 Corinthians 14, where the pattern is set that if an unbeliever or unlearned one comes into your midst, when circumstances are right he will fall down on his face and be convicted. *"But if all prophesy, and there come in one that believeth not, or one unlearned, he is convinced of all, he is judged of all: And thus are the secrets of his heart made manifest; and so falling down on his face, he will worship God, and report that God is in you of a truth."* Hearing this made my heart hungry again as I thought of that chapter in comparison with our services today. I've been in so many services when I didn't know whether God was there or not. He didn't make Himself manifest.

As long as we are content to have nice services I expect we are going to have them. I can't speak with authority now, because I don't know much of it from experience. But I do believe in my heart that a church must be prepared and it must prepare its own heart, break up its own fallow ground, and quit sowing among thorns. Don't expect a crop if the seed falls on stony ground. *Only ground prepared can receive the gospel,* and the evidence of its reception is the bringing forth of fruit unto perfection.

I think God deals with an individual child of His on this same principle. Matthew 5:6: *"Blessed are they which do hunger and thirst after righteousness: for they shall be filled."* Read much of the Psalms which is the highest peak where Old Testament sainthood is manifested. Psalm 63:1: *"O God, thou art my God; early will I seek thee: my soul thirsteth for thee, my flesh longeth for thee in a dry and thirsty land, where no water is."* Psalm 42:1-2: *"As the hart panteth after the water brooks, so panteth my soul after thee, O God. My soul thirsteth for God, for the living God: when shall I come and appear before God?"*

The longer I live the more I know by experience, I think, that the seeking that started when God first arrested you back yonder is to continue. And it must get hotter and hotter all the while until you see the Lord. A Christian is a seeker—he is not somebody that is satisfied and settled down on his lees. He is a seeker, he is a comer. The book of Hebrews describes a child of God as always coming to the Lord. It looks like the Lord would get weary of such a one! Hebrews 10:22: *"Let us draw near with a true heart in full assurance of faith, having our hearts sprinkled from an evil conscience, and our bodies washed with pure water."* See also Hebrews 11:6.

When a little child is hurt it cries, "Mama"; when hungry, "Mama"; or when thirsty, "Mama." Always coming to Mama. That's like a child of God. What do we want as God's people, as individuals? The fullness of the Spirit, insight into the Word of God, power in prayer, to be used as a witness. Then we keep crying to Him for these things.

I think God deals with lost people this way. All the invitations in the Bible are limited to folks who are *hungry, thirsty, or weary.* Not a one of them is addressed to anybody who wouldn't be glad to hear it. Isaiah 55:1: *"Ho, every one that thirsteth, come ye to the waters, and he that hath no money; come ye, buy, and eat; yea, come, buy wine and milk without money and without price."* Somebody says, "I'm not thirsty." Well, *I wasn't talking to you!* Another says, "I am all right." Jesus said in Luke 5:32: *"I came not to call the righteous, but sinners to repentance."*

In the very midst of the temple where the hostility against Christ was the hottest, where in about seven days it would lead to His crucifixion, He turns in that hotbed of hostility and says: *"If any man thirst, let him come unto me, and drink."* They said, "We are not thirsty." Well, I wasn't talking to you! I said, if any man *thirst.* The last invitation of the Bible is to *thirsty people* in Revelation 22:17: *"And the Spirit and the bride say, Come. And let him that heareth say, Come. And let him that is athirst come. And whosoever will, let him take the water of life freely."* We may not believe it but God's Spirit doesn't go around offering water to people unless they are thirsty. You can lead a mule to water but unless he is thirsty you can't make him drink to save your life!

I was on the radio down South and I wasn't able to get a crowd in the meetings, so I thought I would do a little something different because I was desperate. On the radio I said, "Here is five hundred dollars I will pay to the person who phones in or comes to me and tells me where in the Bible it says, "Whosoever will may come to Christ." Well, I got phone calls from folks who thought they were going to get that five hundred dollars. And everyone of them was from the 22nd chapter of the last book of the Bible, beginning at verse 17. I had the privilege of showing them something when they would come to me to get the five hundred dollars. I would say, "Let's read it. It doesn't say that, does it?" Of course, it is true, "Whosoever will may come." God won't say NO. But that doesn't mean a thing for *nobody will come. Nobody will, except thirsty people, thirsty people.* Amen! Let him that is athirst come. Are you thirsty? Would you like a drink of the water of life, that if you drink of it you shall never thirst? Okay, come on. Jesus says in John 4:14: *"But whosoever drinketh of the water that I shall give him shall never thirst; but the water that I shall give him shall be in him a well of water springing up into everlasting life."*

Are you tired of sinning and scared of dying? Come on! Are you hungry, are you tired of eating the husks that the swine eat? Would you like to eat the Bread of Life? John 6:35: *"And Jesus said unto them, I am the bread of life: he that cometh to me shall never hunger; and he that believeth on me shall never thirst."* Come on. Come on! Somebody says, "I'm not hungry." Well, *I didn't say anything to you.* I don't know anything the Lord has got by way of blessing, and I don't know any gift the Lord has for somebody who wouldn't be glad to receive it.

Years ago I went down to Mississippi, Wednesday night through Sunday night at the request of a friend. He said, "I will pay the bill and help you if you will go." So we set it up and I went down. The young preacher, a student of a Baptist college there, met me. He was pastoring a small country church on weekends. So I preached on Wednesday night and Thursday the young preacher, who was a go-getter, came and got me early and we went out to knock on doors. I preached Thursday night and Friday we spent all day knocking on doors and talking to people. We spent all day Saturday visiting around in the community talking with people.

Saturday night after the service was over, I was already gone to bed and a knock came on the door of the room where I was being entertained. I said, "Come in," and that young pastor came in. He said, "Brother Barnard, I don't know what to do. You are older than I am and you are here as my guest. I am just a young fellow but I'm going to ask you not to preach tomorrow. I don't want you to preach for us anymore." He said, "I just can't stand the way you are doing." I asked, "Well, what on earth am I doing that is hurting you so?" He said, "Well, Brother Barnard, in all of our visiting you just talked about the gospel to one person." I said, "Well, I haven't found but one sinner. You see, I am forbidden to sow among thorns; I take that pretty seriously. I am forbidden to give holy things unto dogs." Matthew 7:6 says, *"Give not that which is holy unto the dogs, neither cast ye your pearls before swine, lest they trample them under their feet, and turn again and rend you."*

I remember we had gone into lots of homes and they were all right; some of them would try to come to the meeting one night before it closed, if it didn't rain. Some were aiming to come last night and just as they got ready friends came in. I just heard all the excuses and everybody was just fine and dandy. So all I would do in such homes, I asked if it was all right for us to have prayer. They would say it was, so I would pray to them *and I would preach them a sermon in my prayer on the holy demands of a thrice holy God.* I wouldn't invite any of them to come to the meeting or anything else, I would just leave.

But we came to one place and we talked awhile, then the pastor said we had to go; would it be all right if we have a word of prayer? So he led in prayer, then I prayed, and while I was praying I noticed a woman was crying and I quit praying. I thought the Lord would forgive me. And I said, "What's the matter with you?" And she said, "I wish I could be saved but I can't." I asked, "Why can't you be saved?" She said, "I'm such a big sinner, I have sinned so long there is no hope for me."

Now that is the kind of folks I like to find! And I told her about the pearl of great price, the Son of the living God who came to justify the ungodly. Romans 5:6: *"For when we were yet without strength, in due time Christ died for the ungodly."* Romans 5:8: *"But God commendeth his love toward us, in that, while we were yet sinners, Christ died for us."*

But let me show you something: I was forbidden to tell those *self-satisfied in-for-hell church people* about the Lord. I am not going to sow among thorns. *I preached to them the holy claims of God's law.* And as I explained that to the young preacher, he said, "I understand." I said, "Young man, if you will let me help you—instead of going in homes and trying to get them to take Jesus—do what the Scriptures say. Break up some fallow ground and use the holy demands of a holy God. *No man will ever receive Christ as Lord and Savior until he is stripped and slain and conquered by the claims of God's holy law.* And we are butchers of souls if we ignore the fundamental truth that God gives His best, and that is Christ, to *prepared hearts.*

You know what that boy did? He took me literally and his visiting from then on was scriptural. Where he found nice little secure people, he just shot them with God's holy law! *If God's holy law won't rout you out of feeling how good you are, you will just have to go on to hell.* That is his weapon. And in six weeks after the meeting he had thirty-seven grown people in the little country community come to him asking him: "Is there any hope that we might be saved?"

I am telling you, God gives His best and that is Christ; for Christ is everything to people whose hearts have been prepared. It is so wonderful. Now God says, before you go out to talk to people, spend some time saying, "Lord, You go ahead of me." Are there not many examples of this in the Bible? Don't get you a little tract that has got the same pill for everybody. Take no thought of what you shall say. Luke 12:12: *"For the Holy Ghost shall teach you in the same hour what ye ought to say."* You will never find two persons in the same shape. *Depend on the Holy Ghost to lead you to that portion of truth that would be meat in due season to that person.* If he needs his heart plowed by the Holy Spirit with the claims of the holy law of God, then pray that *the Holy Ghost would do that work for the glory of Christ.*

Chapter Eleven

The Redeemer's Witness

For thou shalt be his witness unto all men of what thou hast seen and heard. —
Acts 22:15

Between the years 1964 and 1968 Rolfe Barnard and his friend, R. T. Kendall, began a joint pen ministry to reach ministers with the message of sovereign grace. Together they formed and published a monthly magazine entitled the *Redeemer's Witness* which was freely distributed by mail upon request. Kendall was a settled pastor and Barnard an itinerant evangelist and both men viewed this periodical as important to the sovereign grace movement which was building momentum. Issues would advertise the annual Sovereign Grace Conferences with a list of speakers, dates, and locations and so this medium of print soon became a welcome ministry to many ministers around the country.

Issues of the *Redeemer's Witness* contained articles by Dr. John Thornbury, Dr. N. B. Magruder, Ernest Reisinger and others. Each issue contained a segment by Rolfe Barnard entitled, "Bread from Barnard"; here are his thoughts on this contribution taken from an early issue from August of 1964:

> Before I set down a "morsel" of bread for this issue suffer a word or two from me to you who read as to the "why?" of the *Redeemer's Witness*. Brother Kendall and I wish to keep the

paper small in the hope it will be read and studied. We hope it shall witness to the one who is working His will in our day.

More detailed insights for the reasoning behind the publication of the *Redeemer's Witness* is seen in the following "opening article" written by R. T. Kendall from the first issue dated, April, 1964:

In this first editorial of our new publication, *Redeemer's Witness*, I should like to set forth some principles that pertain to this periodical. A portion of our readers will recognize this as an extension of our former publication, *Fairview Flame*, which was published in Ohio during my pastorate there. Evangelist Rolfe Barnard joined me in writing weekly articles for better than half of the last year there. I stated in the final issue of the *Flame* that early in 1964, God willing, Evangelist Barnard and I would publish another periodical. So the *Redeemer's Witness* comes to you this month, and will follow every month as God enables us.

Why *Redeemer's Witness*? First and foremost because we want to be the Redeemer's witnesses. We want to proclaim a message which will truly represent *Him*. Moreover, we feel we have the message which makes us ambassadors for Christ, so as to reveal Him as He is both in His person and His work. We do not intend to propagate any label which may identify us theologically or denominationally—but we do intend to proclaim loudly and clearly the beauty and glory and sovereignty of our blessed Redeemer, the Lord Jesus Christ! This publication is not a denominational witness; it is not a witness of proving doctrine, but we will not shrink from theological issues; it is not a witness of the great and godly men of history, but we will not ignore God's mighty visitations in history—but it is the REDEEMER'S WITNESS! It is to assert prophetically what we believe the Redeemer is saying to our generation.

Jonathan Edwards once stated that the task of every generation was to find out in which direction the sovereign Redeemer is moving, then move in *that* direction. The *Redeemer's Witness* will be the story of what we believe to be His direction for our generation. We respect history. So much so that we will refer to it often; but at the same time we do not assume the issues to be exactly the way they were in

Augustine's day, or Luther's, or Calvin's. We do not want to involve ourselves with a controversy that may be five hundred years old. We want to involve ourselves with the issues which confront us *today*.

It is our conviction that God is willing to bring great revival to this earth before the second coming of the Lord Jesus Christ. We know that in the last days the *"love of many shall wax cold,"* and that there must come a *"falling away first"*; but all this being true does not rule out the parallel purpose of God in reviving His people before the end, and also to let the world know Jesus Christ still rules from a throne!

We do not believe revival will come apart from preaching. While some who hope for revival still await some supernatural spiritual phenomena that will by-pass preaching, we still believe that *"it pleased God by the foolishness of preaching"* to accomplish His work. Therefore if God uses preaching as we have stated, it becomes necessary that at least two things are in evidence: (1) The *minister* must be owned of God. (2) The *message* must be owned of God. If the preacher is owned of the Lord Jesus Christ it will prove in turn that he is wholly given to Him. The minister of the gospel must be totally resigned to the sovereign will of God. He must be slain, broken, and utterly committed to Christ's person and work. If he is not, then he is in that multitude of ministers who are where they are only for expediency and gain.

If the *message* is owned of God it will mean that true revival will soon follow. I am tempted to say here that it means the message will be the preaching of truth. This may be true; but hundreds of ministers are preaching truth without God owning their ministry. Theological aptness does not secure a claim on God. *Nothing* secures a claim on God. But a God-owned ministry means revival and blessing. Good examples are the ministries of Brainerd, McCheyne or Spurgeon.

But one thing is certain: the message cannot be owned of God if, first of all, the minister is not owned of God. Our prime concern is not in our sermons but in ourselves. The sermons are products of what we are. On the other hand, let us not take lightly the importance and place of the *content and verity of doctrine*. *"All his works are done in truth."* (Psalm 33:4). I do not concur with a well-known statement, "One thing we can learn from history is that we do not learn from history." We can indeed learn from history. If we don't it's our fault. And one thing we can learn from history is that when God was pleased to visit this planet with true revival it was also accompanied by the preaching of the truth. So let us not underestimate this point. But at the same time while we are striving for theological aptness we can lose the anointing of the Holy Spirit. And we can learn only in proportion to our anointing.

Will you join in prayer with us? If you share a similar burden as we do, let's stay close together. We are in the "perilous times" the apostle Paul said must come. Our only hope of survival is the revelation of the glory of Christ. Let us stay near Him. Let us exalt Him. Let us magnify Him. Let us, like John on the isle of Patmos, fall at His feet "as dead." For *there* are we safe and sure. It is in Christ, and Him alone, that are hid *"all the treasures of wisdom and knowledge."*

R. T. Kendall

The following issues of the *Redeemer's Witness* carried follow-up articles by Kendall on such themes as: The God-Owned Ministry; The God-Owned Minister; The God-Owned Message. Rolfe Barnard composed his articles "on the run," in hotel rooms and pastors' homes as he traveled about the country preaching the topics he wrote about. A quick perusal of "Bread from Barnard" reveal that Kendall was the more gifted writer, but there is much from Barnard's pen worthy of our attention. Space does not permit the re-publication of all of Barnard's articles from this periodical, but since this is the predominate pen ministry of Rolfe Barnard (he authored no books like his colleague Kendall), we will include a good portion of Barnard's nuggets for our study in this chapter.

We are grateful to Wiley Fulton for providing the author with the *complete set* of original copies of the *Redeemer's Witness*, from which the material in this chapter is provided. Before we present some choice "Bread from Barnard" it is interesting to note that Ernest Reisinger had gotten behind Barnard during this time in promoting Rolfe's ministry through the distribution of reel-to-reel tapes to young preachers. In fact, each issue of the *Redeemer's*

Witness contained a box at the bottom of the page with the following caption:

Attention Young Preachers!

The Rolfe Barnard Evangelistic Association, through a friend of the gospel [this was Reisinger, author's note], offers a series of messages on tape for use of preachers. The tapes are not for sale but for use. They may be obtained, four messages at a time, until series is exhausted. The messages are all directed toward instructing young preachers in the how of preaching to lost men. They are the thinking of Evangelist Barnard as a result of 30 years as an evangelist. A small deposit will be required to be returned in full when all tapes have been returned. I express the hope that you who read this will be helped as you avail yourself of these tapes. They may be secured by writing Mr. Ernest Reisinger, 262 Graham, Carlisle, Pennsylvania.

The *Redeemer's Witness* eventually went from a monthly to a bimonthly periodical. Both men were busy with their primary ministries and time and financial constraints (they never broke even on this pen ministry—it was a huge financial cost to them) forced them to reduce the issues to six a year from the original twelve. The last issue of 1967 contained the following words, "Who knows what 1968 will bring forth? With the coming of every new year it is our frequent hope that *this will be the year* of the great revival we are all praying for. By God's help we will continue to proclaim the message to that end!" Unfortunately, this was to be the last issue of the *Redeemer's Witness* for one of the Redeemer's witnesses, Rolfe Barnard, went home to glory in 1969.

We hope you enjoy the following insights of Rolfe Barnard. They are cutting and meant to have an edge to awaken sleeping ministers. Yet, they were meant to encourage also the discouraged pastor who needed fresh nourishment from the "Bread from Barnard" articles which appeared regularly in his mail box. We will begin with the very first issue dated, Volume 1, No. 1 which appeared in April 1964. The turbulent sixties were a time of unrest in America as the social fabric of the nation was changing dramatically. Some of the articles of "Bread from Barnard" are dated to their time (Communism, issues pertaining to the sixties, etc). The following articles were hand-picked for this chapter and are considered "classic Barnard" which typify his ministry from this time period. They need to be carefully read as they are as relevant today as when Rolfe penned them, so we hope you enjoy these selections of "Bread from Barnard."

Bread from Barnard: Volume 1, No. 1 April 1964

G. Campbell Morgan, greatly used Bible teacher of yesteryears trace the gospel as to its content as follows: "You and I are accustomed to hearing the gospel preached along the familiar lines of man is a sinner, he is utterly incapable of securing his own salvation, either by himself or by any means he can create: God in love toward men gave Jesus Christ, who gives Himself for our sins that He might deliver us from this present evil world. But we do not enter into the fulness of the grace of God by any casual act: we do not drift into divine mercy. It requires the decisive action of our will to trust and commit ourselves to Him. If we do this, we get the gift of eternal life; and not only for time but also for eternity is the heart and spirit then secure. If we fail and turn our backs upon the grace of God, then weeping and wailing and gnashing of teeth in the outer darkness is the ultimate portion of the soul.

That in brief says Morgan is the general line. It is not wrong but it is not the message of the gospel as preached by those nearest the birth, life, death, resurrection and ascension of the sovereign Redeemer. Continues Mr. Morgan, "Come to the Acts of the Apostles and you will find that the primitive evangelism was *not* preached like that. The Saviourhood of Christ was never questioned nor denied but the emphasis was His sovereignty. His love was never questioned but God had made that same Jesus whom they crucified both Lord and Christ. The emphasis was on the lordship of Jesus. The challenge concerns the supremacy of God has given the sovereignty that is now His by reason of the salvation that He wrought for you and me on Calvary's cross."

This of course is only the thinking or deduction of one man, but I submit that it is well worth re-reading, until we are willing to face the fact that so little gospel preaching now emphasizes what the early preachers did. The little paper you are now reading is dedicated to the proposition that while Christ cannot be divided, He must be proclaimed as He is now, absolute Lord of all the universe. One of the keenest minds of our day has this to say, "This is a day of revivals that do not revive; evangelism which does not evangelize; salvation which does not save." I am under deep conviction that the statement just given is substantially true, and I am further deeply convinced that the only hope today is a return to preaching the Christ the early apostles and preachers proclaimed: The ascended, ruling, interceding, saving Lord of glory, who got on the throne by way of a virgin's womb, sinless life, a substitution, horrible, bloody death, a mighty resurrection and a glorious enthronement by Almighty God.

This is a day when our Lord Jesus Christ is being challenged concerning His sovereignty and power. Three-fourths of the world have struck tents and humanity is on the march. This lawless spirit is felt in every realm, social, political, religious. This is the time to reaffirm and proclaim the sole authority and absolute sufficiency of the Son of God. There is no middle ground here. The problem is not gray. It is black or white. We must have a Super Church, a Super Government or a Sovereign Redeemer. Of one thing I am certain, it is all or nothing now. It is thorough going orthodoxy or thorough going infidelity. One or the other will survive. They are in a death struggle as I write these words. Methods may be debatable but the message for this hour and every other hour is not. Men are not being confronted these days by and large, with the truth about Jesus Christ, with His absolute authority, His God-given sovereignty. Men will quickly accept a Savior if we soft pedal His absolute authority. No man will accept the Bible Christ apart from the miracle of grace. It is high time we cease to offer men the blessings of salvation divorced from the acceptance, and that gladly, of the rule or authority of Christ in their lives. In subsequent issues we propose to implement the above thinking by a study of the preaching in the Acts of the Apostles.

Rolfe Barnard

Bread from Barnard, Volume II, No. 4 June-July, 1965

There are two things about current Christianity? and present day gospel? preaching that alarm me quite painfully. First: all of a sudden the gospel? has gotten quite popular. One wonders where the offence has gone. Second: this gospel presents a Christ who does not change and transform lives as He touches them. I wonder if many do not share my concern here. The noble, the wise, the mighty are sponsoring the gospel now? "And religious America attends church on Sunday morning and enters hell that night." Faced as I am with the burden and privilege of proclaiming the gospel, responsible for tending with my small potato patch, I have been camping for some time in the first two chapters of Paul's first letter to the church at Corinth. One cannot do this without being brought up sharply against the contrast in Paul's presentation of the gospel and its results and that of our own day. For this and subsequent issues of this page I wish to sit with my readers at the feet of Paul praying for a recovery of his offensive but transforming message, for I deeply believe that if such a message is not proclaimed, the world in our own generation is going to get converted and go on to Hell.

Let us graze around somewhat freely in the passage, 1 Corinthians 1:17 through chapter 2. Let us for this moment look at Paul's preaching that resulted in changed lives. We read as follows in the Authorized Version, these words: *"And I, brethren, when I came to you, came not with excellency of speech or of wisdom, declaring unto you the testimony of God. For I determined not to know any thing among you, save Jesus Christ, and him crucified."* A very literal translation of this passage reads as follows: "As for myself, having come to you, brethren, I came not having my message demonstrated by transcending rhetorical display or philosophical subtlety. When I announced to you the testimony of God. For after weighing the issues, I did not decide to know anything among you except Jesus Christ, and this very One as crucified," or "this very One having been crucified."

Here is brief commentary on apostolic preaching. The whole book of the Acts of the Apostles is found here. How was Christ proclaimed? Note carefully that Paul began with a living Lord and worked backwards. Today most preaching is in the exact opposite direction. Thus the Person who is now alive forever more and who alone transforms men is lost in the journey and the gospel is well nigh exhausted before His person is proclaimed. A word from another is helpful here. The Scottish theologian, James S. Stewart, of Edinburgh comments here, "Such a declaration might appear to justify those treatments of the atoning work which focus all attention on the earthly ministry of Jesus and the cross in which it is culminated, and either omit the resurrection altogether or else bring it in only as epilogue not essential to the drama of redemption. But this would be to seriously misunderstand the apostle's meaning, for "knowing Christ" means here precisely what it means regularly in Paul: the primary reference is not to the Jesus of history, but to the exalted, ever present Lord. Hence the historic phrase, "Knowing Christ and him crucified" indicates the direction of the apostle's thought: it is moving, not as is often supposed, forward through the earthly life to the final act on Calvary, but backward from the risen life to the sacrifice which lay behind it. Christ alive forever: this is the viewpoint at which Paul takes his stand to gaze upon the cross and to preach Christ, the one having been crucified. It is one thing to preach the cross as the last word of revelation. It is quite another thing to preach it as the road traveled once for all by one now known to be alive forever."

What this man is saying is simply this: Paul went to Corinth and confronted men with a living sovereign Lord, alive forever more, reigning at the right hand of the Majesty on high, exalted on a throne forever, given all authority now and forever, having been installed there by way of a bloody tree and in virtue thereof. It is this Jesus that this generation of fact believing church people do not know experientially and thus have not been made new creations in Him.

If we would see lives changed we must recover the proclamation of a living Lord, raised and seated on the throne of power and authority. It is this one who gives eternal life to as many as the Father has given Him, and this eternal life is to know by experience God through Jesus Christ. Multitudes of sincere people today believe in the fact of the glorious death of Christ but have never by faith laid hold of the living Lord and been changed by His powerful touch. But salvation is to be touched.

Someone has said, "A Christian filled with the Holy Ghost is the redemption counterpart of the fanatical devotee of political religion, people consumed by the inner fire of the Spirit are the counterpart in human life of the smashed atom which releases cosmic force. It is necessary that the Word of God become incarnate in my flesh in a spiritual sense, that Christ be formed in me, revealed in me, and not simply to me. What we need, if we are to match this hour is men who are utterly Christian, in whom the full potentiality of spiritual life becomes manifest." Surely today if anything will shake and persuade the mockery spirit of the hour, it will not be our arguments but the degree of our conviction and that depends always upon the reality of our personal commitment to the risen Lord. This is what is behind Paul's, "I determined."

Samuel Rutherford wrote to a friend from prison: "Jesus Christ came into my cell last night, and every stone flashed like a ruby." Here is a Christian. Here is a man who knew a living Lord. This is the result of men being confronted with a living Lord in all the truth of His cross and His throne. This is salvation. This is to be translated from the kingdom of darkness into the kingdom of His dear Son. "So be it, Lord! Thy throne shall never, like earth's proud empires pass away. Thy kingdom stands and grows forever, till all Thy creatures own Thy sway."

We must preach, proclaim, gossip, testify, this living Lord who got on a throne by way of a cross and who gives life to as many as He will. Let men be shut up to a living, vital union with Him or the pangs of eternity utterly separated from His bliss and blessing.

Bread from Barnard, Volume II, No. 6 October, 1965

It is "Repent or Perish" for present day evangelism. These are harvest days. The crop is now being reaped. What we have sown and watered is come to maturity and the barns are full. Behold what we have done. We have spawned this great Religious Monster called Christendom or Christianity? The barns, we fear, are filled with more tares than wheat. The net seems to contain more snails than salmon. Behold thrice religious America; and thrice pagan America. More church members and riots in the streets. A Bibleless, Christless monster on our hands threatening to continue to count noses, while Rome burns. Can it be that the message and method of popular, successful evangelism need to be summoned to the bar and examined as to guilt and accomplices after the fact.

One encouraging sign of the times in our day is that many are seeking to examine the culprit, viz, modern, popular, successful? evangelism. Few are boasting these days. Burdened, almost defeated, pastors and evangelists are almost shut up to honest confession and earnest entreaty. Some are well nigh at the place of resorting to the Bible message and method of obeying our Lord's command to evangelize all nations. It may be that the time is not too far off when the many books will be studied again. In that Book is to be the message to be proclaimed and the methods to be followed. May God hasten such a day.

Just how much responsibility for the "status quo," which is Latin for the "mess we are in," should be laid on present day evangelism is, of course, a matter of opinion. Of one thing I am reasonably certain, the "much" or the "how much" is enough to justify a conviction that we must set ourselves to the task of slaying the evil giants of evangelism today. The preaching of a perverted gospel and the use of man-devised methods which we thought would be so much more successful than Bible methods and message must be challenged, destroyed, and replaced if possible with true evangelism. Let me single out one of these "giants" and if space permits, offer them a word of caution.

The "giant" I thus now expose is as follows: Today's evangelism has become a thing of externalism. This is made manifest by, among others, the following:

A. By legalism on the one hand and antinomianism on the other. Churches today are heavily loaded with people who make their own rules and live by them, and others who have done away with all law in the name of liberty. Pharisees in one corner, thanking God they are not as others and profligates in the other, sinning the more because of abounding grace. Both miss the mark and bring reproach on the name of the Lord. One need not experience the new birth to be either of the two here mentioned. We need a John Wesley and a George

Whitefield to return with their one message of an inward work of grace in man's life which changes also the outside.

B. By a faith which is mere intellectual assent. What a rebuke needs to be administered to us today, who, perhaps in our zeal to simplify the way of salvation, tell the sinner that faith is like stepping onto a motor bus, or agreeing to buy an insurance policy, as though faith had no moral quality and involved no moral decision. The keynote of faith and knowledge must be love. It has always been so. We have disunited faith from love and forgiveness from purity. The soul of true religion is still love, humility and obedience. The true gospel is of the Spirit not the letter.

C. By a widespread tendency in many professedly evangelical circles today, namely, where salvation by grace through faith is quite openly treated as a separate thing from a life of self-denial and cross bearing. Again it must be insisted that Christ can be known only in discipleship.

D. By methods of evangelism, which methods of course must logically follow the perverted message of "another Jesus," wherein physical acts of people, viz, hand showing, signing on the dotted line, walking an aisle, coming to the "altar of prayer" etc., etc., are of more account than humility and repentance. We have succeeded far too well in divorcing justification and sanctification and in our success are sending souls to the judgment seat clothed in the garments of a tight evangelical formula without any inward conformity to the law of Christ. Martin Luther, who was given a copy of the book, *German Theology*, the voice of the pre-Reformation Reformers and then wrote that he owed more to it than any other book, save the Bible and the writings of Augustine, imbibed the spirit of these his predecessors. To him repentance was not the mere overture to salvation, it was the permanent ground and condition of it. The first of his ninety-five theses rang the death knell of all externalism whether found in Rome or modern evangelism. Here it is: "When Jesus Christ in the Gospels says, 'Repent' He means that the whole life be one of repentance." That death knell must be sounded again.

E. By the popular espousal of antinomianism in its worst possible form, the idea that it is possible to "take" Christ as

196

Saviour without also "taking" Him as Lord. This evil giant must be dethroned.

F. By a scrupulous avoidance today of the fact of the inwardness of true salvation and the reality of union with God. At the age of 85, Nicholas of Basle was arrested and burned as a "heretic." The chief crime of which he was accused was that he "audaciously affirmed that he was in Christ and Christ was in him." The preaching of such men as Nicholas was that the union of the soul with God is the ultimate goal and that this can only be affected by the denial and dethronement of self, and the incoming and enthronement of God; godliness is unselfishness: a godly life is the steadfast working out of inward freeness from self: to become godlike is the bringing back of man's first nature. They set forth a living Christ who must be embraced, not merely historically as an article of faith but much more as a principle of life, inasmuch as His highest and full significance lies in the fact that He perpetuates and reproduces Himself anew in man. The life-giving power is not the letter but the spirit, not the work but the disposition. It requires of man to strive after God in Christ, goodness and virtue, not for the sake of reward or merit, but from the purest love and because these are the highest, noblest and most desirable objects. Surely we must have once more this vital note in our evangelism or we perish!

Bread from Barnard, Volume III, No 1 January-February 1966

Four Thoughts on the Lordship of Christ

I. His Lordship Is Real

The basic truth of all truths is *Jesus is Lord*. This is the rock upon which all else rests. The very name "Lord" implies that He is ruler, one who has authority. Therefore all others are His subjects. As Lord he can brook no rivals. Christ's lordship lies in the realm of fact, not of theory. It is a matter of history, not of idea. For one to be Lord does not mean for him to discuss or confer about the ideas of lordship and to persuade people in their minds that his rule is a good thing. It is rather to meet men with terms to be accepted, which if not accepted must be established by action. Lordship is an achievement not an idea. It is a reality not a thought. Here then is much misunderstanding by both friend and enemy. Christianity is not a way of looking at life—a philosophy. It is not a way of living—an ethic. It is not a set of ideas about God—a theology. It involves all these but it is basically other than these. It is an event, a deed, an accomplishment, a victory. Speaking of his own work, our Lord said, *"No man can enter into a strong man's house, and spoil his goods, except he will first bind the strong man; and then he will spoil his house."* In order to establish his lordship, therefore, it was necessary *"that the prince of this world be cast out,"* and that was not done by conference. It was done by costly action on a cross. The gospel therefore is the good news of that costly action. This is not an idea. This happened. The early church believed and preached that God had acted in the behalf of man. Here is the heart of the Christian faith. Paul insists that this was not his "slant" only. This he had received from the others. He held this in common with them. What was it that they held in common? It was that the gospel was the proclamation of a series of events wrought by God in Christ. He brought the new age by dying for sinners, by rising on the third day and by ascending to the right hand of God, where He now reigns in exaltation *"far above all principality, and power, and might, and dominion, and every name that is named, not only in this world, but also in that which is to come"* He will also come again to bring to light the things now hidden in darkness and to disclose the purposes of the heart. Something wonderful has taken place. It is neither theology, philosophy or ethics. It is a simple story of facts. Christ is Lord because these facts are true. His lordship is real.

II. As Lord, Christ Demands Unconditional Surrender of His Subjects

Our Lord demands from men not admiration, sympathy, interest, approval; He demands surrender. To be a Christian is first of all to "bow the knee" to Him, to crown Him Lord of all. Friend, He is as well as counselor, example, guide, but before all these He is absolute Lord. "For the Lord, our God, the Almighty reigns" was the theme song of the early church. Someone has pointed out that in this sense Christianity is not a democracy but a monarchy, and it is not a constitutional monarchy, wherein subject and ruler agree on the limits of rule. It is an absolute monarchy. Men are subject to Him not by a compact they have made with Him, but because they belong to Him. Thank God, His lordship is not capricious or arbitrary for it is exercised as an expression of His gracious nature, but that gracious nature is not of our choice and His kindness is not the result of an agreement which we have forced on Him. It is the free exercise of His own nature. We receive but do not contribute. He reigns over men absolutely in virtue of His lordship. It is our source of blessing that His lordship is graciously enforced. God's people confront the world, therefore, not primarily with an offer to heal its ills or solve its problems. Our first appeal is to rebels who have taken up arms against their Creator; an appeal which is nothing less than the demand for surrender.

III. There Is Therefore No Way of Salvation Open for Men Apart from Unconditional Surrender to Christ as Lord

In this sense at least, Christianity is absolutely intolerant. Both the Old and the New Testaments are clear here. *"For I am God, and there is none else."* What then? The conclusion is inevitable: Turn to me and be saved. If there is no God but one, then He is the God of all men, and there can be salvation in no other. The N. T. says, *"For there is none other name under heaven given among men, whereby we must be saved."* Christ does not simply add to the world's knowledge. He is not the crown of a process. He is not the capstone to be placed on the pillar of other faiths. He does not supplement other religions; He supplants them. Thus our message is absolutely intolerant and adamant. This world belongs to Him. All other efforts at salvation are in vain. All who are saved are saved by Him. He saves men by establishing his rule over them.

Despite criticism from whatever quarter and however intense it may be, this dogmatic message, this absolute call for total surrender, must not be silenced. If God has done what the Bible says He has in Christ, it is not the mark of intolerance to tell men of His great act. He has put all things under Christ our Lord. Let all men hear of this, the one great fact of time and eternity. If one should be in a burning building with many doors, but only one moved open, should not one with desperate demand and command point to that door alone. To keep silent is to shame Christ and bring reproach on

Him. God grant His Spirit of boldness upon us that we may cry aloud to all whom we touch that He is the door, the only door, the way, the only way; the Lord, the only Lord. Bow down in loving, glad surrender and worship Him who is worthy.

IV. The Lordship of Christ Shall One Day Be Manifested in Total Victory at His Reappearing

Now by suasion, then by power men shall bow to confess Him as Lord. That which Christ has begun, He will complete. He was not only the fulfillment of promise; He was also the promise of fulfillment. Since His lordship is real, it is blessedly true that what is true in the heavenly places where Christ is seated at the right hand of God, must be true in the whole created universe which is now in rebellion against Him.

Bread from Barnard, Volume III, No. 2 March-April 1966

There is a nominal Christianity which is accepted and approved of men, but the pure gospel is still despised and rejected. The real Christ of today, among men, is unknown and unrecognized as much as He was among His own nation nineteen hundred years ago. Christ in doctrine, Christ in Spirit, Christ in life; the world cannot endure as King. It is all right for men to chant about Him in cathedrals, or sing about Him in synagogues, or preach about Him in pulpits; but Christ honestly obeyed, followed and worshipped in simplicity, without pomp or form, Christ exalted as prophet, priest, and King (not later, but now) they will not allow to reign over them. It is as a spiritual Lord that Christ claims sovereignty among men.

Somewhere in my reading I came across the expression, "The richness of the ascension." I was struck by the expression because so little is said or written these days about the tremendous act of both the Father and the Son by which the gospel of God concerning His Son is brought to its climax. A gospel that does not speak of an ascended Lord is not the gospel of God. If the gospel is Christ and Christ is the gospel, and surely this is true; we must proclaim a Christ risen, exalted and reigning.

He must be preached where He is now and identified as the pre-existent, virgin born, sinlessly living, vicariously dying, Son of the living God. Always the apostles preached the living Christ and worked backward, a decided reverse from the gospel of today. This is God's good news. How can Christ be preached if He is not preached where He is now? If Christ be risen and exalted, the rest is easy to accept. If not, the virgin birth and everything else cannot be accepted. The whole pattern of the gospel story sinks or swims on the truth or falsity of the resurrection and exaltation. In the classic passage, Philippians 2:9-11, Paul says, *"Wherefore God also hath highly exalted him, and given him a name which is above every name ... that every tongue should confess that Jesus Christ is Lord, to the glory of God the Father."* The word *hupsoo*, which is translated "exalted" is never used of the resurrection. It is the word for "ascension" or "exaltation." Thus it was by His ascension that Jesus was marked out to be Lord, as by His resurrection He was marked out to be the Son of God in power (Romans 1:4). By the resurrection Jesus is seen to be Victor over death and corruption. By the ascension, He is seen to be Lord, with all power in heaven and earth (Matthew 28:18). As sin was shown to be subject to Him by His sinless life; as death was shown to be subject to Him by His resurrection; so all things in heaven and earth are shown to be subject to Him by His ascension. It was not that the ascension effects His lordship any more than the resurrection effects His victory over death. Rather, the ascension is the designation and the demonstration of His lordship. It is the designation in that it is the reward of the Father for His perfect obedience. In His humanity He was subject to His Father. It is demonstration since He ascended of His own will, His own power and in His own right. It is true to say that God raised Him and that He raised Himself. God took Him up and He ascended of His own power.

Peter points out the tremendous significance of the ascension as he comes to the climax of his sermon on the day of Pentecost. He quotes first from Psalm 110, and then says, *"Therefore [in view of the ascension] let all the house of Israel know assuredly, that God hath made that same Jesus, whom ye have crucified, both Lord and Christ."* The climax of gospel preaching *must* be here. This is God's answer and act. Men killed Jesus, God exalted Him. Let us preach this Jesus; Peter writes, *"Who [Jesus Christ] is gone into heaven, and is on the* right hand of God; angels and authorities and powers being made subject unto Him" (1 Peter 3:22). This is true. It is true now, not in some distant future. Where is the crucified Christ now? He is at the right hand of God. All things are under Him now. Brethren, the hour is late. It is long since time that this generation hear the "gospel," not just a part of the chain but all of it. The whole Christ is the gospel, nothing less, nothing more.

The apostle Paul in Ephesians 4:8 quotes from Psalm 18 and portrays a wonderful picture in this connection, *"He led captivity captive."* The ascension is the triumphal return to heaven of the Son of God. He has conquered and He returns with the captives of war. Sin and death, those enemies of man and God, those tyrants which had enslaved men and themselves now subjected and held captive to Him who openly triumphed over them. The power of sin is broken; it shall not lord it over the believer. Death is swallowed up in victory, its reign ended. Christ the Conqueror rules and He shall rule *"till he hath put all enemies under his feet"* (1 Corinthians 15:25). For the apostles here is greatly needed help and hope. They see now that the resurrection proclaimed a King after all. The suffering Servant is enthroned, this same Jesus. His kingdom indeed is and shall be glorious, but it shall not be the glory of this world. He is and shall be victorious, but His victories shall not be achieved through the blood and steel of men. The cross was the decisive and atoning conflict. The resurrection was the proclamation of triumph. The ascension was the conqueror's return with the captives of war which issued in the enthronement of the victorious King.

Away with the preaching of a pitiable, helpless Jesus. He is not an exile hopefully watching to see what happens. He is the enthroned Lord into whose nail-pierced hands the control of all things and all men has been given. It needs to be shouted from the housetops now as perhaps never before that everything depends on a man's union with a living, present Saviour. In the absence of that union, even the gospel of the cross loses its saving efficacy. *"If Christ be not raised, your faith is vain; ye are yet in your sins"* (1 Corinthians 15:17).

Atonement remains impersonal and largely irrelevant until we make contact with the One who atones; and contact of a vital kind is possible only if Jesus is risen, alive and on the throne now. James Denney in his book, *The Christian Doctrine of Reconciliation*, says that, "nothing could be more curiously unlike the New Testament than to use the resurrection to belittle or disparage the death." But we do not disparage the death of our Lord, we simply insist that unless Christ is now enthroned, the death is powerless to save. We insist that without a living, present, reigning Christ, with whom through faith the believer can come into union, all the benefits of His death would have had to stand unappropriated forever. It was on the resurrection and ascension fact that the church was built. This was the gospel of the apostles. It was the experience of union with the risen, exalted, living Lord that made them conquerors. Let their gospel once more be preached.

Bread from Barnard, Volume III, No. 3 May-June 1966

The World's Greatest Debtor

The greatest product of God's redeeming grace, Paul the apostle said, *"I am debtor both to the Greeks, and to the Barbarians; both to the wise, and to the unwise"* (Romans 1:14). The world's greatest debtor! Paul would claim that title. The world's greatest debt! What is it? Without doubt it is the debt that redeemed sinners owe the God who saved them. Paul will say, *"And I thank Christ Jesus our Lord,"* or he will say, *"When it pleased God ... to reveal his Son in me."* However this is a debt that can never be fully paid but this sense of thankfulness and of being forever indebted to the God of all grace will of necessity lead to Paul's statement in our text. Having drunk at the fountain of blessing, he will be all things to all men if by any means he may save some. The apostle, I doubt not, could with zest sing the blessed song, "He Touched Me." Here are the lines:

> *Shackled by a heavy burden,*
> *Neath a load of guilt and shame;*
> *Then the hand of Jesus touched me,*
> *And now I am no longer the same.*
> *He touched me, oh, He touched me,*
> *And, oh, the peace that floods my soul.*
> *Well something happened and now I know,*
> *He touched me and made me whole.*

I can almost hear this blessed man singing,

I never traveled far around the world,
I have never seen the many thrills and sights unfurled,
But I have taken the journey of journeys for me;
Up Calvary's mountain there my Savior to see.
I have been to Calvary, I can say I've seen the Lord,
I have been to Calvary thro' the witness of God's Word.
Each day at Calvary, oh, what a thrill of love divine,
Just to think that the Savior is mine.

Here we are most surely confronted with the world's greatest need. What is it? The answer must be: men who have something in them that drives them to seek to pay their debt to God by sharing the saving gospel with others. One surely gives the lie to his claim of being a "saved one" if he does not feel as this man felt. Mr. Finney said, "If you do not live to save others you are not saved yourself." I wonder if that statement is true. It is a sharp indictment. What does make us (today's Christians?) tick? Why are we what we are and why do we do as we do? Do we share the Redeemer's passion for lost men? Can one be "saved" and not share it? I wonder.

Twentieth century Christianity seems to be quite comfortable, thank you. Never were God's fat sheep more at ease in Zion. Today our church life is marked all too much by two tragic facts; first: we have ignored God's prophets who seek to call us to arms to invade Satan's territory and rescue the perishing—as a result prophets are becoming scarce. Perhaps God is withdrawing His voice and will cease to disturb us anymore. At any rate never were there more comfortable priests and fewer flaming prophets, and the people would have it so. We want blessing but not disturbance, peace at the alarming price of deadness— "Please do not disturb" is our motto.

Second: under comfortable priests we comfortable people have a very comforting religion on Sunday morning that does not challenge our emotions and does not call us to induce inner travail of soul for the sake of gaining spiritual victories. Well nigh totally absent is flaming zeal; men on fire, churches on fire. Our Christianity is not worth shouting about nor sacrificing for by the giving of ourselves to its spread. We have painted sin until it is no longer to be feared. We have made a doormat and a fire escape out of Jesus Christ until the Lord of glory is the "unknown" God of modern Christians. We have made salvation a myth instead of a way of life. Our greatest need is for somebody to come on the scene as a voice crying in the wilderness, a somebody who really believes that men are really lost and Christ is the only remedy. Blessed Gypsy Smith used to say that he hoped the Lord would come again to the earth between the hours of eleven and twelve on Sunday morning, else his people would be greatly embarrassed.

Does someone reading these lines know how to cry aloud to this generation, so at ease, while all hell pops everywhere; while the foundations crumble all about us; while immorality replaces immortality; while lukewarmness overcomes the fire; I wish I did! I will listen to anyone who can come to the kingdom for such an hour as this. In my burden and utter dismay I offer four suggestions that may challenge some of us to get on fire.

(1) Remember the pit from whence we were dug; Paul was often calling on the saints to "remember" how in times past ye were, etc., *"and such were some of you." "But God, who is rich in mercy." "Who was before a blasphemer, and a persecutor, and injurious: but I obtained mercy."* Surely such "remembering" would cause us to have compassion on people who are still in the ditch from which we were snatched by the God of all grace.

(2) Reflect often upon the wonder of God's so great salvation. Burdens were lifted at Calvary, so says the popular song. Peace, sweet peace, the gift of God's love; the life of the Spirit, heaven on the way to heaven; a clear slate, a fresh start. To have been changed with a change that keeps on changing until one is conformed to the likeness of Christ. The wonder of salvation. God grant that the wonder of it all may be restored in hearts and churches. "O, what a wonder, that Jesus found me. Out in the darkness, no light could I see. O what a wonder, He put His great arm under, and wonder of wonders: He saved even me." Surely so to reflect will touch the foundations of the deep and of such touched hearts shall flow again healing waters to bless our parched land.

(3) Reflect often on the actual, real, condition of the

lost. Here the "color" is not grey, it is actually black. There is no in between here; men are lost, blind, hostile, helpless, dead, seeking things but not God, absolutely obnoxious to the judgment of a thrice holy God. Their condition is desperate; their destiny is utterly terrible; their need though unfelt is beyond words to describe. They need not a helping hand, not a push or a shove: they need a Savior who is Christ Jesus the Lord. One who has been rescued must surely get involved in the task of rescuing. Head belief in the Bible teaching about unutterable torment of the lost will not suffice; this must be heart belief and of such intensity that once again it may be true of us that *"They that sow in tears shall reap in joy."*

(4) Ponder much the glory of God's purpose in grace. Salvation is God-purposed not a result of fate or blind chance. There is no maybe-so here. God purposes to save and to save sinners. None are too big or too sinful for God to save. God's record in the past encourages us in the "now." No sinner too vile—abandon hope therefore for none. Where sin abounds, grace doth much more abound. God saved Manasseh. God saved Saul of Tarsus. God saved *you*. He would have no trouble saving the biggest sinner out of hell since he was able to save you.

We preach a saving God; a saving gospel. Be thou encouraged in the Lord.

Bread from Barnard, Volume III, No. 6 November-December 1966

Evangelism

To begin at the beginning let us refresh and sharpen our minds and hearts with a definition of (1) *evangelism* and (2) an *evangelist*. When we have made this venture to the best of our ability, we shall suggest some four obstacles that stare us in the face. If space permits we shall conclude with a brief word about "effectual doors" opened to Christ's church.

Just what, then, is evangelism? No better definition of evangelism is to be found than this: evangelism is the prosecution of Christ's marching orders to His church. We call it the Great Commission.

Invested with all authority by God the Father, the risen, enthroned Lord gives to His church her age long task. Go, preach, baptize, teach. There is no provision for furloughs, rest periods or new tasks. His church is to be everlastingly at this task. There is to be no withdrawal from the world, always it is a going to the world. There is to be no arriving at a position and digging in to hold such position. The church is to be continually on the march, pressing the battle in enemy territory. It needs to be emphasized over and over again that evangelism is the prosecution of all the commission. Not simply winning men to a decision but making rebellious men Christian.

What then is an evangelist? We are told in Ephesians 4, that the enthroned Lord gave gifts, some apostles, prophets, evangelists, and some pastors and teachers. We need to take a new and hard look here. As we do we discover afresh that evangelism is not the task of a few or many "gifted" men, but of the whole church which is the body of Christ. Not to be separated or detached from the whole, the evangelist is seen in the New Testament as having two jobs; first he plants churches. Second, he corrects churches when they get out of order. Such was the ministry of Paul. His authority was to be found in the fact that he was a "gift" of the Lord. His authority was questioned and disputed by some and received by others. Where received, the church was set again in order for her task of evangelism. How far removed from this are we today! The result: churches which employ "gifted" men to do what the risen Lord tells the church to do. The result: churches full of people who pay somebody else to do what all are called to do. The result: churches that are not going, preaching, baptizing, teaching. The result: a world in militant rebellion not being invaded by armies of Christ's church pressing Christ's claims upon all men.

Allow me to present two quotations from our last issue in the context of what I have written thus far. "What will bring them together (people from 106 nations in the World Congress held in Berlin) is their awareness that an hour has struck in the world affairs for a mighty evangelistic offensive again." "But obedient fulfillment of the Great Commission requires every single disciple of Jesus Christ to be a faithful witness." All this brings us to face the tremendous obstacles that must be tackled if a mighty offensive of evangelism is to get off the ground.

It is of course to be taken for granted that Satan and his forces constitute the obstacle we face. Evangelism prospers only and as his power is bound. But I suggest that evangelism is almost hated now and Satan's kingdom flourishes, and this I believe to be true for four reasons. These four cannot be entirely separated but I offer them in order that they may be addressed, faced and overcome in the power of the Holy Spirit who alone makes Christ's power manifest. They are as follows:

(1) The unevangelized church cannot evangelize a lawless world. (2) Mild mannered preachers delivering mild sermons to mild mannered congregations cannot make a dent on a world saturated with the spirit of anti-Christ. (3) A continued presentation of a "gospel" which upon being believed leaves men still in rebellion against the throne rights and claims of the sovereign Redeemer cannot be the vehicle used of God to produce revival in our time. (4) The militant, anti-Christian climate in a world gone mad against the one great, eternal, irrevocable act of God when He raised His well beloved Son from the grave and sat Him down on a throne.

It is agreed that generalizations are always subject to exceptions but the exceptions to the first three obstacles here cited. Now and again a local church and of course that is the only kind we have, gives evidence of obedience to its Head and thus is making some impact on the lawless climate it invades.

Here and there is to be found a prophetic voice crying in the wilderness of churchanity. There is some evidence of a resurgence of the whole gospel of a whole Christ who changes everything and everyone He touches.

However, there can be no exception to the fourth statement given above. The climate in this year of our Lord 1966 is militantly anti-Christian—they are violently opposed to the totalitarian claims of King Jesus. Religion—yes. Churchanity—yes. The Christ of God as Lord of life—no! The one issue of this hour and every hour since the rebellion in Eden's garden is authority. God on the throne; man subject to Him there. Here the battle rages and will until all things are summed up in the Christ. "A mighty evangelistic offensive" must therefore mean the proclamation of the Christ of God whom God has invested all authority and made to be Lord of all and over all.

A gospel that produces a salvation apart from glad subjection to and holy adoration and worship of an enthroned Lord cannot be owned of God in our day. A preacher not under authority cannot have authority (utterance) in our day or any other day. Most of us preachers today say "go" and nobody goes. We lack authority. The word of command is ever the way God works—Let there be light and there was light—Stretch forth thine hand and the man with the withered hand does stretch forth his hand—Lazarus come forth, and a dead Lazarus comes forth. Oh, God, give us men lashed to the truth of the Bible which is the truth of a commanding Christ. Nothing short of this will get a hearing in our day.

Men with a holy fear, moving to warn men who have no fear. Men with tears warning a generation obnoxious to the holy judgment of a thrice holy God. My old "Old Testament" teacher was wont to say often to young preachers: "I want to hear in the future that many of you have been fired because of your preaching the 'holiness' of God." Perhaps a great "ejection" is called for today. In England's history we read of some 2,000 pastors removed from their pulpits. I wish something like that could take place in our day as preachers put on the mantle of God's prophets and with boldness and tears attack the apathy and lawlessness within our churches for something must happen to and in our churches. They must become disciplined armies of the Lord, not rest homes for the tired and hospitals for the sick. May God deliver us from seeking to protect ourselves from the disturbing Christ. This lawless generation must be confronted with the Christ of the covenant in the truth of Him; His cross and His throne. This generation has not been so confronted. This generation is a stranger to the enthroned Lord of glory. The Jesus of our popular "gospel" is not the eternal Son of a living God, not the commissioned one of the everlasting covenant. We have had far too much of Paul's "another" spirit. It is the Christ-given task of the church to confront each generation with the gospel of God, concerning His Son. How can our churches be reformed and reborn? How can we preachers speed the word of command and be heard? There are two questions, I believe, are the living, vital questions of this hour.

Surely our prayer must be "Wilt Thou not revive Thy work in the midst of the years," or, "It is time for Thee to work, O Lord, for they have made void Thy law." Dear Spurgeon would say, "Give me men and women who cannot rest, while the crown rights of our Lord are ignored and rejected." Let us become concerned, under God, for the church which He purchased with His own blood. Let us bewail her flight into the wilderness of apathy, confusion and rebellion. Let us proceed to root up the perverted gospel of our day and preach the gospel. Let us confess our bankruptcy, lament our defeatism and face the fact that we are shut up to an intervention by the One who disturbs that He may heal and kills that He may make alive.

Bread from Barnard, Volume IV, No. 1 January-February 1967

The Whole Gospel for the Whole Man to the Whole World

This as perhaps never before must be the word for this hour. Not a part of the gospel and thus no gospel; not for a part of man (the soul) and thus no gospel; it must and will be all or nothing.

The whole gospel for the whole man for the whole world must focus its attention on the one issue of the ages. Let me write to this statement:

Where a Sovereign is crowned in Britain one part of one part of the traditional service is as follows. A golden orb surmounted on a cross is presented to the Sovereign. The words are spoken, "When you see the orb set under the cross, remember that the whole world is subject to the power and empire of Jesus Christ."

This will serve to focus our attention on the one issue of this and every hour. It is the question of authority. Shall God be sovereign and man subject? God's rule and man's rebellion: Here is the controversy and here is the issue. This is the story of Eden's garden and Calvary's cross. Adam (and the whole race in him) rebelled against God's rule and His right to rule. The rebellion was repeated in the lawless cry at Calvary, "Away with Him, crucify Him and release unto us Barabbas."

Whether it be nation, state, city, home, church, or world, the foundation head of the evils we are experiencing now is the doctrine that we can prosper apart from the sovereign rule of Almighty God. By removing the divine rule of human conduct we lay the groundwork for "other" gods. If we will not have the God of the Bible to be our God, we will find other gods. The whole gospel must not skip lightly over God's right to the throne and His exercise of that right. Herein is revealed the fact that man is not a weakling nor a victim but a rebel against God's throne rights. There is a war going on. A state of enmity is the fact of today. Paul tells us that the carnal mind is enmity (hostility) towards God. It is not that man is God's enemy. It goes deeper. An enemy can be reconciled. Enmity cannot. The carnal mind (whole man) is enmity against God. The occasion of the enmity is the "law of God" or in other words, "God as moral governor of the universe." The enmity is revealed by all who do not gladly submit to God's kingly authority as the Sovereign law-giver. Supreme dominion is essential to God's character. One cannot be a friend to God if His rule is hated. Here is the issue; who shall reign, God or man? Let God drop the reins of government, descend from the throne, lay aside His scepter, give up His law and the enmity will cease. But God can as soon cease to be as to give up His right to dominion. He must assert His claim to the throne. He is bound to maintain the dignity, shield the purity and support the honor of His law. One thing is settled, God exercises His right to rule.

Sin is rebellion against the highest throne in the universe. God has spoken in His Son. He has nothing more to say. Men are to honor Him on the throne. This is the issue. We cannot, we dare not set aside this word from heaven. The essence of all sin is arrogance, setting up the little puppet god of self on the throne of the heart instead of the rightful ruler, Jesus Christ. There can therefore be no New Testament salvation without submission to Him on the throne. The very essence of salvation is the collapse of the regime of self and the enthronement of another King.

The word "believe" today means little more than acceptance of truth which still leaves us uncontrolled and uncommitted. This is not peculiar, not the deeper life, it is the gateway to life, at the cross where self is crucified and Christ enthroned. There is no salvation apart from that. The road to hell is more than skid row. It may be the path that brings a man into church membership without the puppet of self having been dethroned. The commitment of oneself to Christ in accepting Him as Lord and Savior is of course the necessary starting point. But the initial decision must be reaffirmed and implemented in the life which follows. Paul says, *"As ye have therefore received Christ Jesus the Lord, so walk ye in him"* (Colossians 2:6). We must continue to choose between the lordship of Christ and the dominion of sin. It never becomes true that we may somehow serve both God and mammon. We cannot negotiate a special arrangement whereby we can serve two masters. We cannot carry water on both shoulders and get along well enough by "doing our bit" for God, while hobnobbing with the devil. One cannot be a part of His people while giving allegiance to the world, the flesh and the devil.

A mild "religion" must disappear in this our day. It must be glad submission to God's Christ or open flagrant rebellion. There must be no grey, it must be black or white. God's preachers must confront men with an either or. They are under orders to offer the kingdom (rule) of God to all men and command men (all men) to repent of their self righteousness, love of sin and rebellion and receive the message of the kingdom of God as gospel. It is vain for one to speak of faith in Christ as Savior, who is not committed to the lordship of Christ and positively opposing the dominion of lordship of sin in his personal life.

There can be but two reasons why any man is unsaved, whether he has been confronted with the gospel or he is unwilling to accept the conditions of repentance and the discipleship whereby the gospel of Christ may become for him personally *"the power of God unto salvation."* One cannot share His life everlasting apart from repentance toward God. Men today and every day want to be free; free of the lordship of Christ; free from divine restraint; free from holy obligation;

and they are but also free of saving grace, eternal life and all prospect of heaven. Every man is free either of the dominion of Christ and prospect of heaven or of the dominion of sin and fear of hell. Also every man is a slave, of Christ, or Satan. To be free of the tyranny of sin he must accept the lordship of Christ. Take his yoke. No man can have two masters. It must be constantly remembered and everlastingly preached that at the "fall" or the rebellion in Eden's garden two things occurred. First, God's sovereignty was threatened. This issue must and will be settled. It is comforting to look in the back of the book and find the answer. Second, man's wholeness was lost. The natural man now is the unnatural man. Man was made to be governed. Only so is he a whole man. Otherwise he is like a fish out of water. Man was created to be under God. Human personality was designed for something more than self-centered animal existence. Man was made not to stand alone but to be lost in a great purpose. That strange expression, "In whose service is perfect freedom" is still true. Man not under glad subjection to God is not free. Sin is personal slavery instead of obedient freedom. To be free man must be under Him upon whose shoulders the government is given.

Salvation, therefore, is the restoration of God's throneship and man's manhood. From the above assertions I make three observations:

(1) The gospel of God concerning His Son that brings salvation (wholeness) to man is the proclamation of a person in all his offices (prophet, priest, and king) to the whole man, (not three men) but man in a body with a spirit; of a person, I say, in whom and through whom God's sovereignty is restored and man's wholeness regained. God has put all his eggs in one basket. It is Christ over all and Christ in you, the hope of glory; it is man under God's appointed Lord and glad of it. It does not in this life make men perfect but men perfectly happy to be under Him. It is the announcement of a crisis and a process and a crisis by which men are "conformed to the image of God's Son." That is salvation completed.

It is not simply Christ as Savior, but Christ the Savior; it is not Christ as Lord but it is Christ the Lord. It is not the death of Christ, but the Christ who died; it is not the resurrection of Christ but the Christ who was raised. It is Christ, the whole

Christ. It is thus that we are able to understand Paul as he lists the credentials of gospel preaching. In 1 Corinthians, Paul tells us that three things make gospel preaching: *(1)* It is scandalous to the just. *(2)* It is foolishness to the Greeks. *(3)* It is the power of God to the called.

(2) To be "saved" then means to be converted to the rule of God in Christ, to be man under God. It means the consent of the heart to the sovereignty of the Redeemer. Here is wholeness. Christ received with the opened hand but the knee bowed. Men made captives of Christ and thus free. Men most free when they bow to Him. Under His authority is man's freedom and thus his wholeness or salvation and nowhere else. The greatest need of man is to find the right answers to the questions where shall supreme loyalty be given? How may one surrender to someone beyond self? How reign as general manager of the universe? How render up one's sword and swear allegiance to Him? How find freedom by becoming His slave? The usual, self-centered man refuses to recognize the claims of God on his life. He thus attempts to become the ruler of his own life with his will the supreme God. This is sin, the setting up of one's own kingdom in opposition to God. The subject trying to be the sovereign. In a state of open rebellion against God and spiritual deafness to His voice. This is more than an action; it is a condition. Man needs to be saved from this and brought into glad, willing subjection to God in Christ.

(3) It follows therefore that revival, glory, is when Christ is loved on the throne and as Head of the church. Here the battle rages even now. Rebellious church members in a lawless age. Two questions seem to me to be the questions of our hour.

(A) Can a given local assembly be brought to loving submission to Christ? We are shut up to this. Rebels have no message to a rebellious world: how challenging to live in a generation where rebellion seems to be breaking out in a thousand ways within what we call the church. Every public preacher must challenge this condition at whatever the cost.

(B) Can we in our day see men taken captive by Christ? Shall we see a return to a God-centered faith and a departure from man-centered faith? Martin Luther came to see that true faith was not a matter of his needs or desire for peace of mind, but a bowing to God, even if nothing resulted to himself. He thus came to define "salvation" as "the realization of God's will and purpose, whatever that might be rather than the satisfaction of human need." He went so far as to say that those who truly love God "freely offer themselves to all the will of God, even to hell and death eternally" should God so will in order that His will may be fully done. This is strong language. Here the glory of God is central. We could do with some of this stern stuff today.

Holy McCheyne wrote, "Had this evening a more complete understanding of that self-emptying and abasement with which it is necessary to come to Christ. A denying of self, trampling it under foot, a recognition of the complete righteousness and justice of God that could do nothing else with us but condemn us utterly and thrust us down to the lowest hell. A feeling that even in hell we should rejoice in His sovereignty and say all was rightly done."

Solemn stuff! Yes! Maybe this generation needs some of it. God grant that it may be so.

Bread from Barnard, Volume IV, No. 4 July-August 1967

The Problem of the Invitation

After a full lifetime as a traveling evangelist I am deeply concerned about the fact that I, for one, do not yet know how to "give an invitation."

Years since I heard a fellow evangelist, speaking in the old Billy Sunday Tabernacle in Winona Lake, heartbreakingly tell of his soul agony about the matter of the "invitation." I have shared that agony through the years.

A number of years ago, Dr. N. B. Magruder of Louisville, KY, suggested a nationwide conference for the purpose of seeking the "how" of the best possible way of dealing with the problem of the invitation. Such a conference has as yet not been held. I wish it could be. Just recently a friend has sent me a booklet just off the press, by Iain Murray of England. The title of the booklet is *The Invitation System*. The author deals in an objective and I believe Christian way with the popular "invitation system" of today. It is thus fair to say that "invitation" is a matter of deep concern to all who publicly or privately preach the gospel.

Before I write to three facts that have to do with the "invitation" I wish to sincerely invite any and all, whether public preachers or personal witnesses, who read this to write me your thinking on this matter. Perhaps we can learn from one another. I should like to publish this in this column cross sections of opinion on this vital matter.

Here then is my contribution: I shall write to: (1) The importance of the invitation. (2) The content of the invitation. (3) The how of the invitation.

I. The Importance of the Invitation

The invitation must be given and it must be pressed with all urgency, all are agreed here. It is likewise true that all give the invitation after some manner. It is not a disputed point as to whether the invitation is to be pressed. That is settled for us in the Bible. Men must be invited and pressed to scripturally and savingly respond to the message of the gospel. The occasion for dispute is in the manner in which the invitation is pressed. The problem here grows out of three facts as I see it. First, the message (proclamation) and the invitation must be *one*. They are not the same but must not be separated. For instance, justification and sanctification are not the same but they must not be separated. Repentance and faith are not the same but they must not be separated. Salvation and discipleship may not be the same but they must not be separated, etc.

Second, the second fact that makes for the problem of the invitation grows out of the first; namely the invitation must not vitiate or repudiate the message. One must not proclaim that salvation is of the Lord and then invite men to respond as if salvation were of man. This is perhaps the common and popular procedure today. Only the sovereign God knows the awful carnage of souls left in its wake.

Third, the third fact that makes for the problem of the invitation is this: the gospel proclamation comes as a command and demand to men. Repentance and faith are presented as the duty of man, and that right now. All who hear the gospel are duty bound to respond under the main of the judgment of hell for failure so to do. Here is fire, passion, urgency. *"We pray you in Christ's stead, be ye reconciled to God."*

"Woe is me if I preach not the gospel." Sin is raging; death is coming; judgment is real; hell is hot; eternity is long; God's law is consuming. It is repent and believe *now!* The message is the invitation: the invitation is the message; this is important! The problem of the invitation and its tremendous importance are vividly shown in the,

II. Content of the Invitation

Here, of course, we quote the Savior's first gospel invitation. It is recorded in Matthew 11:28-30: *"Come unto me, all ye that labour and are heavy laden, and I will give you rest. Take my yoke upon you, and learn of me; for I am meek and lowly in heart: and ye shall find rest unto your souls. For my yoke is easy, and my burden is light."*

Bible teachers remind us of the "law of the first mention." The first time a truth occurs in the Bible there the meaning of said truth is found and this holds true throughout the rest of the Bible. The first gospel invitation in the ministry of our Lord is here recorded. Here then is the content of the invitation we are to give in His stead. It must not be added to nor deleted. It must be given in its fullness.

The importance of this invitation (and there must be no other given) lies in two facts. First, one cannot come to Christ except by invitation. Here is the glory of Christianity. It is God seeking man! One does not come pell-mell into His presence. One must come by His invitation. It is still true that man cannot by "searching" find God. Thank God for His invitation.

Second, the importance of this invitation, the glory of it, lies in the "One" who gives it. Four tremendous things are revealed about the Savior in the context of His invitation. He is revealed as the Judge of all the earth. Bible teachers call verse 20 of Matthew chapter 11, the continental divide of the ministry of our Lord in the days of His flesh. Here through verse 24, He pronounces, and that for the first time, a judgment on the nation as such, *"Then began he to upbraid."* These verses reveal Him as Judge. He will in verse 28 turn from the nation to the individual.

The die is cast, a nation which rejected Him is judged by Him. It is the Judge of all men who gives the gracious invitation. God pity the man who treats lightly that invitation from his future Judge. He is revealed in verses 25 and 26 as an utter believer in and acceptor of the sovereignty of God. Here He thanks the Father, Lord of heaven and earth, because some things have been hidden from some and revealed to others. From the wise and prudent (in their own esteem) the truth of Himself has been hidden. To the babes these things are revealed. The Savior bows to this hard truth by simply saying, *"Even so, Father: for so it seemed good in thy sight."* Here is unquestioned acceptance of the character of God. The unexplainable is bowed to. This is the One who gives the invitation.

In verse 27, two profound things are claimed by the Savior. First, there is the matter of commitment. *"All things are delivered unto me of my Father."* The declared prime minister of the Godhead is the One who invites. He to whom the conduct of the world has been given: He who controls the destiny of everything that wriggles, man included, is the One who invites. How gracious that He does invite. How utterly damning is the failure to respond.

The second claim of this verse is as follows. It is the matter of revelation. *"No man knoweth the Son but the Father; neither knoweth any man the Father, save the Son, and he to whomsoever the Son will reveal him."* Man is a goner after all is said and done except the Son reveals the Father to him and He reveals the Father to whomsoever He will. Here is hard doctrine. It certainly can be rejected but if accepted a hard fact is before us and that fact is, man must have revelation. Salvation is not man's decision, it is by the Savior's revelation. Here is the very center of the battleground around the invitation. The problem arises from the content or nature of the invitation. Four things are involved here. First, what is it to *"Come unto me"*? Second, what is it to take *"my yoke"*? Third, what is it to *"learn of me"*? Fourth, what is this *"rest unto your souls"*? All of these impressed by the kind of people invited, namely, laboring, heavy laden ones. The old proverb has it that you can lead a mule to water but you can't make him drink. Only thirsty, weary ones will drink or seek rest. All these are involved in the manner of "giving the invitation." By all means let us be sure that the message and the invitation are one in view of these facts.

In inverse order, consider them briefly. The message and invitation must address the condition of the hearer. Who will consider himself invited, unless he be weary and worn and in need of rest. The old song, "All the fitness He requireth is to feel your need of Him" is verily true. But this is a generation of secure people who, if they believe in their heads in God, live as if there were no God, no death, no eternity, no guilt and no need. How to preach to and invite such people is our question.

Again there is the matter of the yoke to be taken and the school in which to be enrolled. Do we need to be reminded that this is part of the Savior's invitation? Sometime since I listened to a much revered Bible teacher as he proved to his own satisfaction that the words, *"Come unto me, all ye that labour and are heavy laden, and I will give you rest"* are addressed to the unsaved. Then the words, *"Take my yoke upon you, and learn of me"* are addressed to the saved. The matter of the yoke and the school are optional according to this good man. More the pity his interpretation fits quite nicely the popular invitation today. Modern day evangelism has divorced the Saviorhood and lordship of Christ. One trust Christ as Savior and if convenient sometime may receive His yoke and begin to learn of Him. No wonder, we have a generation of "saved" people who know nothing of commitment and still less of rest for the soul.

Surely the message and the invitation must comprehend the whole of the content of this invitation. *"Come unto me"* and *"Take my yoke upon you, and learn of me"* without doubt are speaking of the same thing. What does it mean to "come" to Christ? It surely means to receive His yoke and begin to learn of Him. He rests people by putting His yoke on them. We are not to change His invitation either by dividing it as with our Bible teacher or by adding to it. Here we are at the very heart of the problem of the invitation. What does it mean to invite men to "come to Jesus Christ"? How to be true to men by refusing to tamper with the Savior's invitation. There is a great deal involved in "coming to Jesus." This leads to my last word.

III. How to Invite Men to Saving Response to the Savior's Invitation

Here three things confront us.

(1) As to content, all the invitations of the New Testament must agree with this first invitation, given in our text. There are not several invitations; there is just one. It must be that *"Come unto me," "repent ... and believe," "whosoever shall call upon the name of the Lord," "Believe on the Lord Jesus Christ," "If thou shalt confess with thy mouth the Lord Jesus,"* etc., it must be, I repeat, that all these mean the same thing. How best to summon men to this response is our problem. That it is not a physical act is of course self-evident. That it is a spiritual matter is agreed. Here is the danger in "giving" the invitation. Whatever the method used by different groups and in different times we are faced with the fact that men must be urged to respond and at the same time warned not to trust in the form, whatever the form of "physical" action may be. For instance, men are not saved by praying, but at the same time men are not saved apart from praying. Men are not saved by a "mourner's bench" but one must have a mourner's bench in the heart. Men are not saved by an inquiry room, but men must be instructed in the "truth of Christ."

(2) It is, I believe, true that one method of "giving" the invitation may be better than another but that is about as much as one can say. As for me, after some years of living in agony of soul about this matter, I have occasion to fall back on the grace of God more and more. To me the deepest meaning of "grace" is "in spite of." God blesses, uses, saves, heals, etc., "in spite of" our poor message and poorer invitation. Men are saved (some) in our big campaigns "in spite of" all the error. Men are healed, "in spite of" all the error. God uses men "in spite of" themselves. This is not I hope an alibi, it is a fact in which to rejoice.

(3) When the "wind" blows everything seems to work. When the wind (Holy Spirit) does not blow, flesh kills everything it touches. Thus I have written without answering the question, "How best give the invitation?" May a gracious

God pour out His Spirit upon us as we labor in dry fields in these desperate days.

Chapter Twelve

The Man and His Message

To whom God would make known what is the riches of the glory of this mystery among the Gentiles; which is Christ in you, the hope of glory: Whom we preach, warning every man, and teaching every man in all wisdom; that we may present every man perfect in Christ Jesus: Whereunto I also labour, striving according to his working, which worketh in me mightily. — Colossians 1:27-29.

Rolfe Barnard is proof that a man who believes in sovereign grace and then takes those great doctrines and preaches them evangelistically in obedience to the Great Commission, and who sincerely loves lost sinners and desires their conversion to Christ to such a degree that he is willing to weep real tears over them in intercessory prayer, and who is willing to be a daily witness for Christ and aggressively proclaim the full gospel, with all its claims and demands, and call lost sinners to their duty of immediate repentance and faith in Christ, that person will be greatly used of God in the salvation of men.

Rolfe Barnard took the doctrines of grace and proclaimed them in all their beauty and authority and used them as a double-edge Claymore to cut deep into all self-reliance and self-righteousness and brought the sinner to be shut up to God and God alone for mercy. Barnard knew the Holy Spirit had to take those doctrines and make them come alive and incarnate in the sinner's heart and plow up the soil of the heart to receive the Lord of glory. Barnard also knew that if a preacher takes these same great doctrines and merely rejoiced in them and taught them academically as a essay to be considered, or an argument to be won, that the result was *dead formalism*. The main thing that killed Barnard was not disease of his heart but heartbreak over the grace men who would not do what Christ commanded them to do in regard to effectively preaching these truths and living a life of holy obedience to them. He knew that academia was for the classroom and evangelism is for the street corner and he agreed with the apostle Paul's words, *"Who also hath made us able ministers of the new testament; not of the letter, but of the spirit: for the letter killeth, but the spirit giveth life"* (2 Corinthians 3:6). Rolfe Barnard was a man who lived what he preached to the glory of God. He knew that if one was saved by grace and knew it, they would have no choice but to live in obedience to the commands of Christ in proclaiming this same mercy to lost sinners because being the recipient of mercy would propel you to want to see others become the recipients of that mercy as well. Barnard could not understand churches who claimed to be sovereign grace churches and did not have a proactive evangelism which ignited all members from pulpit to the back pew. He had a passionate love for his sovereign grace brethren but with that love came reprimand, if he felt they were not doing what they should in accordance to the grace they had received. Read carefully his comments from a sermon he preached to a sovereign grace audience; it is taken from his sermon, "The Recovery of True Faith":

> People need to give diligence to make their calling and election sure. And the promise is if you do this you'll not fall ... evidently this is just not a verse for us Calvinists to quote. It is fraught with warning. I am reminded of the fact that a perverted understanding of the doctrine of election led to the crucifixion of the Son of God. That' right. There is nothing on earth that plays such havoc with heaven and earth as a doctrine out of place or out of joint! Or a half truth about it. Or a perversion of it! And the whole conflict between my Lord and the leaders of the Jewish people when He was here in the days of His flesh was over the doctrine of election. They said, We have Abraham our father. He said, If you were Abraham's

children you'd have two things. What? His works and his faith. And neither of which you have. There is WARNING and there is DANGER in this one doctrine that so sums up the whole Bible. If you find one word that describes the whole Bible, the whole Old Testament's concerned with the election of a people as a nation. And the whole New Testament is wrapped up in the election of individuals; that's the whole Bible. People that tell me that they do not believe in election have thrown the whole Bible away. Everybody has to believe in it. And bless God, the Pharisees and Scribes they dead sure did. They were as orthodox as all get out and before they changed their conception they crucified the Lord of glory over a perverted conception of the hard truths of the entire Word of God.

I've been asking myself this question, several questions lately, why did Israel lose their election, for she dead sure did. She's been cast aside for awhile. We might differ for how long that while is, but right now she's on the shelf. Lost her calling and election! I've been trying to find out if this is one of the things that were given as an ensample for US lest we follow in the same tracks. Can we learn anything as ministers of God's grace, from the reasons why Israel, the elect covenant nation was cast aside and lost the privileges and forfeit the responsibilities of God's election. Israel was called on to hear God's revelation, listen to God. Israel was called on to reflect God's whole character. And Israel was called upon to be God's missionary agency! And they failed of all three of them. When Jesus, who is God's revelation came, Israel who was charged to hear, didn't hear. And turned down God's revelation. And Israel who was charged to reflect the character of God, turned in on itself and wouldn't even STOP; so busy were the priest and the Levite in their religious course they wouldn't even stop and minister to the man fallen by the wayside. And Israel REFUSED to be God's missionary light and God's missionary agent. Ichabod is written on the DOOR of multiplied thousands of churches, some of them grace, sovereign grace churches—if you please—that don't listen to God. They read John Owen. And they don't reflect God's character! They're antinomian. And they're not INTERESTED IN BECKONING ALL MEN TO COME TO THE SAME FOUNTAIN FROM WHICH THEY DRANK AND HAD THEIR THIRST WONDERFULLY SUPPLIED ... Nothing on earth so terrible as a so-called Calvinist who doesn't have tears in his heart and a passion in his soul to be a little like Christ and give of themselves so others may drink of the eternal fountain. Israel failed. I want to ask you this question, I don't know the answer, can a church lose its election? Where is the missionary zeal? I'm not interested in what the other fellow does that's wrong; God knows, let's do what's right.

Rolfe Barnard could be harsh with those he loved but he did so to *stir* them out of their slumber and to challenge and exhort them to do as Christ would do. Barnard loved people enough to tell them what was wrong with them from a biblical perspective. This stance cost him dearly but he would not back off from what he felt was the truth in the life of a church.

Rolfe Barnard was a theologian and a defender of the faith. He fought hard to defend the Bible and the God of the Bible! It disturbed him greatly to be living in a day when the "old paths" were a forgotten memory as far as evangelism was concerned. He *hated* modern day evangelism. He was known as an enemy of evangelism. And indeed he was in the sense that he stood against what was considered evangelism of his day and a gospel that misrepresented the Christ of the gospel. He often used the following example to sum up the gospel and evangelism of his day (again from his sermon, "The Recovery of True Faith):

A Sunday school teacher in class in a Southern Baptist church, was asked this question by a student: "Was Hitler a Christian?" And the product of some generations of methods as a substitute for the power of the Holy Ghost, of which we've all been guilty and suffered greatly. This Sunday school teacher in all seriousness said, "We do not know, we can only hope that he accepted Jesus when he was a little boy but he sure didn't act like one." That's a pretty good parable of what's passed for the gospel in your day and mine."

What was the message that Rolfe Barnard preached? Did he have just one message? It was said of him that when he preached in Arminian churches he would preach on election and reprobation for a week! When he ministered among Calvinists he would preach on the duty of evangelism and holy living. In other words, often his audience determined his message. He believed in the doctrines of grace as a *means to salvation*. His whole ministry focus was evangelism. He had the apostle Paul's passion for souls. Perhaps because he, like Paul, did so much damage to the church before salvation; Paul persecuting the church and Rolfe damning his fellow college students when he was the president of the infidel club. The fact that the memories of both men haunted them spurred them on with a true sweetheart love for Jesus Christ!

Rolfe Barnard preached a gospel message which many of his peers chose not to preach. He preached a message which, rather than bring him popularity and mass acceptance, brought him great opposition and rejection. It was a message out of date with his generation. His message was the message of Jonathan Edwards and George Whitefield, Charles Spurgeon and Asahel Nettleton. The pulpits of America, for the most part, disregarded the gospel of the New England Puritans. Unfortunately, in America during the twentieth century, the majority of pulpits proclaimed a different gospel from that which made this nation a Christian nation and gave it its independence to a newer, more acceptable gospel which gave no offense to lost man. A gospel which gave all ability to man to be saved or lost; for the most part, God was removed from it entirely other than in His beneficence offering heaven to those who would chose it.

Rolfe Barnard's gospel was the gospel of God's glory in the salvation of men. In the gospel which Rolfe preached man was not in control of his destiny—God was. God could save you or damn you. A sinner possessed no ability to turn to God in repentance and faith—that ability had to be given him through grace. Rolfe preached that man's duty in accordance to the gospel was immediate repentance. Man was a sinner who needed to be reconciled to God by the shed blood of Christ through repentance and faith. Rolfe Barnard preached about a bloody cross with a crucified Savior who was a substitute for sin, incurring the wrath of God while on that bloody cross in the place of sinful man. Rolfe's gospel was a *scandal*. It spoke of a *scandalous cross*. Rolfe's gospel proclaimed the sovereignty of God in the salvation of man. Whereas the gospel of Rolfe's day stated, "God did His part, now you do your part."

Rolfe's gospel was a God-centered gospel rather than a man-centered gospel. Rolfe Barnard believed that the popular gospel of his day was a *perverted gospel*. It divided Christ from His absolute totalitarian authority and His lordship as a living reigning Redeemer. The popular gospel said that one could receive Christ today as a Savior and then at a later date perhaps take him as Lord. Rolfe's gospel stated that JESUS IS LORD. You don't make Him Lord. Your responsibility is to bow to Him now in repentance and utter surrender or some future day He will place His foot on your neck and make you bow to Him then!

Rolfe's gospel upon close examination against Scripture is of course the gospel of the Word of God. It is the gospel which God in former times seemed please to bless with spiritual awakening and revival. It is the gospel which gives glory to God for the gift of His Son. Rolfe Barnard knew that the Holy Ghost had to prepare the heart to receive Christ. It grieved him deeply to see Southern Baptists in particular take salvation out of the hand of God and give it solely to men. It grieved him to hear Baptist pastors omit the need for repentance in their presentation of the gospel. He knew things had to change! He did all he could in his generation to point the church, which he dearly loved, back to a God-centered evangelism which focused on the sovereignty of God and the lordship of Jesus Christ. It broke his heart to witness the deterioration of Southern Baptist ethics and he preached against lawlessness in the life of a believer. He preached on the utter strictness and severity of the law of God with all its attendant claims and demands.

Rolfe Barnard was a prophetic voice to his generation, and as a prophet, he was for the most part rejected as all true prophets are along with their message. He was primarily responsible for the resurgence of Calvinism in Baptists in America during his life and that influence is still felt today—though most Baptists are completely unfamiliar with Rolfe Barnard. In this chapter we will study in depth the doctrines that he preached for they bear great importance, not only to the spiritual health of church life, but to the impact the life of the church has upon its own community in the proclamation of the gospel of the glory of God.

There is an old adage for preachers: that they are either to comfort the afflicted or afflict the comfortable. Barnard seldom comforted his hearers. He was a disturbing preacher and he could get you mad at the preacher and even madder at God! Many a Baptist deacon informed him, "the God you preach isn't the God I worship. My God wouldn't do like that!" To which Barnard would reply, "Yes suh! I reckon you're right. *Your god wouldn't* but the God of the Bible would!" Barnard preferred whip over balm when he preached. Was he too harsh at times? Yes. Even his wife Hazel would ask him to "tone it down some and go easier on them"; and he would for a time but for not very long. He was a scrapper and he enjoyed a good fight! He consistently preached for three things: (1) He would get you mad. (2) He would inform you of your duty to repent. (3) He would call you to believe in a living Lord in all His claims of lordship.

Rolfe Barnard was a bull dog when he preached. He came at you fierce and hard. Few could fall asleep during a Barnard sermon! Barnard often stated that evangelists were God's gift to the church. And he was right. God will occasionally give a generation a man fit for that generation out of His kindness and mercy. Rolfe Barnard was such a man. We will now study the message which Rolfe Barnard preached, all to the glory of God.

Repentance

Rolfe Barnard's primary message was repentance. You would have thought that his primary message would have been the doctrine of election but it was not. He preached hard on man's duty to repent and to do so immediately! He preached a series of four sermons over the radio on "John the Baptist Comes to Town" and they are corkers! And in each sermon the primary message is the need for sinners to repent before a holy God. He preached that man was not sick or diseased but a rebel! And a rebel against God. And it was man's duty, right now, to surrender to a sovereign King. His often comment was in a meeting: "Sinner stack arms! Throw down your shotgun!"

Barnard saw a generation of preaching that omitted the doctrine of repentance from the pulpit. He knew the omission of the need for repentance in evangelism would produce antinomianism in church life. He had seen it time and time again. Church members seated on the throne of their heart where only Christ should reign, lawless living in the lives of church members because they never had repented of their sins to God. Many had merely accepted a historical Jesus who died on a cross and they knew nothing of a vital union with a living Lord which produced a life of holiness.

We turn now to his own words on the doctrine of repentance, from his sermon, "The Sermon That Cost a Preacher His Head":

> You know, my friend, from the beginning of John the Baptist's ministry throughout the lids of the New Testament, repentance is the watchword of the hour. Every prophet and the Lord Jesus Christ Himself in His prophetic ministry, down through John the Seer who wrote the last book of the Bible, rings the charges on the truth that God is a holy God, that His demands have not been lightened, and that men are still called upon to repent toward God and believe in the Lord Jesus Christ. Immediately we open the Word of God—whether in the Old Testament or in the New—we find that the subject that is paramount is REPENTANCE.
>
> In the Old Testament the prophets were all the time, forever and eternally, calling on the people to give up their sinful ways and to live a righteous life. When John the Baptist hit the deck to prepare the people's hearts to receive Jesus Christ, he immediately announced (in Matthew 3:2), *"Repent ye: for the kingdom of heaven is at hand."* The first sermon the Lord Jesus ever preached as a prophet, He *demanded repentance.* The apostle Paul is the author, as the Holy Spirit gave him utterance, of that eternal command as recorded in Acts 17:30: *"And the times of this ignorance God winked at; but now commandeth all men every where to repent."*
>
> It is God's command, and back of God's command is God, the character of God and the requirement of God. In the Bible, my friends, the word repentance, the act of repentance, the duty of repentance, the command repentance, the gift of repentance is the first step. (I don't like that term "first step," but I don't know how to put it any better!) There is no use for us to deny that God Almighty demands repentance. He commands repentance. The duty of all men, Paul says—now

since Christ has come God doesn't overlook anything now and ignorance is no excuse—the first duty of men and women is to repent ...

A generation or two ago, I remember even when I started to preach nearly thirty-three years ago, a generation ago it meant something to stack arms, to throw down your shotgun, to repent, to surrender, to come into the presence of the living Christ in such a way as to be saved. In that day and time this Christian walk and this Christian way was a pilgrimage. Men and women walked in enemy territory as a pilgrim and walked the tight rope, seeking the will of God. In those days this business of walking with God was an eternal conflict—it was an agonizing struggle. In those days coming to Christ meant an honest attempt to do eternally the will of a sovereign God. In those days coming to Christ in what we call repentance meant, if necessary, the cutting off of the arms or a plucking out of the eye.

In the Word of God we are told about a cross and about taking it up and about denying self. In those days coming to Christ in repentance meant being willing to be a fool for Christ's sake. In those days coming to Christ in repentance meant walking alone if necessary. It meant a willingness to be hated for His sake. Now, God help us, it is more or less a picnic—it is a social—it is a mockery! May God open our eyes!

Repentance holds the field until our Lord Jesus Christ recalls it, and He has not done that up till now and so I preach it. John the Baptist preached it. It cost him his head. And I preach it, and failure to obey it will cost you your soul. Luke 13:3: *"Except ye repent, ye shall all likewise perish."*

God's Holy Law

Rolfe Barnard preached the holy law of God and its demands on all men. He believed, like George Whitefield, that a sinner must first be confronted with the awfulness of Mt. Sinai before seeing the beauty of Mt. Zion. Barnard knew from his own experience as an infidel that a rebel against God must be confronted with his ruined condition and perilous position before a holy and just God. Barnard believed in preaching law before grace and he often mentioned how

John Wesley did the same. He highly recommended the journals of John Wesley. Barnard knew the law was a schoolmaster which led a sinner to Christ by shutting men up entirely to God for their salvation. He firmly believed that the gospel must be preached in its proper order.

Rolfe Barnard also believed that the law was a rule for life. He often preached against the lawlessness so prevalent among church members who felt that because they were "saved by grace" could live a sinful life and abuse that grace. Barnard firmly believed that in preaching the gospel it was his objective to get *men lost.* Man had to realize his lost condition against the holy requirements of Almighty God. He often mentioned the old minister who came to him with the fatherly advice of: "Son, you can catch more flies with honey than with vinegar." To which Barnard replied, "Yes suh. I have heard that all through the years of my ministry. And I believe it is true for catching flies, but I am not out catch flies but to KILL MEN!"

The following sermon extract will provide Barnard's thinking on this subject. It is from his sermon, "The Message and Method of the Apostle Paul":

> It is amazing how many of God's people support certain well-known nationwide preachers who have done everything in their power to take the only club the Holy Spirit has got to beat a man down where he would have the slightest interest *in the shed blood of Christ and the holy law of God.*

> It is amazing how in the name of fundamentalism we have reduced the gospel until it is so slick you can swallow it and never know it. *The law and grace are not enemies. Where no law is preached, there can be no gospel preached; because the gospel can only be preached in the context of God's holy law.* It was the Bible teachers that discovered you could separate them! And thus ignored the fact that all through the Bible God constantly reminds us that *He is a God who kills and makes alive.*

> Deuteronomy 32:39: *"See now that I, even I, am he, and there is no god with me: I kill, and I make alive; I wound, and I heal: neither is there any that can deliver out of my hand."*

And He never separates the two. All through the Bible it is crystal clear that since the fall the only way by which God can make a man whole is to *kill him,* then raise him from the dead—not improve him, but kill him. *"I kill"*—that is what the law does, it kills everything it touches. So, we must preach the gospel in its proper order. And the order is: *"O LORD ... in wrath remember mercy!"*

Nobody in this day could possibly feel any need of leaning his whole weight on Christ dying for him, as we listen to the nice little gospel of today, with all of its teeth taken out. Paul said, *"We warn people."* As far as I can see *Jesus Christ is the incarnation of God's holy, perfect law.* I think I am preaching law, when I am preaching Christ. He is the only One of whom if could be said in Hebrews 1:8-9: *"But unto the Son he saith, Thy throne, O God, is for ever and ever: a sceptre of righteousness is the sceptre of thy kingdom. Thou hast loved righteousness, and hated iniquity; therefore God, even thy God, hath anointed thee with the oil of gladness above thy fellows."*

That is the law, perfect righteousness, and perfect hatred of sin, that is it; that's all God asked for, that's all God is. He hates and He loves. Paul said he warned men night and day with tears for three years. I haven't done a good job, but I have done the best I knew how at that time; I am telling you the truth. I have done my best to scream against this steam roller evangelism that comes out of zealous men. *And it produces false professions and deceived people that call themselves Christians. They do not know my Lord, because He has not been pleased to reveal Himself to them.*

God warns us about false preachers that preach another gospel (in Galatians 1:6-9): *"I marvel that ye are so soon removed from him that called you into the grace of Christ unto another gospel: Which is not another; but there be some that trouble you, and would pervert the gospel of Christ. But though we, or an angel from heaven, preach any other gospel unto you than that which we have preached unto you, let him be accursed. As we said before, so say I now again, If any man preach any other gospel unto you than that ye have received, let him be accursed.'*

The beginning of a Christian life in a sinner, the preparatory work, is to bring him to crying out, *"Depart from me, for I am a sinful man.'* There must be a holy woe on the lips and in the heart of a man. That is where it has to begin. For thirty years most pastors have refused to give the Spirit of God a chance to produce that holy woe. And they have been getting people to believe they are saved before they ever spent one moment in godly sorrow for their sins and repentance. Now we are reaping an awful harvest of deceived souls. *O God, give us of Thy Holy Ghost with broken hearts to preach the gospel in its purity and it its proper order* until somebody gets lost. Men are lost, but they don't know it apart *from the Holy Ghost conviction of sin.*

The Lordship of Jesus Christ

Rolfe Barnard lived what he preached and he expected his hearers to do the same. It disappointed him when he felt he had church members "bucking him" on the truths which he proclaimed. One of the biggest battles he fought in churches was the issue of the lordship of Jesus Christ. The churches in America had come to accept the teaching that a person could receive Jesus as Savior but not Lord and still go to heaven. That the issue of the lordship of Jesus Christ was for those who desired victorious living *after they were saved.* This concept was not new. It had emerged from the British Keswick meetings of the nineteenth century and had for its teachers such giants as F. B. Meyer and Graham Scroggie. Victorious living books appeared on the scene to add fuel to the Keswick Conferences; in 1884 Evan Hopkins' book *The Law of Liberty in the Spiritual Life* was widely received among holiness devotees. Keswick teachers proclaimed that a life of victory awaited any believer who was willing to submit to the lordship of Christ in their lives and experience the power of the Holy Spirit for holy living. An illustration which typified the Keswick Movement went like this: "As believers, Jesus can be *reigning* in our lives (by the indwelling of the Holy Spirit) but not *ruling.* In England there is a Queen and it is indisputable that she reigns—but she does not rule. Likewise, the Christian can assert self on the throne and deny Jesus His rightful place as Lord. We must step down from the throne of our hearts and make Jesus Christ Lord!" This teaching made Rolfe Barnard's skin *crawl.*

Rolfe Barnard believed that a person had no biblical standing for salvation if they did not surrender to the lordship of Christ with all His claims upon them *at the time of their coming to Christ in salvation.* He fought against the concept that one could have Christ as Savior and not as Lord. Barnard felt strongly that the Bible stated clearly there was no salvation for any man without a complete and utter dethronement of self and an enthronement of Christ as Lord of *all.* To come to Christ savingly one had to come in total surrender to all the claims of Christ's lordship. Christ must be a total Master. Your life is not your own you were bought with a price and that was His shed blood. Your money is not your own; your time is not your own; your body is not your own—Christ must be Lord of all— you are His bondslave. But the key to understanding Barnard's preaching on the lordship of Jesus Christ is to understand that he meant the sinner did this surrender *at the time of salvation—not at a later date after salvation.*

Barnard fought an uphill battle on this subject all his life because the lordship of Jesus Christ led to a life of holiness— church members fought him on that one! He knew that even among the sovereign grace churches there was a battle to be fought here. Everybody wanted Jesus as Savior but few wanted Him to rule as Lord.

When Rolfe Barnard was the president of the infidel club which he formed during his college days, he fought God on this very issue of lordship and it delayed him coming to Christ for he knew he would have to *surrender* to a life of preaching if he were to be saved. He wanted to become a big shot lawyer and make plenty of money not be a little ole' preacher living on cornbread and water, poor as a church mouse and despised by many! Rolfe knew that the one thing keeping him from coming to Christ was his refusal in this matter of lordship. He knew if he were to be saved he would have to throw down the shotgun of his rebellion and submit to the utter and total claims of Christ on his life and he fought it! Finally God won and we know the rest of the story. But Barnard preached that

God will cross the sinner at his place of rebellion and for him the place of rebellion was the fact that he did not want to be a preacher. But God crossed him there at that rebellious point and Rolfe was saved. Jesus was Lord in his life from that day forward.

This doctrine of the lordship of Christ was a hot topic near and dear to his heart and he preached it with everything he had! Observe his comments on this very thing from his sermon, "Who Is the Lord Jesus?":

> You know, my friends, there is no middle ground in this business. You either have accepted this rejected Christ and taken up the cross and living a life of denying yourself and following Him, all out for Him or you haven't at all. Christ must be all in all or He will not be Lord at all! I say it with a sob in my heart that our preaching today much of it is preaching another Jesus and another gospel. The apostle Paul warned of that in his days. I have been going up and down America for years now, saying that we are mighty close to preaching not the expected Christ of the Old Testament prophecy, not the rejected Christ of the Jewish nation of His day, and not the accepted Christ of the early Christians. But *most preachers have preached another Jesus and another gospel.* I have had to pay a little price for this, oh, I wonder if I am right. I wonder if in the popular preaching of the gospel today, as we call it, everybody talks about accepting Jesus Christ as your personal Savior. And nobody says anything much about surrendering to Christ's absolute authority in your every day living.
>
> I wonder if we haven't got another Jesus, this One we separated His Saviorhood from His lordship. I hear it preached now that we are saved if we accept Jesus as our Savior, and when I say the Scriptures don't talk like that, people say I am not preaching the gospel. Oh, my soul! You mean to tell me this Jesus the Old Testament prophesied of was prophesied just as somebody to keep you from going to hell? No sir! It was prophesied of Him, that He would have the voice of authority, it was prophesied of Him that He would sit on an eternal throne, and that the heathen and the nations have been given Him as an inheritance and a possession. It was prophesied of Him in Isaiah that every knee should bow and every tongue confess and Paul refers to that in Philippians

2:9-11: *"Wherefore God also hath highly exalted him, and given him a name which is above every name: That at the name of Jesus every knee should bow, of things in heaven, and things in earth, and things under the earth; And that every tongue should confess that Jesus Christ is Lord, to the glory of God the Father."*

The only Jesus the Word of God talks about in the Old Testament and announces His arrival in the Gospels, and as the preachers told the significance of His life, His death, His resurrection, and His present reign in the Epistles. *He is the One who has throne rights in our lives everyday.* And I tell you to accept Him as Savior without facing the fact that He speaks with authority and His sheep hear His voice and He rules them, and they will not listen to another fellow's voice. For to do that is at the peril of your soul.

Observe Barnard's comments on the lordship of Christ from his sermon, "The Lordship of Christ":

The lordship of Christ is a reality. It is not a matter of speculation, it is a matter of fact. The most sublime statement in the Word of God is the statement the apostle Peter made in Acts 2:36: *"Therefore let all the house of Israel know assuredly, that God hath made that same Jesus, whom ye have crucified, both Lord and Christ."* The lordship of Jesus Christ is a fact, because it is an act of the triune God. Men do not make Christ Lord, God has made Him Lord of all.

In Barnard's sermon, "The Living Lord" he makes the following comments:

The Christ of the Bible is Lord of all and a salvation that does not so enthrone Him is not God's so great salvation. In other words, a Christ whom men believe in and have their sense of guilt thereby relieved, but who leaves men knowing nothing experimentally of a living Lord, is not the Christ of the Bible. The Christ of the Bible must reign—all hell can't stop it! He must reign in human hearts and He must reign the world over some of these days.

Now my friends, I believe that the issue of all issues in lost American Christianity is this: I believe that churches must be evangelized before they can speak to the anti-Christ spirit of this hour. Surely a church or an individual not bearing about them the marks of the lordship of Christ can only mark time as we seem to be doing now. It is time to demand not only that men come to Christ with an open, empty hand to receive His mercies; but it is time that men must be bidden and demanded to come to Christ on bended knees with surrendered lives.

Maybe it is time for us to make sure that our converts are really converted before we take them into our membership, before we hold them up to the unconverted as examples of what Christ does for a man. Maybe it's time we stress emphatically that the Christian life is more than an acceptance of Christ as Savior—this business of men knowing a Christ who has relieved them of their sense of guilt but leaves them knowing nothing about a living Lord is a delusion and a false hope."

Holiness

Holiness unto the Lord. Rolfe Barnard believed that salvation, in its biblical understanding, meant that when a man experienced the new birth he lived for Christ in a life of holiness pleasing to Him. That if a believer professed to know Christ but their life was a contradiction to this then they never did posses Him. Some of the fiercest opposition Barnard faced in evangelistic campaigns was this issue of holiness. In a tent meeting in Kentucky where God was moving and people were coming to Christ, Barnard faced great opposition from other ministers in that city and they preached against this man Barnard who said, "You can't be a Christian unless you are living holy lives!"

Barnard believed that Christ saves a sinner from the penalty of sin and the *power* of sin. Rolfe would say publicly that he knew he wasn't saved as a young man because he knew he did not possess *life* in here (pointing to his heart). He said, "When the devil crooked his finger I went right along with him because I had no *power to resist.*" He had assurance of his salvation through the knowledge and appropriation of that inner supernatural power of Christ in the man through a vital living union with Him by the Holy Spirit. Rolfe Barnard did not preach the doctrine of perfection but he did preach the doctrine of holiness. We see his comments on this from his sermon, "What Is Holiness?":

Christ died to make men HOLY, holy. Salvation is in Christ; it's in Him, not in what He did apart from who He is. I believe the most damning fundamental preaching that is taking place in the South land today; it is the preaching that leads people to think they have an interest in the death of Christ, without being vitally joined to Him in their daily walk. We've been preaching salvation through a representative that we never came into contact with. I want to lift a voice from time to time and say that you can't have any interest in or benefit from the perfect life and glorious death and resurrection and present intercession of our Lord—except as you are *vitally and really and experimentally and actually joined to the Lord Jesus Christ*. The limit of His salvation is found in Matthew 1:21: *"For he shall save his people from their sins."*

God Almighty is not going to try to improve on their old wicked hearts, for their hearts are represented in the Scripture as incurably sick. God Almighty is not going to try to improve old Rolfe Barnard's sinful nature! The only thing that He is going to do is to deal it a death blow and give Rolfe Barnard a new nature—and in that new nature the principle of holiness is planted within the heart of an old rotten sinner.

We want to show how the Holy Spirit baptized and identified His people in the virgin birth of the Lord Jesus Christ. And that everybody who is ever saved gets in the family of God by being born of the Spirit just as supernaturally and just as miraculously as the Lord Jesus Christ was born out of the womb of Mary. The most humbling thing I ever faced in the Word of God is how the Holy Spirit planted a Divine Seed in the womb of a natural woman and out of that a Holy Thing. That is exactly was what regeneration is: the implantation of the divine nature of God in the old dirty cesspool heart of Rolfe Barnard, that out of the heart of old dirty Rolfe Barnard shall come that which is holy, a new nature that, BLESS GOD, will result in a new way of walking that is pleasing to God ... Christ died not only that we might be reckoned perfect as God looks on us in Him, but Christ died that our lives should be lives of daily victory over sin. Praise God, when a man is born again, the power of sin is broken, and sin can't lord it over that child of God anymore. That is all in the purpose of God.

There isn't anything about which there is more ignorance

that what Bible holiness is. And yet there isn't anything that is closer to the heart of God or the heart of the gospel than this simple statement: Christ didn't come down here to save people from hell; but He came down here to make a people who had been given Him by the Father, to make them where they might live like kings!

Will you let Brother Barnard help you? We are chosen unto *holiness.* To call oneself a saved person while living in sin and enmity to God is downright foolishness. And a man who calls himself a child of God who does not have the *evidence that the work of grace is real in the heart, and that evidence is practical obedience to the will of God—a man who doesn't have that evidence, doesn't have any evidence! That is the evidence that God saved you.* That is the evidence that you are one of God's children. This is working in your life. Without holiness, no man would be capable of serving God in heaven. Without holiness, no man would be capable of beholding the glories of Christ here. Without holiness, no man can serve God, now or later! Without holiness, no man can have fellowship with God now or then. We are chosen, not because we are holy, but that we might be made holy.

Election

If there was a doctrine central to the ministry and life of Rolfe Barnard it was the doctrine of election. Election was the theme by which he breathed and lived and served his precious Redeemer. Rolfe knew his own wicked heart and what a cesspool the heart of man was and that there was nothing in man that would desire God. God had to put that desire there. Saving faith was a gift. Rolfe knew man was saved by grace and he had come to embrace the doctrines of grace while still a student at Southwestern Seminary.

The doctrine of election was the subject which divided churches where he ministered. It split more churches wide open than anything else! People would leave a Rolfe Barnard meeting upset and mad at the preacher and mad at God. People would leave the meeting split and go home believing in two gods: some would go home believing in the God of the Bible and the others would go to their houses believing in their god who was not the God of the Bible. Rolfe preached that God was a sovereign God in the salvation of men and that people were saved because God saved them. Rolfe preached that it was man's duty to repent—but he would not repent. He preached that it was man's duty to turn and come to Christ and believe—but he would not do it! He would not *because he could not.*

A Rolfe Barnard meeting would come to a head when he began to preach up the doctrine of sovereign grace. He would catch more heat on this topic than any other he preached and it was continually a wonder to him that the churches that were "bucking him" most on this issue were Southern Baptist churches. From the time in seminary where he was greatly influenced by the "ten cent book" of B. H. Carroll he knew that salvation came to man no other way other than by sovereign grace. It was the doctrine of election which spurred Rolfe Barnard on in evangelism because he *knew* there were men waiting to be saved and that the God who "opened the heart of Lydia" would continue to do so under the preaching of His Word of the gospel of the glory of God. Rolfe would often comment to a group of "grace preachers" that when he was laboring in a church and began to preach on sovereign grace the church members would turn their heads toward the pastor to see what *his reaction was.* If the pastor was in agreement it would soften some of them, if the pastor was turning red in anger they would get madder too!

He addresses this issue in his sermon entitled, "God's Call":

> It is crystal clear that anybody on God's earth who is raised from his spiritual grave, who is brought out of his darkness, and who is born into the kingdom of God—that happens by God calling, quickening, converting, regenerating, justifying, and sanctifying that soul! God does the calling, God does the quickening. Men have to be called, thank God. God calls. He calls all who are exposed to the gospel in such a powerful way that they are left without excuse. Not all who are exposed to the gospel when it is preached, but all who could hear it. They have an opportunity, but they don't avail themselves of it. I have to answer to God for the light I have from God, and the light I had an opportunity to have. You see this is serious.
>
> I was down here in Union, South Carolina several years

ago and after I had preached a week, the pastor came to me and said, "Brother Barnard, would you meet with the congregation Sunday afternoon and let us ask you some questions? You have just torn up our playhouse, and you have got us in awful shape."

I said, "Certainly, if the people don't want to argue. I will argue with nobody, but I will talk with anybody that wants to talk. If I can I will answer any question, I want to help and not hurt." So they met and the whole outfit was there, and they never did get to but one question. The pastor asked it, and it was the heart of their difficulty. He got up, and he meant business, and he was speaking for his whole congregation. He said, "Brother Barnard, doesn't God give everybody a chance to be saved?" And I said, "No, young man, God doesn't save people by chance, not by chance. *He saves people by GRACE.*"

And I said, "Tell me what chance has God given a heathen who lives in the deepest jungle of Africa, and lives all the days of his life, and never heard tell of Jesus Christ? I don't know the answer, do you?" This generation has been taught to believe that God owes salvation to people, and that God has got to come across and give everybody a square deal. And if God owes salvation to any human being, then He owes that human being the death of the Son of God. And if He owes the death of the Son of God, He is a monster. No, do you see the blasphemy at the heart of church members who are blowing the smoke of their rebellion and lawlessness in the face of God by saying they believe the gospel of a God who has to treat folks "right" and give them a chance?

No! No! God doesn't owe anybody salvation. He didn't hang His Son on a cross because He was in debt to this old godless world; He put His Son on a cross because He so loved the world. John 3:16: *"For God so loved the world, that he gave his only begotten Son, that whosoever believeth in him should not perish, but have everlasting life."*

God does not save men by giving them a chance. *He saves them by calling them.* Salvation is not by chance. *Salvation is by the grace of God*, and if God owes grace, then it isn't grace; that's debt. And God ought to pay His debts, if He owes man anything, but God does not owe mankind anything, except justice. And if He deals with every human being with justice, He would send everybody to hell.

When Rolfe Barnard preached the gospel he often had to defend the character of God. He felt that the average church goer in America had little concept of who God really was and few really knew Him in a saving way. When Barnard would begin a evangelistic campaign in a city or church he often had to preach a "high view of God" because so many of the church members who heard him maintained a "small view of God." We see from his comments much on this subject from his sermon, "Sovereign Mercy":

> The gospel is not the gospel if it does not treat God as a God who is gracious to whom He will be gracious. The gospel is not the gospel of God if it doesn't preach about a God who shows mercy to whom He will show mercy. Long since I learned that it isn't doctrine that is the center of controversy. I learned that we have come to the hot issue whether or not we shall preach a gospel that leaves men and women with one thing they can brag about; or whether we will preach a gospel that fills churches full of men and women who can say from their heart, *"But God forbid that I should glory, save in the cross of our Lord Jesus Christ."* The gospel that allows one person to glory one bit is not the gospel of the glory of God"

Rolfe Barnard believed that sovereign grace was the mainspring from which all Christian life transpired for it made the saved sinner indebted to the grace of God which would result in a life lived in service to God and holiness unto Him. Even the title of some of Barnard's sermons are apologetics for the doctrine of election. Read his comments from his sermon, "Why We Preach the Gospel and Particular Redemption":

> I want to bring out the difference of the old gospel that proclaims a saving God and the new gospel that proclaims the news about a salvation that has been made possible. Today I want to give you the conception of what preaching the gospel is. I begin by saying that only Almighty God knows how desperately we need in this generation to be set free from the degenerate faith and preaching of this hour. And only

God knows how we need to be set free to preach publicly and privately. I believe that every child of God is to be a witness of what you have seen and heard from God ...

And as we proclaim this gospel which is truth from God, we bring forth four great facts to the attention of men and women.

(1) We tell all men that they are sinners in the sight of God, and they cannot do anything to save themselves. That's preaching the gospel. Every human being is a sinner in the sight of God, and no one can do one thing to save himself. This is truth from God.

Instead of telling an old sinner that God loves him, and Christ died for him, we need to spend that time in the Word and preach the cross. And the first message of the cross is that it was sin that nailed Jesus Christ to the cross. And it was sinners who drove the nails. Judgment is coming and God must punish sin. We proclaim to them as truth from God what all men are bound to believe. Nobody will ever get saved by somebody telling him that God loves him and Christ died for him. A sinner doesn't care whether God loves him or Christ died for him; he is not interested in knowing that, for that is just something we argue about.

We are to tell all men on the authority of God and His Holy Word that they are willful rebellious sinners, obnoxious to the judgment of God, and responsible to God in that awful pit that they dug themselves. They cannot change their awful sinful nature and they are condemned by God's holy law. They are taken captive by Satan, they sit in darkness in the prison house. *God Almighty has to perform a miracle if they ever get out.* We are beginning to preach now.

(2) In the second place, we are to tell men that Jesus Christ, God's Son, is a perfect Savior for sinners, even the worst sinner that ever was on the road to hell. We are to tell men with assurance of the Word of God that God's Son, Jesus Christ, is a suitable and a perfect and all-sufficient Savior for sinners. Oh! My friend, what that old sinner needs to hear first of all is not that God loves him and Christ died for him. He needs to stick to this fact that Jesus Christ saves sinners; He came down here to save sinners. Everybody in the sight

of God, before he is saved, is just an old sinner. The one who God is going to save and God knows He is going to save him. He looks at him as an old sinner. In Luke 5:32, Jesus says, *'I came not to call the righteous, but sinners to repentance.'*

So we tell all men that they are sinners and they can do nothing to save themselves. And if they will believe that, we tell them that Jesus Christ, God's Son, is a perfect Savior. Not a possible Savior, but a perfect, suitable and available Savior for sinners, even the worst sinners.

(3) And then as we preach we tell sinners in the third place that *God the Father and God the Son has promised that all who know themselves to be a sinner, and put their utter confidence in Christ, shall be received into favor, and none shall be cast out.* This is something I can't understand, it is too deep for me. I can tell every sinner in the world and it is true according to the Scriptures; John 6:37 says: *"All that the Father giveth me shall come to me; and him that cometh to me I will in no wise cast out.'"*

Christ died for those who would believe. Christ died for those who do believe. Oh! What grace it is. God and the Son have promised in grace that every sinner who will face the fact that Jesus Christ is a perfect Savior for sinners, so He must be a perfect Savior for me.

(4) Then God tells him in the gospel that He and the Son hath promised grace. This is condescension, this is glory, alleluia! That all who know themselves to be sinners and put their faith in Christ and rest in Christ shall be received. He won't be rejected. Every sinner who his faith in Christ, the promise is, he will never be cast out. Then we are to tell sinners these four things and when we do, we are preaching the gospel. *(1)* All men are bound to believe that they are sinners. *(2)* All men are bound to believe that Christ is a perfect Savior for sinners. *(3)* All men are bound to believe that God promises in the gospel that all who see and know themselves to be sinners, and *(4)* look away from themselves and look in perfect confidence to Him, rest in Him, they shall be received.

And then we conclude by saying that God Almighty has made repentance and faith a duty, requiring of every man who hears the gospel. A serious full resting and rolling of the soul upon Christ, in the promise of the gospel as an all-sufficient Savior able to deliver and save to the utmost them that come to God by Him. Ready, able and willing through the preciousness of His blood and the sufficiency of His death to save every soul that shall freely give up themselves unto Him for that end.

We are all eternity-bound men and women, and unless God Almighty is pleased to perform a miracle in you and reveal Christ in you, you are doomed to hell.

Rolfe Barnard also preached on the perseverance of the saints; the duty of believer to fulfill the Great Commission through a life of active witness; and other subjects. But the main messages he preached have been highlighted in this chapter. Rolfe Barnard preached hard on the doctrine of total depravity. He would comment, "This is the big question that needs to be answered: was man totally ruined in the fall or just partially disabled?" He said that Arminians believe man was merely "wounded" in the fall and not totally ruined. The following sums up his thoughts on total depravity, taken from his sermon, "Sinner's Substitute":

I want to talk to you about God's provision to relieve the awful misery and distress of sinful men, and to cleanse those awful and perverted hearts, and to *make willing* that awful will of yours that is free to do evil but *absolutely unable to do right.*

Rolfe would at times finish a meeting by singing a song in his deep baritone voice. A favorite of his reflected his indebtedness to sovereign grace, it is called "A Sinner Like Me" and we provide it here for it personified his theology in song:

A Sinner Like Me

I was once far away from the Savior,
And as vile as a sinner could be;
I wondered if Christ the Redeemer,
Would save a poor sinner like me.
I wandered on in the darkness,
Not a ray of light could I see,
And the thought filled my heart with sadness:
There's no hope for a sinner like me.

And then, in that dark, lonely hour,
A voice whispered sweetly to me,
Saying, Christ the Redeemer has power
To save a poor sinner like thee.
I listened and lo! 'twas the Savior
Who was speaking so kindly to me.
I cried, I'm the chief of sinners,
OH save a poor sinner like me!
I then fully trusted in Jesus,
And Oh what a joy came to me.
My heart was filled with His praises,
For saving a sinner like me.
And when life's journey is over,
And I the dear Savior shall see,
I'll praise Him for ever and ever
For saving a sinner like me!

C. J. Butler

Chapter Thirteen

Personal Recollections

Wherefore I will not be negligent to put you always in remembrance of these things,
though ye know them, and be established in the present truth. Yea, I think it meet,
as long as I am in this tabernacle, to stir you up by putting you in remembrance;
Knowing that shortly I must put off this my tabernacle, even as our Lord Jesus
Christ hath shewed me. — 2 Peter 1:12-14

Fortunate were the individuals who heard Rolfe Barnard preach and knew him personally. In this chapter we will provide statements about Evangelist Barnard from those who knew him. Unfortunately, many of Barnard's associates are in glory—it has been forty-three years since Rolfe Barnard passed away—and their recollections of him have been lost to posterity. Most of the remarks in this chapter have been collected from the introductions to his three volumes of sermonic material. A couple have been recently provided for this book.

Here now are those personal recollections on the life and ministry of Evangelist Rolfe Barnard. The first is from Carlyle L. Zeigler:

> I would speak for the precious few of us who sat under Rolfe Barnard as he ministered as our pastor for a few years in the 1950s. He taught us that every member had a function in the body of Christ and a mission field in the world. In the light of that teaching, I believe that Brother Barnard was grateful to

all that supported him with their provision, presence, prayers and perseverance, and he would give a special thanks now to Sister Bullock and those who have helped her put three volumes of his sermons in print.

The highest praise and gratitude belongs to our sovereign Lord who called us by His grace, and who put our brother into the ministry. It could well be said that "for such a time as this" Brother Barnard "came to the kingdom" (Esther 4:14). In one of his messages a few years before his home going, he said, "I have given my life in the controversy of the Gospel. There is just one Gospel, but it has a different thrust in times of crisis." He also felt that good and sincere men preaching a perverted Gospel were preparing the religious world to welcome the Antichrist with open arms.

The greatest enemy of the Gospel is preachers and church people who are using the devil's tool, a little Gospel Truth mixed with error. The Gospel with barbed wire will not be tolerated today, but an easy-believes that "accepts" a Savior on a cross to keep us out of hell—this will be accepted. There must be a fight to recover the Gospel that presents a sovereign Lord of absolute authority! Our Brother Barnard did this as he preached the "utter strictness of God's Law" and an "utter commital to Christ as Lord." This sort of preaching causes men to fear God, give Him glory, and worship and love the Christ of the throne.

Carlyle L. Zeigler
Pastor Emeritus
New Bethel Baptist Church
Tobaccoville, NC

The following remarks about Brother Barnard come from W. R. Downing:

When I was a young student an old preacher told me there are only two types of preachers—the one you CAN listen to and the one you HAVE to listen to. Rolfe Barnard was a preacher you HAD to listen to! In over twenty-five years in the ministry, I have heard educated men, gifted men and very extraordinary men in the pulpit. But no one has ever riveted my attention and moved me as deeply as Rolfe Barnard. He was unique. He was a man sent with a message from God, conscious of his Divine mission, bowed down with a sense of that "burden of the Lord." He knew that "the Word of the Lord had come expressly unto him" and was conscious that "the hand of the Lord was upon him." His hearers often sensed the same! "The Word of God was as a fire shut up in his bones" and he could not remain silent. To say that his preaching possessed a "cutting edge" would be an understatement! He simply cut through all the elements of usual ministerial niceties and dealt directly with the eternal issues at hand. He declared the Truth of God simply, directly, fully, faithfully and without apology in his own unique way. He preached hard and cut deeply. He preached with conviction and for conviction. The Word of the Lord through Hosea fitly describes Brother Barnard's ministry: *"I hewed them by the prophets; I have slain them by the words of my mouth"* (Hosea 6:5). Although his preaching was piercing and even aggravating to many, there was yet much evidenced humility, genuine sincerity, sympathy and compassion in the man himself. This, indeed, seemed to put a sharper edge on the thrust of his preaching.

Brother Barnard was not a man out of step with his times, but rather a man fitted for those times by God! He saw the decadent spiritual state of fundamental Baptists and evangelical Christianity at large. He had witnessed the decline and woeful absence of doctrinal preaching and the rise of modern "easy-believes" with its attendant methodology and failure. As did our Lord and His apostles, Rolfe Barnard preached against the popular and accepted religion of the day, exposing its falsehoods and failures, and then faithfully and boldly declared the glorious Truth of God. He was a modern Jeremiah, whose God-called and necessary ministry it was *"to root out, and to pull down, and to destroy, and to throw down, to build, and to plant!"* (Jeremiah 1:10). His ministry was that of John the Baptist—denouncing sin, declaring the certainty of impending judgment, stripping his hearers from every false hope and then pointing them to Christ alone! (Matthew 3:1-12). His was an awakening ministry that stood in the true biblical succession of the prophets and apostles!

The preaching of Rolfe Barnard was not only direct and piercing, it was further characterized by certain major and recurring themes largely lost, forgotten or denied in Baptist pulpits and in both fundamental and evangelical circles. He constantly preached on the absolute sovereignty and holiness of God and the strictness of His holy law. He understood that the moral nature and character of God determine the nature of the Gospel and the character of repentance, faith, conversion and the Christian life! He saw repentance as a complete and continuous turning not only from sins, but from sin as the dominating power of the life. To him saving faith "was the response of the whole man to the whole Christ." Here he again departed greatly from rationally accepted teaching to declare the "totalitarian claims" of Jesus Christ as Lord. Finally, he both believed and preached boldly the Truth of free and sovereign Grace. His purpose was to be faithful to God in the ministry of the Gospel, to preach without compromise of Truth, to stir up God's people to prayer and scriptural fervency, to awaken unsaved church members and mere religious professors and to shut sinners up to Christ alone for salvation!

Unlike many who knew Rolfe Barnard personally over the years and could write much by way of spiritual experience, personal relationship and anecdote, I met him only a year before his home going and heard him preach several meetings in Texas. He also spoke for two weeks in a Bible school where I taught. We spoke on occasion and he gave me much personal encouragement. Although our relationship was relatively short, I profited much from his preaching, influence and counsel. His taped sermons have been my constant companions for these past twenty years and their inspiration, influence and help have been blessed to me greatly.

I must write a few things about Brother Barnard's influence as I know it. In addition to his living ministry, his influence since his home going has been very great. I have met and heard men in the pulpit at meetings around this country and many bear the mark of Rolfe Barnard upon their preaching. His taped sermons have been sent out to untold thousands and have been the means of encouragement to ministers and churches and been used in the conversion of many. The testimonies are many and blessed! He "being dead, yet speaketh."

W. R. Downing

The next testimonial of Brother Barnard's ministry comes from the lady who was saved under his preaching and who prepared and published his sermons after his death. Eulala Bullock painstakingly transcribed Brother Barnard's audio sermons and then had the tenacity to get them published! We are grateful for her labor of love which has been a means of blessing to so many through the years—blessed be her memory!

Dear Friends:

I love the Lord because He hath heard my voice and my supplications, because He hath inclined His ear unto me; therefore I will call upon Him as long as I live. This was David's testimony, and by God's Sovereign Grace and Mercy it is mine. Mercy is God's favor that holds back from us what we deserve. Grace is God's favor that gives us what we do not deserve.

I made a profession when I was about 12 and thought I was saved, but I was deceived with this easy-believe stuff that is being preached today and deceiving the multitudes. But God was pleased to be longsuffering, not willing that I should perish. Praise the Lord, He sent Brother Rolfe Barnard in 1951 to preach two weeks for Pastor B. B. Caldwell in whose church I was a member.

One night when Brother Barnard was preaching in the power of the Holy Ghost, God was pleased to prick my heart with the Word, and reveal to me that I was a guilty lost sinner, and put me under Holy Ghost conviction of sin. And I became a seeker of the Lord and a beggar for mercy.

A few days later I was on my knees at home begging God to have mercy and save me. When I was enabled to surrender to Jesus Christ as my Lord to rule over me, He spoke peace to my troubled soul and revealed to me that He is my Lord and Saviour. Praise the Lord! I became a member of the Body of Christ when I was 40 years old. That is a miracle that only God Almighty can perform. Titus 3:5: *"Not by works of righteousness which we have done, but according to his mercy he saved us, by the washing of regeneration, and renewing of the Holy Ghost."*

It is of the Lord's mercies that we are not consumed, because His compassions fail not. They are new every morning: great is Thy faithfulness. The Lord is my Portion, saith my soul; therefore will I hope in him. **Salvation is of the Lord.**

I have over 100 tapes of Brother Barnard's preaching; they are a blessing to me, and I have learned more Truth by hearing him preach than any other preacher. I believe that he was the greatest evangelist of our day and the best preacher I ever heard. He warned people to flee from the wrath to come, and he exposed the error that is being preached by most preachers. Today's preachers are deceiving people by telling them to "accept Jesus as their Saviour and they are saved." My Bible doesn't teach that. No one is saved unless Christ is revealed to him and he is baptized into the Body of Christ. 1 Corinthians 12:13, John 17:3, Luke 10:22, Galatians 1:15-16, Titus 2:13-14, Titus 3:4-7. **It is a miracle that only God Almighty can perform!**

Eulala Bullock

The next personal recollection of evangelist Barnard comes from the pen of well-known Christian author, Dr. John Thornbury. Dr. Thornbury was converted under Brother Barnard's ministry in a tent meeting in Ashland, Kentucky in the early 1950's. Here is his description of Rolfe Barnard's preaching ministry:

God crowned his labors with revival blessings in many places in the fifties and sixties, the meetings in Ashland being one example. He preached all over the South, Mid-west, and in Canada, and there are thousands today who can testify that God used him to bring them to salvation. Quite a number of preachers were converted to a belief in the sovereignty of God.

Many unusual things happened during his evangelistic meetings and anecdotes could easily fill a volume. Barnard was endowed with a powerful set of lungs and a good voice of medium range. He was an excellent singer and often sang special songs in his evangelistic meetings, accompanied by his wife, Hazel. Occasionally he violated all rules of elocution by shrieking at the top of his voice during a sermon. He did this not by an interjection of some kind but during a sentence. For example, he might say, "The purpose of the cross is the glory of God." On "glory" he might say "gloooo" at the top of his vocal capacity. He did this when his emotions reached a high pitch and he felt very, very strongly about something. Needless to say, such outbursts were ear-splitting and did devastating things to gauges on electronic recording equipment. No one, I suppose, could possibly recommend this as a method, generally speaking, but I can say that this peculiar individualistic trait did have a startling and awakening effect upon an audience. As a rule, it was very difficult for people to sleep when Barnard was preaching.

I have heard Barnard preach many times. There were occasions when his preaching was ordinary and unimpressive. But in the right context, he was one of the most powerful preachers I have ever heard. In the midst of an awakening, when the powers of heaven and hell were visibly in conflict, he had a peculiar unction that cannot possibly be described. Like Finney, whose style he followed, and Nettleton whose theology he accepted, he could hold an audience spellbound in such times.

Rolfe Barnard's gifts were not primarily pastoral. He seemed ill-fitted for a settled type of ministry. He once said, (quoting C. T. Studd), "Some like to live within the sound of a chapel or church bell. I want to run a rescue station within a yard of hell."

He was not a builder, he was a trailblazer. He was not a Timothy, charged to take care of the house of God, he was a John the Baptist crying in the wilderness. He emphasized greatly the lordship of Christ and repentance. One of his few printed messages was entitled, "John the Baptist Comes To Town." It is a characteristic sermon, and I count it one of my personal treasures.

Although Barnard was often misunderstood, and disliked by many, he was a man, I believe, who had an uncommon love for the souls of men, especially sinners. His messages, many of which are available on tape [now online, author's note] demonstrate plainly that he had a fervent desire that lost people submit to the claims of Christ. In some of them, Calvinist though he was, he literally begs them to lay down their arms of rebellion, "stack arms" he would sometimes say, and receive God's forgiveness through repentance! Out of the pulpit Barnard was, as a rule, withdrawing yet friendly. In relaxed, social circles he had a way of badgering his friends, but in a way that was always taken good-naturedly. I recall one occasion when I became the object of his teasing. In 1963, I, along with several other people, was visiting his home in North Carolina. I had just been married and was making plans to go to the Philippine Islands as a missionary. While at his house I wrote a letter to my new bride. When Barnard discovered it, he said, "John, I understand you want to be a missionary. Before you leave my house I feel I ought to do something to help you. I want to pay for your letter to your wife." With this remark, he handed me a postage stamp! Thus did Barnard support my missionary deputation! This, of course, brought a round of hearty laughter.

Dr. John F. Thornbury
Author and Pastor

The following insights on Rolfe Barnard are supplied by Wylie Fulton, who helped in the publication of Barnard's three volume sermon set.

What made Rolfe Barnard the unique evangelist of the 20th century? He was variously known as a fundamentalist, a sovereign gracer, a conservative, a Southern Baptist and a hitchhike evangelist. But Rolfe Barnard was different in many ways from other individuals and groups who carry those names.

Rolfe Barnard *was a prophet.* His message came as a burning fire from the bones, as an urgent life-or-death word that he was under a Divine summons to bring. Every time this brother preached, there was a division—not a division created by the speaker, but his preaching was simply so searching, so Spirit-blessed, so discriminating that it revealed the division already existing between those who merely professed and those who truly knew the Lord!

Brother Barnard was not content for people to go through

the motions, hear a message and go away the same. His great love for people would not allow him to be cruel, but he always said he'd rather make people mad with the truth than leave them utterly unmoved.

Rolfe Barnard was a dynamic speaker. His words on paper cannot portray the power of his spoken message. Brother Barnard and his ministry came into my life at a critical time—a time when I was being disturbed about the shallowness of religion in general and the lostness of my own soul in particular. I was just a teenager then, but I'm glad to testify that the Lord's true servant pointed me away from all mere religious profession, and away from all the works and pride of the flesh, and bade me as a lost sinner to look unto the only One Who is "Mighty to Save!"

Wylie W. Fulton

The last two contributions come from two men close to Rolfe Barnard and are provided especially for this biography. The first, anecdotes, come from Pastor Drew Garner.

I will give you just two of many anecdotes of our dear brother Rolfe Barnard. He was preaching at my church (where I was the pastor) and he noticed a lady in the congregation chewing gum while he was preaching. He paused, looked at the lady, and said, "Ma'am, why don't you take that gum out of your mouth and stick it in your ear!" He said this good-naturedly of course!

Then there was a time he was again preaching at my church and a teenage boy had fallen asleep on his father's shoulder while Barnard was preaching. Noticing this, he stopped preaching, addressed the father with these words, "Sir, wake up your son before he sleeps his way to hell!"

Evangelist D. (Drew) Mason Garner
Houston, Texas

The last recollection comes from a minister who spent perhaps the most time with Rolfe Barnard than any other minister; they were close friends and labored together for many years. Here are Henry Mahan's recollections of his dear friend:

I met Bro. Barnard at Ashland, KY, April 1950! I heard him preach the Gospel of God's Grace for two weeks—morning and night. "The Lord revealed His Son in me." Rolfe and I were dear, dear friends for nineteen years. We walked together, spent many hours together in my home, my church, and on the road together in *many* meetings and I love him very much. He was my teacher, my friend and a *faithful servant* of our Lord Jesus Christ. He preached the Gospel of God's wonderful Grace. Rolfe was a very *private* person—He loved *one Master,* preached what others would not preach, was honest, faithful and kind and generous!

John 1:19-23 describes Rolfe as well as he could be known—, when they asked, "Who art Thou? That we may answer them who sent us?" He replied, *"I am the voice of one crying in the wilderness, Make straight the way of the Lord."*

I would simply say to anyone who asks, "Who is Rolfe Barnard?" Listen to his *sermons* and you will know *who he is and what he believed!*

Henry Mahan

Chapter Fourteen

His Homegoing

Or ever the silver cord be loosed, or the golden bowl be broken, or the pitcher be broken at the fountain, or the wheel broken at the cistern. Then shall the dust return to the earth as it was: and the spirit shall return unto God who gave it. —
Ecclesiastes 12:6-7

Rolfe Barnard often preached from Ecclesiastes chapter twelve. He believed it was the only place in the Bible that described a funeral procession. As a young preacher in the oil town of Borger, Texas he preached from that text in a saloon and from that sermon seven men knelt and professed Christ that day. They became the first seven deacons of his Baptist church!

Rolfe Barnard was out of town when he died. He was away in a series of meetings in Prairieville, Louisiana. Fortunately, these last Barnard sermons are available on SermonAudio.com and they attest that he preached what he always preached right to the end— sovereign grace, the lordship of Jesus Christ, and the necessity of immediate repentance. He had been "in the saddle" as a hitchhike evangelist for more than forty years and he died the way he wanted to die—actively serving his Redeemer amidst a preaching engagement. While at a pastor's home Brother Barnard rose to go to the evening meeting and fell to the floor. He was rushed to the local hospital where it was determined he had suffered a massive heart attack—the next morning the hitchhike evangelist passed into the presence of his Redeemer.

Rolfe Barnard did not die like D. L. Moody, with his loving

family gathered around him in his own favorite bedroom in Northfield, Massachusetts. The hitchhike evangelist died alone, in a strange hospital, in a Southern town far away from his own home in Winston-Salem, North Carolina. The faces of strangers were the last ones he saw on the morning of January 21st, 1969, when he died from heart failure. Some say it was indeed a matter of the heart which killed him—although not entirely physical. But Rolfe Barnard died of a broken heart over the condition of the American church; a heart broken over what generally passed for evangelism and the gospel of his day. Barnard did not merit a large funeral with 4,000 in attendance like his fellow ex-lawyer-turned-evangelist Sam Jones. No, Rolfe Barnard went out with no fanfare—oddly, he did not even rate a public death notice in his denomination. He died as he lived, unnoticed by the masses. If one could compare his last days with another much-used evangelist it would have to be the great Asahel Nettleton of the nineteenth century. Nettleton fought the same battles Barnard did; both men witnessed the deterioration of orthodox religion in their day and were isolated by their peers for their defence of it. Very few today are familiar with the name of Asahel Nettleton and fewer still of the name of Rolfe Barnard. Yet both these men lie among the mighty dead. Their preaching at its best made grown men quake under the burden of their sins as they were confronted with eternity and the Almighty God of that eternity. Their obscurity is odd for they both contributed much to the furtherance of the doctrines of grace in their day. Their similarities are striking. Their usefulness for God amazing.

The following death notices for Rolfe Barnard came from three of his dearest friends. We present them now for they are reflective of what his colleagues thought of him.

The first is from R. T. Kendall, who at the time of Barnard's death, was a pastor of a Baptist church in Fort Lauderdale, Florida. This notice was printed for his congregation:

> A few words from the pastor's desk ... As I was preparing to write these words I received a phone call from my close friend and our recent evangelist, Henry Mahan. I know he had been trying to reach me all day and I knew it would be a good reason for him to call. I was to receive some of the

saddest news I ever expect to hear. "Brother Barnard died this morning." The news broke my heart. Rolfe Barnard, 64, was the greatest evangelistic preacher I have ever known. He had the fire of a John the Baptist. He once estimated to me that approximately 100,000 had responded to make some kind of a commitment to Christ in his 40 years of preaching. Brother Barnard and I published a paper for four years known as "Redeemer's Witness." It went into over 40 states. I gave this ministry up when I became Pastor of LMBC. I consider it a truly great honor to have served with him for those years. He was a Southern Baptist evangelist. But his ministry took him into many other churches as well. I know of several city-wide meetings he held that will never be forgotten, some of which were instrumental in the conversion of some of my closet friends ... my ministry could not conceivably be the same without his influence. Nothing could keep me from being at his funeral. I shall fly to Winston-Salem Thursday and come back Friday. I hope some of his mantle will fall on me.

The next death notice is from close Barnard friend, Henry Mahan, then pastor of the 13th Street Baptist Church in Ashland, Kentucky.

ROLFE BARNARD

Our good friend, Brother Rolfe Barnard, passed away quite suddenly last Tuesday morning. He was in Louisiana in a meeting. Bro. Rolfe preached both services Sunday and was sitting in the pastor's home Monday evening preparing his message for the service. He stood, walked to the door to go to church and collapsed. He was rushed to the hospital, where it was diagnosed as a massive heart attack. Rolfe died at 9:30 CST Tuesday morning. Many of our preacher brethren mean much to us and have been a blessing to this church. But no one has been a greater blessing to us than Rolfe Barnard. He was the greatest preacher of his time. Hundreds of preachers and believers all over this nation call him "My father in the faith." We are going to miss him very much; but the task is now ours to perform, and the banner of Redeeming grace is ours to carry. I'm sure if Rolfe had chosen the way he wanted to leave the field of battle, this would have been "his way." He died preaching the gospel he loved and serving the Lord who loved him. He was away from home and alone when he died, but this was the way he had spent the past 35 years. He used to call himself "the hitch-hiking evangelist." Well, the gallant, devoted, hitch-hiking evangelist has gone home—we'll miss him.

The last notice of his death for our perusal is from his close friend, C. O. Jackson, Jr., President of the Texas College of Theology and pastor of Greenwood Baptist Church of Houston, Texas.

A PRINCE FALLEN IN ISRAEL

"And the king said unto his servants, Know ye not that there is a prince and a great man fallen this day in Israel?" (2 Samuel 3:38).

When David spoke these words, it was in praise and respect for a loyal son of Israel. Abner had been loyal to his king and had demonstrated heroism on the field of battle many times. He would be greatly missed. On January 21, a great man and a mighty prince, Bro. Rolfe Barnard, departed this life of pilgrimage and went to be with the Lord. His absence will be greatly felt. I attended his funeral in Winston-Salem, NC on January 24, and listened to Bro. Henry Mahan of Ashland, KY, as he brought a most timely message of "farewell" from all present, until we meet again where there'll be no tolling of the bells. Bro. Barnard was one of the most noted preachers and evangelists of our day. He knew the heartbeat of a pastor, as he had served in that capacity. He was a combination of scholar and evangelist—a rare treat in this age. His message was both doctrinal and practical. He knew how to rebuke, reprove, and exhort with all longsuffering. He could exalt Christ and his lordship to the extent of which he had no peer. His preaching was God-anointed. He knew the value of an educated ministry. He was a preacher's friend. His evangelism touched the shores of America from east to west. He was in full-time evangelism for some forty-five years. He started the first Baptist church in Borger, Texas, and pioneered that work in the midst of hardship unimaginable. Yet God's hand was upon him and blessed his ministry with the salvation of many souls. He was a Bible teacher and church historian. Truly a brother of his caliber will be greatly missed. It is a solemn but true fact that one by one, God is calling His great prophets home. One writer of another generation warns that a sure sign of reprobation is when God calls His prophets home and raises no one up to fill their place. I pray this is not the case with America. This is a time for solemn reflection and prayer that God will raise up more men faithful to the Gospel.

— C. O. Jackson, Jr.

Rolfe Barnard was a mixture of prophet and evangelist. He lived so that others *might live.* He rebuked church members when they needed it and faced the consequences. He preached about the God of the Bible and His gospel of the glory of God—and faced the consequences. He warned sinners to repent to avoid an eternal hell in a day when other preachers avoided such unpopular subjects—and he faced the consequences. The consequences were many—more than we will ever know. But the only thing of any real consequence was *things eternal* and Rolfe had laid up plenty of gold, silver, and precious stones for review on That Day.

One thing was unarguable about Rolfe Barnard—he was a man jealous for the glory of God and the gospel of Almighty God! When one studies Christian biography, one finds a common denominator in each person mightily used of God. Each person, had he chosen a secular career, would have been enormously successful in his endeavors. D. L. Moody, had he remained a shoe salesmen, could have easily ended up owning the company. He was so driven and talented he would have been a great success in the business world. John Wesley, had he entered secular life, would have commandeered well, as president, of any academic institution. He had all the qualities to succeed in that endeavor. Rolfe Barnard, had he remained a lawyer, would have risen to the top of his profession. He possessed all the qualities that make a successful legal professional. But instead of fancy cars and a big house and a table laden with steak and lobster, he chose rather, a life of cornbread and water, lonely hotel rooms and obscurity. He was *God's* hitchhike evangelist and that counts for something. For to labor in a God-owned ministry as a God-owned preacher is the most *important* work in the world. Rolfe Barnard loved to sing and he had a gifted singing voice which was pleasing to the ear. A favorite song of his which he dearly loved to sing was "A Sinner Like Me." And Rolfe Barnard, God's Hitchhike Evangelist, preached the gospel of God's glory to the very end until he actually realized the last stanza of his favorite song:

> *And when life's journey is over,*
> *And I the dear Savior shall see,*
> *I'll praise Him for ever and ever,*
> *For saving a sinner like me.*

APPENDIX

SERMON BIBLIOGRAPHY

The following sermonic material of Rolfe Barnard can be found in print and on the Internet. We hope the following bibliography of Brother Barnard's sermons is helpful to those interested in his life and ministry. Those who partake of these rich resources will be greatly blessed!

PRINTED SERMONS:
Three volumes of Barnard's sermons are available through Revival Literature, at 1-800-252-8896.

Volume One:
1. Judgment's Coming or Should God Punish Sin?
2. When the Lights Go Out on the Road to Hell
3. The God Nobody Is Mad At
4. Hell
5. Who is God or the Covenant of Grace?
6. The Message of the Cross
7. Seeking the Lord
8. The Purpose Why Christ Died and Rose Again
9. What Does It Mean To Be Saved?
10. God's Rejection—Reprobation
11. Paul's Testimony Part 1—Chosen in Him
12. Paul's Testimony Part 2—When It Pleased God
13. Running Scared
14. Five Marks of a False Prophet
15. The Difference in the Old Gospel and the New Gospel
16. Why We Preach the Gospel and Particular Redemption
17. A Thankful People in a Reprobate Age
18. Why Christ Died
19. Sovereign Mercy
20. The Ascended Lord

Volume Two: (arguably the best of the three volume set)

Volume Three:

Audio Sermons of Rolfe Barnard on SermonIndex.com (184 sermons)

John The Baptist Comes To Town, Part 1
John The Baptist Comes To Town, Part 2
John The Baptist Comes To Town, Part 3
John The Baptist Comes To Town, Part 4
6 Things We Face in Preaching the Gospel
A Burden for Souls
A God That Keeps Records
A Great Revival is Coming
A Hindrance to God's Mighty Works: Unbelief
A Man Who Is Known In Hell
A Sweetheart Love For Jesus Christ
An Exhortation to Church Members
Anathema Maranatha
Are There Few That Be Saved?
As The Days Of Noah Were
Bible Holiness
Casting Pearls Before Swine
Christ Came to Seek and Save
Christ The Lord
Christ The Demander
Claims Of The Lord Jesus
Dead Men Tell No Tales
Dead Orthodoxy and How God Brings Men To Salvation
Death, And After This, The Judgment
Do You Know God?
Do You Know God? Have You Put Away Your Idols?
Doctrine of Election & Man's Free Will
Does This Offend You?
Enter In The Strait Gate
Facing Reprobates With Their Destiny
Four Proofs of the Utter Severity of God's Holy law
Gift Of Eternal Life
God Confirming His Word
God Is Without Any Darkness Within Him
God Saves Lost People
God Uses Earthen Vessels
God's Bloodhound
God's Call
God's Call In Electing Grace
God's Decision vs. Man's Decision
God's Glory And Our Motives
God's Sovereignty & God's Glory
God's Will In Electing Grace
Have You Touched The Lord Jesus In Faith?
He That Being Often Reproved
Hell
Ho, Everyone That Thirsteth
How Can A Sinner Come To Christ?
How Do You Measure Up?
How God Brings Men To Salvation
How God Gets Men Lost

How God Gets Men Lost Saved
How God Save Me From Infidelity
How To Come Savingly To Christ
How To Prepare Your Heart For The Word
How Zaccheaus God Saved
If Any Man Love Not The Lord
If The Foundations Be Destroyed
If The Trumpet Shall Sound
If You Love Me, Keep My Commandments
Is Your God Dead?
Issues Involved in Preaching Grace
Judgment for This Generation
Judgment Is Bound To Come
Judgment Is Coming
Let Him Be Accursed
Looking Unto Jesus
Making Fun Of God
Marks of a False Prophet
Message From Psalm 2
My Experience As A Chaplain—Part 1
My Experience As A Chaplain—Part 2
No Gospel For Me!
Often Reproved
On His Head Are Many Crowns
Order of the Concerned
Paul's Gospel
Paul's Gospel Messages 2&3
Paul's Gospel Messages 4&5
Paul's Meeting With The Lord
Preparing Your Heart To Receive The Truth
Radio Messages on Lordship
Recovery of the Gospel
Revival in the Church
Running Scared
Salvation Is Of The Lord
Save Yourselves From This Untoward Generation
Saving Faith
Saving Mercy
Seeking The Lord
Seeking The Lost
Sent Unto The Lost Sheep
Shall Not The Judge Of All The Earth Do Right?
Should God Punish Sin?
Sinful Praying
Sinners In The Hands Of A God Who Keeps The Books
Sinning Away Your Day of Grace
Sovereign Mercy
Sudden Death
Sweetheart Love For Jesus Christ
Thankful People in a Reprobate Day
The Battle Cry Of The Early Church
The Bible Meaning of Predestination

The Bible Versus Your God
The Character of Hell
The Cross of Christ
The Death of a Believer & Unbeliever
The Depravity of Sinful Man
The Discipline Of Jesus Christ In The Local Church
The Doctrine Of Election And Man's Free Will
The God Nobody Is Mad At
The God of the Bible Kills People
The God of the Bible Must Punish Sin
The God of the Bible vs. the God of Today 1 of 2
The God of the Bible vs. the God of Today 2 of 2
The Gospel For The Days Of Noah
The Gospel In The Days Of Anti-Christ
The Gospel's Invitation
The Great Need of the Hour
The Heart Of Evangelism
The Invitation: Come Unto Me
The Lordship of Christ In The Local Church
The Lordship of Jesus Christ
The Lost Doctrine of the Bible
The Man Who Was Known In Hell
The Marks of Reprobation
The Meaning Of The Cross
The Message and the Method of the Apostle Paul
The Message Of Baptism
The Message Of The Cross
The Message Wherein Ye Stand
The Methods of the Holy Ghost
The Missing Presence of Christ
The One Issue
The Preaching of the Cross
The Reign Of A Sovereign God
The Revival At Pentecost
The Savior's Invitation
The Seekers of The Lord
The Solemn Thought
The Three-fold Vision of Evangelism
The Thrust Of The Gospel
The Utter Severity Of God's Holy law
The Whosoever Wills of the Bible
There is a War Going On
Three Results Of Paul's Commission
Three Unscriptural Expectations
Three Ways A Sovereign God Saves
Try To Determine
Two Things God Promises to do For His Church
Upon His Head Were Many Crowns
Utter Committal To Jesus The Christ
Utterance
Warning Against Rebellion
Watching Men Die

We Will Not Have This Man Rule Over Us
What A Sinner Can Do To Be Saved
What Is A Church?
What Is Saving Faith?
What Is Saving Faith?—part 2
What is the Issue?
What It Means To Be Lost
What It Means To Be Saved
What It Means To Be Under Discipline of Christ in the Church
What the Early Church Preached
When The Lights Go Out On The Road To Hell
When The Saints Shout Hallelujah
When The Saved Shout Hallelujah As God Sends People To Hell
When Will Revival Come?
Who Jesus Is
Who Will Follow Jesus?
Who Will Follow Jesus? 2
Whose Son Is Jesus
Whosoever Wills Of The Bible
Why Christ Died And God Raised Him From The Dead
Why Glory In The Cross
Why God Kills Christians
Why I Believe Many Are Now Reprobate
Why People Stay With Christ
Witnessing A Good Confession
You Can't Resist The Holy Ghost and Get By

Audio Sermons of Rolfe Barnard on SermonAudio.com are courtesy of the Rolfe Barnard Library. This wonderful resource has the lion share of Barnard material with 270 sermons—some with dates and locations.

Do You Know God? Have You Put Away Your Idols and Are You on the Way to Heaven?
Utter Committal to Jesus the Christ—A Life and Death Issue
John The Baptist Comes To Town—Turn or Burn!
John The Baptist Comes To Town—The Sermon That Cost A Preacher His Head
John The Baptist Comes To Town—Calling Men To Come Clean With God
John The Baptist Comes To Town—Preparatory Work
The God of the Bible Kills People
Death
Death, And After This, The Judgment
Shall Not the Judge of All the Earth Do Right?
Hell (Fear Him Which Is Able To Destroy Both Soul And Body)
The Who-so-ever-wills of the Bible
Does This Offend You?
Why God Sends Men to Hell
God's Rejection, Reprobation
God's Bloodhound
Why I Believe Many Are Now Reprobate
Your God vs. the God of the Bible
How Almighty God Brings Sinners To Himself
God's Sovereignty and God's Great Glory
Sovereign Mercy

Judgment for This Generation
The Character Of Hell
The God Nobody Is Mad At
The Marks of Reprobation
A Look at the Cross
Revival Series—How Satan Will Be Bound
The Offense of the Cross
The One Controversy Between God and Man
Sovereignty of God
Oh, For a Passion for Souls!
Most Urgent Task Today—Recovery of the Gospel of the Grace of God
The Real Issue of Revival
Luke 19:10
God Commands Men to Repent
Reality of Hell & Will God Punish Sin
The Ascended Lord
The Gospel for the Day of Anti-Christ
The Gospel for a Day of Lawlessness
Paul Learns Election
The Necessity of Holiness
How Will Revival Come?
God's Saving Mercy
God's Decision vs. Man's Decision
Take Time to Seek the Lord!
Our Lord and Saviour and Why He Died
A Thankful People in a Reprobate Age
Christ's Death as Preached by the Early Church
Christ, God Manifest in the Flesh, Died for Sin
Seekers After God
The Message of Hell
Depravity II
Depravity I
Who Is Jesus
The Gospel of The Glory of God
The Refusing Christ
Watching Men Die—Preached in Texas
Who is Going to Heaven?
False Refuges
How To Be Saved
How Revival Will Come
Judgment For This Generation
The Sudden Death of Dixie
How May I Know That I Love the Lord?
Fellowship of the Concerned
How Can a Man Know that He is Saved?
Death and Judgment
Seeking the Lord in Salvation
Five Marks of a False Prophet
How God Brings Sinners To Himself
How God Gets a Sinner To Know He Is Lost
The Gospel Must Be Preached in All its Purity
God Uses Earthen Vessels

The Covenant of Grace
Battle Cry of N. T. Church—JESUS IS LORD!
Awakening is From the Lord
Have You Touched The Lord Jesus in Faith?
The Recovery of Saving Faith
Paul's Testimony 2 When It Pleased God
Paul's Testimony 1 Chosen In Him
Three Ways a Sovereign God Saves
When I Preached My Father's Funeral
A Burden For Souls
The One Issue
Why I Believe That Many Are Now Reprobated
Why Men Don't Come To Christ
Reality of Christ's Lordship & God's Judgment
Three Short Messages on Revival
Christmas and the Shed Blood
The Preaching of the Cross
The Character of Hell
Real Nature of Christian Hope
A Description of God's Preachers II
We Cannot Give All Sinners The Same Message
God of the Bible vs. the 'God' of Today
God's Substitute for Sinners II
Utter Corruption of the Natural Man I
A Description of God's Preachers I
Honest People Will Not Go To Hell
Sent Unto The Lost Sheep
Teaching God's Electing Grace
The Methods of the Holy Ghost and Evangelical Eschatology
Awakening—Exhorting—Comforting, in Our Apostate Days
Who Jesus Is
Mr. Baptism and His Message
DEATH! And After This The Judgment
Four Things This Generation Must Hear
What a Sinner Can (and Cannot) Do To Be Saved
Spurious Belief or True Faith
Revival at Pentecost
Go In His Authority
A Living Lord
They That Hear Shall Live
Going To Hell in Droves
The God of the Bible Kills People
What is Holiness? Preached under the Gospel Tent in a Rain Storm
How God Will Deliver His People
Do You Want To Be Like Christ?
The Company of Heavenly Worshipers
The Disturbing Presence of Christ
What Does it Mean to be a Christian?
Glorying in the Cross
Watching Men Die
Remember Now Thy Creator—Ecc. 12:1
Christ On The Throne

God Manifested in The Flesh
How God Gets Men Lost
The Narrow Way
God's Last Call
Why God Elects Men to Salvation and to Service
If The Foundations Be Destroyed
The God of the Bible Must Punish Sin
Seeking The Lord
The Word Of God About Hell
What Kind of God Do You Know?
Noah's Day
Who Shall Ascend into the Hill of the Lord
Three Marks of Reprobation
A Message On The Cross
The Old Gospel vs. The New Gospel
National Election
Christ Could Not Do Mighty Works
Save Yourselves from This Generation
Jesus Is Lord
Utterly Committed To Jesus Christ
Many Crowns
Beware of False Prophets
The Severity of God's Law
The Fear of the Lord
Baptized into The Spirit
John the Baptist
The Whosoever-Will Gospel in a World of Whosoever-Won't
Gift of Eternal Life
How Do You Measure Up?
Anathema Maranatha
Claims of the Lord Jesus Christ
Enter in the Strait Gate
The Revival at Pentecost
Judgment Is Bound To Come
When Saints Shout Hallelujah
He That Being Often Reproved
Making Fun of God
God's Call
Whosoever Wills of the Bible
Why Christ Died & God Raised Him From The Dead
What is Salvation?
Is Your God a Dead God?
Saving Mercy
Sudden Death
A God That Keeps Records
No God For Me!
Why We Preach The Gospel
Sovereign Mercy
What Must I Do To Be Saved?
Lord, What Wilt Thou Have Me To Do?
Will God Punish Sin?
The Condition of Man

Preparing One's Heart To Receive God's Truth
How God Gets Men Lost and Saved
How God Gets Men Saved
The Message Of Hell
What Is Gospel Faith?
My Experience As An Army Chaplain
Sinners in the Hands of a God Who Keeps The Books
The Battle Cry of the Early Church
Warnings Against Rebellion
Dead Men Tell No Tales
When The Saints Shout Hallelujah
Why People Stay With Christ
The Gospel For The Days of Noah
Witnessing A Good Confession
God Confirming His Word
How Can I Know That What Christ Did Was For Me?
The God of the Bible vs. Your God
How To Come Savingly To Christ
Running Scared (Ashland)
Looking Unto Jesus
Message From Psalm Two
What It Means To Be Lost
Christ, The Demander
God's Great Demander
Seeking The Lost
The High Crime of Inviting Men to Church
What it Means—Come Unto Me!
The Samaritan Woman
How Does God Get Men Saved?
How Does God Get Men Lost?
What is Saving Faith?
What is Saving Faith 2
How Zacchaeus Got Saved
Why God Puts Up With Wicked Men
When Will Revival Come?
The Three-Fold Vision of Evangelism
Try To Determine the Way a Man Should Go in His Day
Watching Men Die
Three Result's of Paul's Commission
God's Bloodhound
How Can I know Christ Died for Me?
Why Christ Died
6 Things We Face in Preaching the Gospel
The Message of Baptism
Do Men Have Choice of Accepting or Rejecting Christ?
God's Glory and Our Motives
The Message, Wherein Ye Stand
When the Lights Go Out on the Road to Hell
Do You Know God? Have You Put Away Your Idols and Are You on the Way to Heaven
Utter Committal to Jesus the Christ—A Life & Death Issue
John The Baptist Comes To Town—Part 4 Turn or Burn!
John The Baptist Comes To Town—Part 3 Sermon That Cost a Preacher His Head

John The Baptist Comes To Town—Part 2 Calling Men To Come Clean With God
John The Baptist Comes To Town—Part 1 Preparatory Work
The God of the Bible Kills People
Death
Death, And After This, The Judgment
Shall Not the Judge of All The Earth Do Right?
Hell (Fear Him Which is Able To Destroy Both Soul And Body in The Everlasting)
The Who-so-ever-wills of the Bible
Does This Offend You?
Why God Sends Men to Hell
God's Rejection, Reprobation
God's Bloodhound
Why I Believe Many Are Now Reprobate
Your God vs. the God of the Bible
How Almighty God Brings Sinners To Himself
God's Sovereignty and God's Great Glory
Sovereign Mercy
Judgment for This Generation
The Character of Hell
The God Nobody Is Mad At
The Marks of Reprobation
The God of the Bible vs. the God of Today 2 of 2
The God of the Bible vs. the God of Today 1 of 2
Often Reproved
The Marks of Reprobation
What It Means To Be Under Discipline of Christ in the Church
When The Saved Shout Hallelujah as God Sends People to Hell
Do You Know God?
If Any Man Love Not The Lord
The Bible Meaning of Predestination
The Message and the Method of the Apostle Paul
God's Call
Sinning Away Your Day of Grace
Preparing Your Heart to Receive the Truth
Thankful People in a Reprobate Day
God's Sovereignty and God's Glory
Four Proofs of the Utter Severity of God's Holy law
Why I Believe Many Are Now Reprobated
If The Foundations Be Destroyed
If The Trumpet Shall Sound
Dead Men Tell No Tales
How Can A Sinner Come to Christ?
Two Things God Promises to do For His Church
The Lost Doctrine of the Bible
The Depravity of Sinful Man
Exhortation to Become Involved (2)
Bible Holiness
He Could Do No Mighty Works Because of Unbelief (2)
God Is Without Any Darkness
Your God vs. The God of the Bible (2)
Who Will Follow Jesus?
Marks of a False Prophet

What is The Issue?
The Unpardonable Sin (3)
If the Foundations Be Destroyed
Three Things God Cannot Do
The Unpardonable Sin (2)
The Note of Extremism and the Thrill of Expectancy
If You Love Me, Keep My Commandments
There is a War Going On
You Can't Resist the Holy Ghost and Get By
Ho, Everyone That Thirsteth
Why God Kills Christians
Who Will Follow Jesus? (2)
Order of the Concerned
Christ the Lord
The Sovereign Redeemer's Invitation
Is Your God Dead?
Teaching God's Electing Grace
God Uses Earthen Vessels
Running Scared
Sinful Praying
Revival in the Church
The Meaning of Baptism
Four Results of Heart Faith in Divine Election
A Hindrance to God's Mighty Works: Unbelief

Forsyth Memorial Gardens

Home in Winston-Salem

"Borger, Texas - World's Greatest Oil Field"
1920s

Borger Street Scene 1926

Southwestern Baptist Seminary, 1928, with some of Rolfe Barnard's professors, including W.T. Conner, L.R. Scarborough, I.E. Reynolds, and H.E. Dana

Meeting House Near Rolfe Barnard's Home in Winston-Salem

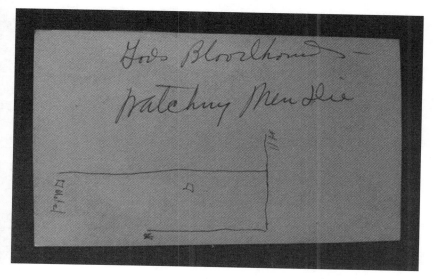

Some of Rolfe Barnard's Handwriting

Meeting Invitations

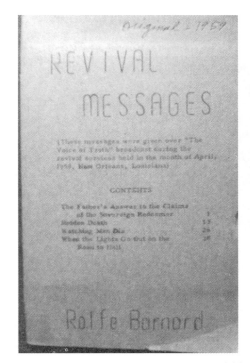

**Younger Picture
of
Rolfe Barnard**

L.R. Shelton, Sr., Rolfe Barnard, 1959

Sketch of Rolfe Barnard

INDEX